August 11th

To my Elly,

who inspires me with the powerful Word of God from her lips, and the powerful faith of her heart. You reflect the message of the Reformation with your gifts of preaching, teaching, and loving! I love you so very much. You carry on the tradition of "women of the Reformation" because you are a beautiful woman of the Reformation, the continued renewal of Christ's church.

Chip

WOMEN OF THE REFORMATION
In France and England

WOMEN OF THE REFORMATION
In France and England

ROLAND H. BAINTON

AUGSBURG PUBLISHING HOUSE

MINNEAPOLIS, MINNESOTA

WOMEN OF THE REFORMATION
IN FRANCE AND ENGLAND

MANUFACTURED IN THE UNITED STATES OF AMERICA

Contents

To

Elisabeth Langerbeck

with gratitude for her

admirable translations

Preface

In *The Women of the Reformation in Germany and Italy* I ventured a reflection on the effect of the Reformation of the sixteenth century on the role of women in society. The suggestion was that the dropping of monasticism in Protestant lands made for the exaltation of the home, the especial domain of the wife, as the sphere for the exercise of the gentler virtues of the Sermon on the Mount. In Catholic thought these have been called the counsels of perfection to be observed by monks. Protestantism made no distinction between the counsels to be observed by the few and the precepts binding upon all. The entire Christian ethic was held to be incumbent upon every believer. Nevertheless there was a distinction of areas. Political man was given a different code and in time economic man also. The shift is evident in Luther who exalted the home as the area where there is neither mine nor thine. Apart from Luther I have not found a direct statement of this principle and I suspect that the only way to test the thesis is to look at the literature of the ensuing centuries.

7

The work on this volume has prompted another surmise, namely that the religious cleavage contributed to the decline of family made marriages in the western world. Both confessions insisted on marriages within the faith and by faith they did not mean a nominal adherence to one or another confession. The Huguenots in particular and likewise, of course, the English Puritans demanded a heartfelt commitment. As the crisis became more acute, so also did the Catholics. That being so, children could not be betrothed at the age of two with any assurance that after reaching the marriageable age they would still be of the faith. Thus the individualizing of faith made for the personalizing of marriage. Again direct statements bearing on this point are only occasional in the present study. Once more, the thesis must be tested by the outcome. A recent book on the Puritan period discovers a shift from progeny as the primary end of marriage to companionability. The chief text is no longer "Be fruitful and multiply" but rather that "God saw it was not good for man to be alone." Marriage was then not just a legal contract but a spiritual covenant into which the partners had to enter by their own consent and commitment. (James T. Johnson, *A Society Ordained by God*, Nashville, 1970)

The present work makes no pretense of completeness. All along the line one encounters allusions to women prominent in the reform movements whose careers might have been explored. Research in this direction is under way. The *Archiv für Reformationsgeschichte* LXII (1972) has three pertinent articles by Miriam Chrisman for Strasbourg, Nancy Roelker for the women of the nobility in France and Charmarie Blaisdell on Renée de France. Pearl Hogrefe is working on the English women, though not with a particular eye to their religious views. There is a sketch of Archbishop Matthew's wife by Mrs. Edith (Weir) Perry, *Under Four Tudors* (London, 1940). A noted Catholic martyr is treated by Mary Claridge, *Margaret Clitherow* (New York, 1966). I would have included her had I not at the end encountered limitations of space. Brief sketches are given of the women named in the examination of Anne Askew by John Gough Nichols, ed., *Narratives of the Days of the Reformation* (London, 1859), pp. 311-13. Some readers will complain that I have not given more on the women in the middle brackets of society. There is a paucity of material. I have not found very much on the wives of ministers. Diligent search would undoubtedly disclose more.

For general background in this volume I have relied on chronologies, maps, and accounts embedded in the narratives. Those who wish connected surveys may consult my *Reformation of the Sixteenth Century* (Boston, 1953); Owen Chadwick, *The Reformation* (Penguin Books, 1964), A. G. Dickens, *Reformation and Society* (London, 1966).

PART I

WOMEN OF THE REFORMATION IN FRANCE

la feü roine de nanarre
margueritte

Marguerite of Navarre

1.

Marguerite of Navarre
(1492-1549)

Marguerite of Navarre had two great passions, love for God and love for her brother. He was her baby brother and her king, Francis I of France. When a grandson arrived and was given his name, she wrote, "He has your nose. May he have all your other virtues." [1] Her brother was to her the perfect knight, the paragon of excellence, the chosen of the Lord, the savior of France. When Marguerite's delivery ran overtime during the absence of her brother, she explained that the baby would not venture to be born without the consent of its king.[2] For Francis, Marguerite was willing to traverse seas and mountains and to outride men. She and her brother corresponded in verse like Michelangelo and Vittoria Colonna, who, by the way, was an admiring friend of Marguerite. Francis called his sister *Ma Mignonne* and entrusted to her, along with their mother Louise of Savoie, much of the administration of the kingdom during his absences in war and captivity. After the death of Louise in 1531 Marguerite added the role of her mother to her own. Statesmen like Cardinal Wolsey visited her. Ambassadors called upon her. The oppressed entreated her. The king heeded her.

Yet there were two points on which he did not altogether incline to her wishes. The first had to do with Navarre. By her second marriage to Henri d'Albret she became the Queen of Navarre. The kingdom had at one time included both flanks

Marguerite playing chess with her brother, Francis I

of the Pyrenees but Spain had gobbled up the southern portion. The king and the queen of Navarre were constantly contriving to recover the lost province. One way was through negotiation with Spain but this would mean ceding something else by way of compensation and at the expense of France. The other way was for France to make war on Spain. Francis was not averse to war with Spain but not over Navarre. Marguerite was to bequeath the problem to her daughter Jeanne.

The second point had to do with religion and involved Marguerite's passion for God. She wanted to reform the church because God willed it. Francis wanted to reform the church because he controlled it. The reform should not disrupt the structure. By a concordat with the pope, the king enjoyed the dis-

posal of ecclesiastical patronage to the extent of 93 archbishop-
rics and bishoprics, some 500 abbeys and any quantity of pre-
bends and priories.[3] He might have retained all this had he
nationalized the church like Henry VIII but in that case he
could not have counted on the pope as an ally against the
emperor. Consequently Francis played the game warily. He
would make a military alliance with the pope and would seek
a theological accommodation with the German Lutherans with
an eye to such an alliance. He would tolerate innocuous reformers in France and clamp down on those who rocked the barque
of St. Peter.

Marguerite tried to win his clemency for moderates by assuring him that she was no radical.[4] She did not condone the
smashing of images and the posting of scurrilous placards. She
too, desired the extermination of heresy and had never tolerated
Sacramentarians in her circle.[5] One wonders whether she understood the meaning of the word which was applied to the reformers of Zürich and Strasbourg with whom those of her entourage were in the closest rapport. Marguerite could be gracious
to Cardinal Pole on his way to assist Mary Tudor in the restoration of Catholicism in England[6] and at the same time exploit
every device to save some poor wretch from the flames, not so
much because she endorsed the opinions of the martyrs as that
she hated the flames.

A point of agreement with his sister inclined Francis to grant
her greater leeway in dealing with those incriminated for deviations from the faith. The king and his sister were devoted to
the new learning. He was a prince of the Renaissance and flat-
tered himself in the role of a Maecenas to scholars, artists and
poets. He invited Erasmus to head a college in Paris, brought
Benvenuto Cellini to embellish the court and gave support to
Marot and other poets that they might give luster to the land
of the fleurs de lys.

Marguerite was a lady of the Renaissance who read Dante in
Italian, Plato possibly in Greek,[7] and Luther to a slight degree
in German.[8] When Pope Paul III heard her in conversation
at Lyons with Cardinals Sadoleto and Contarini he marvelled
at her saintliness and erudition.[9] She was a poetess of distinc-

Guillaume Briçonnet Euesque de Meaux, et Abbé de S.t Germain des prez lés Paris

Bishop Briçonnet

tion and originality. A literary critic of our own day has said that she is unique in French literature for her recital in verse of the Christian drama of redemption. To find a parallel in any tongue one must turn backwards to Dante and forwards to Milton,[10] which is not to say that she equalled their quality. Not a few of the heretics whom she befriended were literary figures. Francis was much readier to condone in them dubious opinions than in the case of a carder of wool.

Marguerite's absorption in the love of God comes first to light in her correspondence, commencing in 1521, with Guillaume Briçonnet, the bishop of Meaux.[11] She was then 29 years old. He was a Christian mystic who believed that man can rise in the hierarchy of being until united with the Ineffable.

> To this end the good Lord has given us ladders on which ravishing contemplations from Him to us and from us to Him can descend and ascend. . . . By His grace we are made god, like unto Him, so that it is possible to discern

in us only luminous divinity, proceeding not from us but from the true fire which transforms us into Him. This will be the true and indubitable union without darkness or shade.

Self love stands in the way and must be overcome by mortification.

Then, Madame, the supercelestial, infinite, sweet, lovely, only true light by its excessive and insuperable love will blind and enlighten you so that in blindness you will see and seeing will be blind. You will arrive at the pathless path of seeing without seeing, of knowing without knowing, of darkness in which this sweet and infinite light is hidden and makes its dwelling place.

One finds here a blending of strains from medieval Christian mysticism and from the newly revived Neoplatonism. There is an indisposition to describe God in personal terms except in so far as Christ is God. There is a penchant for paradox and an intense anti-intellectualism in favor of an ardent piety of the spirit. Briconnet is especially fond of the imagery of fire.

The flame of the ardent fervor of love descends upon him who embraces it and causes him to shine as the stars in the firmament by an exemplary life and this true fire does not consume the soul as material fire burns the wood.[12]

Marguerite, like Briçonnet, eschews personal language about God and calls him "He that is," or "the All." He is the circle whose center is everywhere and circumference nowhere.[13] But by way of compensation Christ is intensely personal and to him may be applied all the imagery of the bridegroom and the bride. Marguerite draws not only from the rhapsodies of Briçonnet but from the *Paradiso* of Dante the *Banquet* of Plato, the sermons on the Canticles of Bernard of Clairvaux, from the paradoxes and mathematical symbols of Cusa and the rapture of St. Francis before the crucified.

Here are excerpts from her poems voicing themes which she held in common with Briçonnet. They need not be pinned down as to date because these notes are recurrent.

The Paradox of Mortification

Make me blind that I may see,
Crippled and bound to walk and run.

Drown me in nothingness that I may be
Whole and complete and all in Thee.[14]

The Rapture of Divine Love

Perfect love—would that it were known!—
Bestows a pleasure that can never end,
And every breath of bitterness is blown.

Perfect love, it is the eternal God,
Which sheds abroad in hearts its charity
And raises up the whole man from the sod.

He who by love is brought to utter naught
Loves only that which is naught
And thereby to wholeness he is brought.

I did not know. I would not have believed,
That love by dying can increase.
But now I know, for now I have received.[15]

Briçonnet was anything but a mere contemplative. He was extremely active in the reform of his diocese. He had under him some 200 parishes to which he appointed preachers obligated to stay in residence. These preachers clamped down on indulgences, stopped genuflecting before candles, gave up exhibitions of relics, excluded the *Salve Regina* (Save O Queen) from the hymn to the Virgin, recited the Nicene Creed in French and commenced sermons by reciting the Lord's Prayer instead of the *Ave Maria*. They would allow representations of Christ but not of the Trinity, because pictures of one head with three faces or one body with three heads suggested three gods. The reform took hold with the common people. Carders, weavers and women began to hold conventicles.[16]

Briçonnet aspired to reform the church throughout France. This was a moment of intense optimism with respect to reform and in France the time was propitious because the country was cool toward the papacy. Bishop Briçonnet enlisted the services of a circle of fiery young men who later appeared in varied roles. There was William Farel of whom it was said that no one bellowed more vociferously. Oecolampadius, the reformer of Basel, urged him to tone down.[17] Farel was later to be the Reformed pastor at Neuchatel in Switzerland. No less intrepid was Pierre Toussaint, who was to be the Reformed minister at Montbeliard. Michel Arande and Gérard Roussel were tremendous preachers, who thought best to foster reform by becoming bishops, and conducting their sees after the manner of Briçonnet. Mazurin and Caroli were fiery at times but wavering at others.

Then in addition, Briçonnet brought in scholars whose writings would help to disseminate the reform throughout the whole of France. One was Jacques Lefevre. He was sixty-five but as enthusiastic as the young. He rejoiced to be alive in that day which should renew all things in the advent of Christ.[18] Farel said that he had never seen a man conduct prayers with such devotion.[19] Lefevre was a biblical scholar who commented on the New Testament and made a translation into French. He was scrupulous in his scholarship and devout in his piety. "O, good Jesus," he exclaimed, "the way, and the truth, deliver our ignorance from the lies of deceivers, snatch us from the mouth of him who seeks to devour. If we turn to Thee we shall be saved from the fiery dart of the evil one, for thou, O Christ, art the only true and more than true Savior of all." [20] Briçonnet had been a pupil of Lefevre and offered him a spot of tranquility when Paris had grown uncomfortable after Lefevre had incensed the conservatives by claiming that three references to Marys in the New Testament are not to the same person but to three. He was assisted in biblical studies at Meaux by the Hebraist Vatable.

This group never could reform the church in all of France without the help of the government which controlled the patronage. Therefore Briçonnet addressed himself to Marguerite as the sister of the king. He assumed also the role of her spiritual director telling her that a fire must be kindled, "and I do not see any sparks coming from your finger tips."[21] She showed his letters to her brother and mother who were in tears.[22]

Then came an incident in which they were in a position to take a hand. Arande, preaching the gospel of Briçonnet at Bourges, was interdicted by the archbishop. Marguerite was quite ready to have the king interdict the archbishop. "Better not," [23] was the advice of Briçonnet. What he wanted from the crown was the appointment of better archbishops and bishops in the first place but not interference with their jurisdiction after they had once been appointed. Such intervention by the state, however good the cause, might prove highly dangerous should another ruler prove hostile. Better then, said Briçonnet, to endure the meddling of the archbishop with patience.

The case was different when the reformers were dragged before the courts. There were three agencies qualified to deal with heresy. The Inquisition, was, of course, one. Another was the Parlement, not a parliament, but a court with jurisdiction over deviations from the faith. The president was Pierre Lizet, whom the Protestants satirized by comparing the tint of his nose to the hue of a cardinal's hat. The third was the theological faculty of the Sorbonne, spurred by the inflexible Noel Beda, who was worried that Erasmus would be damned hereafter and Erasmus was sure that he was a damn fool already.[24] This theological faculty could determine what was heresy and then commit the culprit to one of the other agencies for punishment. Briçonnet was speedily in trouble when he incensed the Cordeliers, a branch of the Franciscans in his diocese, by his refusal to let them have a statue of St. Francis with the stigmata.[25] They reported him to the Parlement. Marguerite exerted pressure and he was exonerated.

The atmosphere grew more tense when in 1521 the works of Luther began to infiltrate into France. The Sorbonne had lately condemned his teachings. French translations of a number of his works were made in Strasbourg and sent directly to Briçonnet and his friends including Marguerite. She had read the *Babylonian Captivity* and herself had translated into French verse Luther's meditation on the Lord's Prayer.[26] The doctrine of justification by faith was accepted by Lefevre and the group at Meaux, though they could readily enough have derived it from the Apostle Paul apart from Luther. In the poetry of Marguerite we find expressions of three tenets characteristic of Luther and for that matter of Calvin, namely the primacy of Scripture, justification by faith, and the doctrine of election. Here are examples:

The Primacy of Scripture

Encased in lambskin is the sacred Word
Embossed with markings of a deep blood red,
Sealed with seven seals may now be heard
By those who find that law and grace are wed.[27]

Justification by Faith

To you I testify
That God does justify
Through Christ, the man who sins.
But if he does not believe
And by faith receive
He shall have no peace,
From worry no surcease.
God will then relieve,
If faith will but believe
Through Christ, the gentle Lord.[28]

The Doctrine of Election

God has predestined His own
That they should be sons and heirs.
Drawn by a gentle constraint
A zeal consuming is theirs.
They shall inherit the earth
Clad in justice and worth.[29]

The rosy nose of Lizet sniffed and the acute ear of Beda detected heresy at Meaux. Lefevre was brought up for inquiry. His offense was that he had translated the New Testament into French and at that not from the Latin Vulgate but directly from the Greek. King Francis was not going to have his scholar snuffed out and quashed the proceedings. Then another distinguished humanist scholar was under attack, Louis Berquin. He did not belong directly to the circle at Meaux, but was sympathetic. His quarters were searched and he was found to have works of Luther and Melanchthon from which he had translated portions. He had also done passages from Erasmus. A book came out which blended excerpts from Erasmus, Luther and Farel. Berquin was suspected, but whether guilty or no he had done quite enough in any case. Beda tried to circumvent the king's predictable intervention by having the case turned over to the Parlement or the bishop of Paris. Francis cut the ground from under him by committing it to his own council. Berquin was exonerated.[30]

At Meaux in the meantime Briçonnet subscribed to the Sorbonne's condemnation of Luther's teaching and then went blithely on with his own variety of reform. But Mazurin and Caroli were forced to make public abjurations and on the very day when Briçonnet was released a man named Jean Vallière was burned in Paris.[31] The provinces likewise were affected. The Queen Mother and Marguerite happened to be at Lyons. In this area a man named Sebiville was arrested. He said he had been delivered by "secret friends." One suspects the hand of Marguerite. It was quite evident in the case of a man named Meigret. When he was arrested a Swiss reformer wrote to another, "Meigret is in prison. The Duchess is there, thank God." The Duchess was Marguerite. The case was transferred to Paris and he was saved.[32]

Now came two events which played into the hands of those determined to extirpate heresy. The first was the Peasants' War in Germany. In spite of Luther's violent denunciation of the ravaging hordes the belief could not be dispelled that his revolt against ecclesiastical authority had created a state of civil anarchy.

The second event was the removal of the king and his sister from the scene. Francis started out to wrest northern Italy from the emperor. The Queen Mother and Marguerite accompanied the troops as far as Lyons. Marguerite's first husband was a commander in the army of her brother. She awaited the news of a glorious victory for she was sure that God would not desert

the most Christian king. But the Holy Roman Emperor had no
less a claim on divine assistance and he won at Pavia in February
of 1525. Francis was made a prisoner and taken to Spain.

Marguerite's husband saved his contingent by a retreat. Shat-
tered in health and remorseful that he, too, was not in captivity,
he came to Lyons, where Marguerite nursed him without reproaches until his death a few months later. Then, as soon as
a safe conduct came from the emperor, she hastened by sea and
by land, outriding the men, to the bedside of her brother, too
ill to recognize his *Mignonne*. She saved him for France but not
from a humiliating treaty.

During the king's absence his mother was the regent. The co-
hort of implacables tried to wrest from her the government by
vesting it in the Parlement. She thwarted that. But the Sorbonne
forbad even the discussion in private of Luther's opinions.[33] The
Colloquies of Erasmus were condemned. Berquin was again arrested. Caroli and Mazurin were to be tried once more. Lefevre,
Briçonnet, Caroli, Roussel, Toussaint, Arande and all the rest
of the circle were to be brought to Paris for investigation. They
scattered and fled mostly to Strasbourg where they were enter-
tained by Capito. Briçonnet remained under severe intimidation. A sympathizer, Joubert by name, was executed at the Place
Maubert. Farel, already out of the country, reported that in
France the reformers remaining were as "silent as a fish." [34]

Francis, hearing of all this, sent word from his captivity that
the proceedings should be suspended until his return.[35] When
he did come back Berquin was again saved by his intervention
and the exiles returned. But the circle at Meaux was smashed.
Individual members were saved by attaching them to the court.
Lefevre was given a post at Blois. Toussaint was employed at
the court. Arande was made a bishop. Roussel became the al-
moner of Marguerite. Caroli was allowed to preach in Paris
with the approval of the bishop.

But the intransigents did not subside. Berquin, moreover,
was far from discreet. He tried to turn the tables by indicting
Beda for heresy. To no avail. In 1528 the truculent reformers
enflammed public opinion by mutilating an image. Francis took
part in the expiatory procession and Lizet shouted, "Kill them

all!" Berquin was arrested again. Francis was absent. Marguerite was at Blois. Before word could be gotten to them Berquin was burned. The reformers saw no recourse but to lapse into silence.[36] Marguerite saved Mazurin by making him a penitentiary at Notre Dame. Caroli fled to Geneva. Lefevre took refuge in Marguerite's territory at Nerac.

Then after 1530 came another lull. Du Bellay, the bishop of Paris, was inclined to the reform. Roussel was able to preach in

Francis I in a procession to atone for the mutilation of a statue of the Virgin

Paris to audiences of 5,000. The king and queen of Navarre were in attendance.[37] But the intransigents kept up the attack. They accused even the bishop of Paris of heresy. Francis quashed that. Then, Beda had the audacity to make charges of doctrinal deviation in the *Mirror of the Sinful Soul,* a poetical work composed by Marguerite herself.

Let us glance at its content. Some literary critics have said that it lacks structure. But there is structure. It is the structure of Psalm 42, with the recurrent alternation of "Why art thou cast down O my soul?" and the answer "Hope thou in God." The preface announces the themes. "When God pleases to justify the heart he confers the gift of faith by which one has knowledge of His goodness, wisdom and power. One is filled with love and charity and has no longer fear. This gift of God allows itself no repose until man is made into God. No one can understand this save the one to whom the gift is given." Here we find the doctrines of justification by faith, sanctification, deification and election.

She dilates on her unworthiness. She is a naked worm, proud, indolent, dissembling and thereby increasing sin. "O, who shall deliver me from the body of this death?" The answer is not simply that she will be forgiven, as Luther would have said, but that she herself will be made divine. This assertion of a mystic is given a startling turn when she calls herself the mother of God. "Take not offense, sweet Virgin Mary," she says, "I am of no mind to detract from your preeminence. But did not Christ say that he who does the will of God is his brother, sister and *mother?*" But there is more involved than this. Marguerite, filled with God, felt herself to be a bearer of God. At the same time she was the sister and the bride of Christ, for did he not say, "Thou hast ravished my heart, my sister, my spouse" (Song of Solomon 4:9). The forgiveness of sins is set in this context. "A father," she says, "will have compassion on his son. A mother will never forget her child. A brother will cover the sin of his sister. But what husband ever forgave the faithlessness of his wife? I am the bride of Christ. I have been faithless to him. And he has forgiven me." [38] "O charity, to make me a new creature, to make me beautiful! Dost thou not give me a sceptre and crown in thy kingdom?" Then comes an expression of rapturous longing for death.

> O my God, that death is fair
> Which takes me from this fetid air.
> By death I'm victor in the race.
> By death I look upon Thy face.
> By death I am to Thee conformed.
> By death I languish for my king.
> O sweet death, where is thy sting? [39]

The Sorbonne would scarcely have sensed heresy here had not Luther arisen to emphasize justification by faith. After all, this doctrine is in Paul and he has never been condemned as a heretic. The affirmation that the Christian can be "godded" is in the medieval mystics. Heresy might be detected in the omission of any reference to the intercession of Mary and the Saints, and in one edition a prayer to the Virgin was recast to make it refer to Christ. The king demanded of the Sorbonne to know precisely at what point the heresy lay. The president reported that no heresy whatever had been discovered. The offense lay in publication without permission. The case was dropped and the printer went to the stake.[40]

Marguerite made her response by pillorying Beda and probably Lizet as well in a satirical playlet entitled *The Inquisitor*.[41] This personage enters saying, "I must destroy the new teaching. This would be easy if I had to deal only with the ignorant. I spare no one except for a fee. If an innocent man is burned he will fare better in heaven." He then notes some children at play and tells them to go back to their books. A dialogue ensues:

> *Inquisitor:* Who is your father?
> *Jacot:* The same as yours.
> *Inquisitor:* No, by St. Peter, we are not brothers. How do you get him to come?
> *Jacot:* He always comes without being called. He lives far away.
> *Inquisitor:* Give me the house, street and number.
> *Clerot:* All the children know him, but you don't.
> *Inquisitor:* Is he a gentleman, merchant or mechanic?

The Inquisitor, from a woodcut of 1541

Thienot: Don't try to find him. You won't know him if you do.

Inquisitor: Is he the father of all of you or does each have a different father?

Janot: He is *our Father.*

Inquisitor: Why doesn't he make you go back to your books?

The children then start to sing the third Psalm in the French translation of the poet Marot:

> O Lord, how they increase
> Who seek to work us woe.
> They take the field and smite us
> And they would strike us low.
> Thou art, O Lord, our helper.
> Thou art, O Lord, our shield.
> Thou art, O Lord, our glory.
> With Thee we need not yield.

The Inquisitor tumbles to the meaning and continues:

Inquisitor: What do you call God?

Child: Papa.

Inquisitor: What do you want from Him?

Child: Dodo.

Inquisitor: What is He like?

Child: Bon Bon.

Inquisitor: What does He give you for being good?

Child: Ba-a-a-a

The Inquisitor perceives that the wisdom hidden from the wise and prudent is given to babes, and proclaims squarely his adherence to the doctrine of justification by faith.

But the battle had grown too grim to be won by satire. Now came the posting of the Placards. The story has been told in the previous volume in connection with Renée of Ferrara, but may be here briefly repeated. In the year 1534 on the 17th and 18th of October Paris awoke to find posters in public places describing the mass as frightful blasphemy in the eyes of the Lord. Someone even affixed a placard to the door of the king's bed-chamber at Amboise. This was an insult not only to God but also to the sovereign. Francis was enraged. A penitential procession wound its way through the streets of Paris with all the dignitaries of church and state, Queen Eleanore on a palfrey bedecked with cloth of gold and Francis barefoot carrying a taper. After a non-penitential banquet the day was topped off by the burning of six heretics. Some fifty fugitives were proscribed, including the poet Marot, who took refuge at Marguerite's court in Navarre and by her was forwarded to the entourage of Renée at Ferrara.

After this shock Francis hardened. He envisioned the specter of a land ripped apart by fanatics. Stamp them out. On this score Marguerite was increasingly unable to temper his asperities. But in other respects her influence for a time increased. The Queen Mother had died in 1531 and Marguerite added her role to her own as adviser to the crown. Ambassadors still waited upon her. Both sides in the religious controversies looked to her. The Swiss cities appealed to her intervention on behalf of the persecuted. But Calvin wrote a friend, "Our greatest hope is in the Queen of Navarre but we cannot place on her too great reliance." [42]

The pope suggested to Cardinal Pole on his way to England to assist Mary in the restoration of Catholicism that he call upon the Queen of Navarre to enlist her support for the cause of orthodoxy. But Pole said that he did not enjoy talking with her because she was always "soaring into the bosom of God." [43] and that did not greatly help orthodoxy. She would not come out flatfootedly for either side, but would curb the violence of both. She had no taste for the posting of defamatory placards and the smashing of images by the Huguenots and much less for the burnings by Catholics at the Place Maubert.

Still she was able to save a few of those endangered. Rabelais at Lyons was snatched from the jaws of the Cardinal Tournon.[44] Dolet was a humanist printer at Lyons. Assailed by a thug, he killed his atacker, fled to Paris, and secured exoneration thanks to her plea. But her ability to save was diminishing. Dolet was in trouble again, this time for his opinions, and it proved easier to rescue a murderer than a heretic. He is usually classified as a free thinker. He was a free publisher who would bring out works on both sides of the disputes. He perished at the Place Maubert.[45]

She was successful, however, in the case of Bonaventure des Periers, the author of a book called *Cymbalum Mundi*. He was no frivolous spirit and had collaborated with Olevitan in the translation of the New Testament. Des Periers complained of the Catholics and Protestants alike. He ridiculed those who debated whether garments should be colored green and red or yellow and blue. This was a crack at the habits of the monastic orders. As for the other side, he used fictitious names not too difficult to identify. *Drarig* was a transposition of Girard, the name of Erasmus. *Melancheres* was obviously Melanchthon. *Theridamus* in Greek means a subduer of horses. The word in German for subdue is *zwingen* and this suggests Zwingli, and so on. The Philosopher's stone, said Des Periers, has been broken into fragments. Each one collects as many pieces as he can and boasts that he has more than any other, but what does it all matter? The pieces are all alike. Did he mean that the differences between the Catholics and the Protestants were not worth a tinker's damn or that no religion was better than another? Marguerite quashed the proceedings against him but his printer was imprisoned.[46]

Then came the affair of the Vaudois. This was the name given to the Waldenses in the south of France. Their founder, Peter Waldo in the twelfth century, had incurred the displeasure of the church because as a layman he would not desist from preaching and teaching the Scriptures. His followers, despite many persecutions, survived in northern Italy and southern France. When the Reformation began they perceived affinities with their own views and sent a delegation to Basel to confer with Oecolampadius. Such association with the Protestants may have incensed the Parlement of Province at Aix to pass the *Decret* of Merindol, the name of their chief town, by which the heretics were to be burned, their goods confiscated and their houses razed. Francis I several times intervened on their behalf until he was told that the Vaudois were in armed rebellion, fifteen thousand strong. Then he gave the order for the execution of the decree. Twenty-two villages were razed and none were spared. When the news was brought to Francis and Marguerite he is said to have laughed and said, "Serves them right," but his sister was in tears.[47]

More than ever she felt herself to be futile and withdrew to her province of Navarre where she and her husband for the most part resided. We have already seen how on more than one occasion she made her domain an asylum for the religious fugitives. Lefevre transferred his residence to her neighborhood. He is said, shortly before his death, while dining with her, to have expressed remorse that he had not openly announced his adherence to the reform.[48] Whether to do so or not was becoming a subject of acute disquiet. There were many who did not see that the cause was being advanced by dying and those with families found emigration very difficult. Many of them so spiritualized the church that its outward forms appeared to them indifferent. Consequently they were able to conform to Catholic practices, while cultivating a religion of the spirit in their hearts and by gathering in secret conventicles.

Calvin might also have recognized that Nicodemites, too, might came to Jesus only by night. He wrote several tracts against them. Marguerite felt that he was striking at her and her friends and told him in effect that it was all very well for him to talk in this fashion from the security of Geneva. What would he do if he were in France? Calvin replied:

> Do not think I am insensitive to the plight of the brethren in France, Italy, England and Flanders. I do not reject them. Out of compassion I can find excuses for them. But I must in conscience speak for their salvation and having done so fall on my knees and pray God to give them comfort. I praise God I have never been put to the trial of prison and torture. If I were what would I do? I hope I would be constant. What would I advise them to do? Go into exile. They reply, "Yes, but we have a father, a mother, a household and cannot leave." In that case I say confess to God that you are sinners and wait for a chance to go.[49]

A modern writer has suggested that Calvin had an ulterior motive for insistence on exile. He wanted the refugees to come to Geneva. He had five thousand of them there and upon them his control of the city depended. He would certainly never have admitted to himself that such a consideration had any weight, but he might have perceived what the Nicodemites did for the cause of France. At Paris, for example, during the days of the severest repression, Landry kept alive an underground congregation, and incidentally composed a catechism which Marguerite used for her daughter. There were other such underground churches and when the wars of religion began and the Huguenots were able to come out in the open, France was amazed to discover their strength.[50]

Calvin might also have recognized that Nicodemites, too, might be martyrs. There was his old friend Roussel, at whose conduct Calvin was absolutely aghast when he allowed himself to be named by Marguerite the bishop of Oléron. In this role he carried on after the manner of Briçonnet in the beginnings at Meaux. In his diocese was a parish among the Basques. He preached to them himself and inveighed against the cult of the saints. A parishioner leapt forward with an axe, severed the support of the pulpit and gave him such a fall that he was incapacitated for life.[51]

There was another and even more serious rift between Calvin and Marguerite because she harbored Poque and Quentin, whom Calvin called *Libertins Spirituels,* Spiritual Libertines.[52] Calvin told Marguerite that as a dog must bark to defend his master, so must he denounce these seducers for the honor of God.[53] They held that a Christian could become a Christ. Marguerite could speak of her brother as a Christ.[54] They believed that man can be deified and so did she. They believed that a deified man cannot sin because God cannot sin. Calvin thought this meant that whatever they chose to do would not be sin. He took especial umbrage at their claim that if one party in a marriage were not of the faith the other could separate and be joined afresh. This was an extension of Calvin's practice in allowing one whose partner refused to go into exile for religion to take another.

Calvin thought these "Libertines" were advocating promiscuity to gratify the flesh.[55] He might have considered the case of

Claus Frey of Strasbourg, who left his wife and six children to be joined to a spiritual partner. The town council gave him the choice of returning to his wife and family or drowning. He chose to be drowned and did not thereby gratify the flesh. We are not to assume that Marguerite endorsed all of these views. She was faithful to two husbands who did little more than tolerate her religious convictions. The point is that she would not dismiss these mystics because they were disowned by the outstanding leader in the Protestant camp.

The rift with Calvin increased her sense of isolation. In her own domain she spent much of her time visiting her subjects and especially the hospitals, some half dozen of which she had founded, modelled on the one which she had initiated in Paris.[56] These charities were harder to keep up after the death of her brother, because his successor, Henry II, her nephew cut down her stipend and thereby curtailed her philanthropies.

As she was carried about in her litter on these visitations, she began to think out and record a collection of tales with the title *Heptameron.* The title at once suggests Bocaccio's *Decameron.* The words mean seven days and ten days respectively, that is so many days of story telling. In her book, as in his, the tales have to do with love, love unrequited, love jilted or betrayed, love unfulfilled and resolved only in the cloister or the grave. She is indulgent toward the youth swept into indiscretion by a rapturous kiss and scornful of the cleric who contrives to lure a maiden into sin. There is a chuckle for the monks nearby who hearing of these recitals conceal themselves in a thicket that they may overhear. Each tale is followed by a discussion in which reproval is bestowed on the improperties which have been relished in the telling.

Of course one must remember that this was a society in which the king's mistress was a recognized institution. Marguerite was on friendly terms with her brother's favorite. Writers of the previous generation could not understand how any one could so write of earthly love and yet be enraptured by the love of God. But that was her point, for "How can he love God whom he has not seen if he love not his brother whom he has seen?" (1 John 4:20). The earthly love rises in the scale of being until it becomes the heavenly. This is Platonic. But then all the warblings of the lovers in the Song of Solomon become the words of the Savior to his earthly bride. Some of the tales are altogether decorous. There is the one of a sailor, neglectful of his wife, who sends a diamond to his sweetheart. She sends it as if from him to the wife. A reconciliation follows and of course everlasting happiness ensues.

There is another little piece called *The Coach* [57] which strikes a deeper note. The authoress withdraws from the frivolous world (The accompanying woodcut shows only a very proper picnic in the woods.) and retires to a sylvan glade where she encounters three dolorous dames whose laments voice the languishings of courtly love. The first two can neither love nor be loved. The third loves and is loved. Her grief is separation, but a deeper grief is that she cannot shake off concern for the pangs of the other two. She has learned that the Christian can never enjoy undiluted bliss so long as others suffer. The discussion is cut short by a minor calamity. A pelting rain drives them to their coach and provides a subject for a charming woodcut.

Woodcut from *The Coach*

A devastating calamity was in store for the queen. Her brother Francis was on the point of death. Her days were spent in agonies of prayer. For two weeks his death was concealed from her. Then, entering a church, and hearing the sobbing of a peasant woman, she went over to give her comfort. The woman said, "Madame, I am not weeping for myself, but for you." [58] For three months Marguerite isolated herself in meditation and prayer. Then found expression for her grief in a dialog between herself on earth and her brother in heaven.[59]

> *Francis: Ma Mignonne,* my darling sister, why is your face so pale? Why not put off your weeds? Why not laugh as once you did to cheer me up?
>
> *Marguerite:* Francis! It is your voice. Would God that I were dead. When you were here my life was milk and honey, now gall and wormwood.
>
> *Francis:* But sister, my Pearl (Marguerite means pearl) have you forgotten the pearl of the gospel? I am a Christian. I am here with the Lord and with the saints.
>
> *Marguerite:* The half of me is dead. My laugh is withered

Woodcut from *The Coach*

at the root. Fifty and two years we were together. I did not
know that love could grow through death. But now I know.
Francis: Don't wear out the angels with your cries. A little
weeping is all right. But don't overdo. If you wait in patience
you will be doubly blessed. Here my soul is bathed in light.
Love is the light and charity the fire. He who was hated
now is loved. The peasant is ennobled and the proud king
brought low. The old dream dreams. The untutored preach.
He who knows the love of God knows that for love of us
He sent His Son to hell. If the golden dart of love had
pierced your heart other loves would die. Blessed am I and
blessed you, if you can sense my felicity. I am a citizen of
heaven. Close the eye of the flesh. Open the eye of the spirit
and we two shall be with our Lord conjoined and dwell in
the circle of the saints.
Marguerite: Yes, my brother, I know that you are sitting
at the banquet of the Lord, but I am not there. I ought to
rejoice in the spirit, but my frail clay cannot rejoice when
yours is ashes. You came last into this cruel mortal maze and
you have been taken first to the garden of the Lord. I will
drink my cup and sip my soup, but God, let me not forget
my perfect prince. If to love too much is a sin then I
have sinned. Forgive me, but forgive me more that I have
not loved enough. I have not loved the good which dwells
above and dwelt in him. I know we shall all be resurrected,
but I just can't wait.
Francis: Sister prepare for death. Use your cross as a ladder.
Goodbye dear sister. We shall meet in paradise.

The greatest literary work of the queen of Navarre came in
the waning years of hopes belied. The alchemy had been reversed and the gold converted into lead. She had lived through
the burnings at the Place Maubert, the massacre at Merindol,
flights of exiles and returns and flights again, stately processions,
sumptuous repasts and the shrieks of burning men, prisons, tor-
tures and the stake and all for the love of Jesus and of God. Her
longest and her greatest poem, entitled *Prisons,* is a recital of
the vanities of earth's delights, truly delights, but prisons in the

end, tarnished by greed, lust, ambition and the love of self.
Even the very church with mystical allure is not without alloy.

> Churches entrance me with their ancient towers
> Triumphant portals and chimes that mark the hours
> Altars within, with silver marked and gold,
> Given lavishly by those of old.
> They hoarded not their goods and lands but gave
> As if by prayers perpetual mankind to save.
> The candles flicker and the torches flare,
> While bells harmonious reverberate in air.
> 'Paradise is this,' I say to me,
> 'Chants melodious, organs with holy glee
> Reverent priests with sermons that console
> To bring the seeker to his cherished goal.
> I am in rapture, Lord, my altar Thou.
> My pilgrimage in Thee is ended now.'
> Then in my fancy comes hypocrisy
> With sweet seduction she entices me.
> For honor says I should a church endow.
> Or give a fee to break my wedding vow.
> Let me devote some of my sordid gain
> To house a relic brought by Charlemagne.[60]

"Vanity of vanities!" So is it with life's every charm, the "spacious firmament," the starry sky, gardens, woods and flowering nooks, games and the diversions at the courts of kings, all give but a momentary flush of mirth, then wither or are tarnished by the sons of Cain. Only in the realm above this mortal flesh, above the strivings vain and lust of power, only beyond the last frontier shall we find peace, merely approximated now as we the naught are drawn into the Whole, in the rapturous union of the bridegroom and the bride, in loss of self within the Savior's wounded side.

Joyfully she awaits the order of release:

> Lord, when shall come the festal day
> So ardently desired
> That I shall be by love upraised
> And seated at Thy side,
> The rapture of this nuptial joy
> Denudes me quite.
> Seductions of love and fame
> No more delight.

Assuage my streaming eyes
And hear my sigh.
And may I have a gentle sleep
When I shall die.[61]

Her wish was granted four days before Christmas of the year
1549. Scarcely could it have seemed to her that there were yet
seven thousand who had not bowed the knee to Baal. But she
had so harrowed the soil of Navarre that it became the most
fruitful field of the Huguenot movement to be spearheaded by
her daughter, Jeanne d'Albret.

CHRONOLOGY

1492	April 11. Birth of Marguerite.
1494	September 12. Birth of Francis.
1509	Marriage to Charles duc d'Alençon.
1519	Luther's writings infiltrate into France.
1521	Marguerite begins to correspond with Briçonnet.
1523	First arrest of Berquin.
1524	Sebiville and Meigret preaching at Grenoble and Lyons.
1525	Peasants' War in Germany.
	Battle of Pavia. Francis captured and taken to Spain.
	Death of Marguerite's husband. She follows Francis to Spain.
	Scattering of the circle of Meaux.
1526	Return of Francis and Marguerite and some fugitives.
	Second arrest of Berquin.
1527	Marriage of Marguerite to Henri d'Albret. She is Queen of Navarre.
1528	Birth of Jeanne d'Albret.
	Mutilation of an image of the virgin.
1529	Berquin burned.
1531	*Miroir de l'Ame Pechereuse.*
	Death of Louise of Savoie.
1533	The Sorbonne sniffs heresy in Marguerite's *Miroir.*
1534	The Placards. Severe persecution.
1536	Marguerite's *Inquisiteur.*
1545	Massacre of the Vaudois.
	Calvin writes her against the Nicodemites and *Libertins.*
1547	March 31. Death of Francis I.
1549	December 21. Death of Marguerite.

BIBLIOGRAPHY

WORKS OF MARGUERITE OF NAVARRE

The Heptameron is in many editions and English translations.

Les Marguerites de la Marguerite. ed. Felix Frank, 4 vols. (Paris, 1873).

A facsimile of the edition at Lyon, 1547 in *Classiques de la Renaissance en France* (Wakefield, Yorkshire, 1970).

Dernières Poésies de Marguerite de Navarre. ed. Abel Lenfranc (Paris, 1896).

Théatre Profane. ed. Verdun L. Saulnier (Paris, 1946).

In the series *Textes Litteraires Français,* Droz, Geneva 1971.
La Coche, ed. Robert Marichal.
Chansons Spirituelles, ed. George Dottin.

Lettres de Marguerite d'Angoulême, ed. F. Genin (Paris, 1841).

Nouvelles Lettres de la Reine de Navarre, ed. F. Genin (Paris, 1842).

Répertoire analytique et chronologique de la Correspondance de Marguerite d'Angoulême . . . (Paris, 1930). With some new letters.

Herminjard, A. L., *Correspondance des Réformateurs,* 9 vols. (Geneva and Paris, 1886-97). Gives several to and from Marguerite and many references to her in the letters of her contemporaries.

Calvini Opera, Corpus Reformatorum, several letters. For references to her see the index in volume XXII. (Abbr. *Cal. Op.*).

See also Becker below.

Biography:

Jourda, Pierre, *Marguerite d'Angoulême,* 2 vols. (Paris, 1930).
Reviewed in detail by Augustin Renaudet, "Marguerite de Navarre à propos d'un ouvrage récent," *Révue du Seizième Siècle* XVIII (1931) 272-308.

Ideas:

Lenfranc, Abel, "Marguerite de Navarre et le Platonisme de la Renaissance," *Bibliothèque de l'École des Chartres* XLIII (1897), 258-292 and LIX (1898), 712-757. Documents her indebtedness to the various strains in the Platonic tradition.
Les Idées réligieuses de Marguerite de Navarre (Paris, 1898). Shows the affinity of her thought with that of Calvin.

Becker, Ph.-A., "Marguerite Duchesse d'Alençon et Guillaume Briçonnet," *Bulletin de la Société pour l'Histoire du Protestantisme Français* (Abbr. *BSHPF*) 393-477 and 661-667. Extensive quotations with comments. A full publication is projected by Christine Martineau and Christian Grouselle who have made a beginning in the *Bibliothèque d'Humanisme et Renaissance* XXXII (1970), 559-577.

Sckommodau, Hans, "Die religiösen Dichtungen Margarets von Navarra," *Arbeitsgemeinschaft für Forschung des Landes Nordrhein-Westfalen* XXXVI (Köln, 1954) with additional quotations from the manuscript correspondence.

General Background:

Imbart de la Tour, Pierre, *Les Origines de la Réforme,* III *L'Évangélisme* 1521-38 (Paris, 1914).

Moore, W. G., *La Réforme Allemande et la Littérature Française,* (Strasbourg, 1930).

Contemporaries:

Berquin, Louis: Nathanaël Weiss, "Louis de Berquin son premier proces 1523," *BSHPF* (for full title see under Becker above) LXVII (1918), 162 ff.

Margaret (Mann) Phillips, "Louis de Berquin et L' 'Enchiridion' d'Erasme," *Revue du Seizième Siècle* XVIII (1931), 89-103 and 309-323. She discovered a translation of Erasmus together with passages from Luther and Farel.

Bonaventure des Periers: Adolf Cheneirère, *Bonaventure des Periers* (Paris, 1886).
Cymbalum Mundi, ed. Felix Frank (Paris, 1873).

Farel, William: Comité Farel, *Guillaume Farel* . . . (Neuchatel, 1930).

Meigret, Aimé: Henry Guy, "Le Sermon d'Aimé Meigret," *Mélanges Offerts à Alfred Jeanroy* (Paris, 1928), 583-595.
Nathanaël Weiss, "Le Réformateur Aimé Meigret," *BSHPF* XXXIX (1890), 245-253.

Roussel, Gérard: C. Schmidt, *Gérard Roussel* (Strasbourg, 1845).

Sainte-Marthe: Caroline Ruutz-Rees, *Charles de Sainte-Marthe* (New York, 1910). Important because his funeral oration gives a brief and vivid sketch of Marguerite.

Toussaint Piere: *Jean Viénot, Histoire de la Réforme dans le pays de Montbéliard*, 2 vols. (Montbeliard, 1900). See volume I, chapter 1.

Recent editions of several works of Marguerite are reviewed by Jules Gelernt in the *Renaissance Quarterly* XXV, No. 4, Winter, 1972, pp. 464-467. These appeared too late to be utilized here.

NOTES

1. Frank, *Marguerites*, III, 206.
2. Génin, *Nouvelles Lettres*, No. 50, 906.
3. Imbart, *Origines* III, 238.
4. Lenfranc, *Idées*, 109.
5. Herminjard, *Correspondance*, VII, No. 1084, p. 391.
6. Jourda, *Marguerite*, I, 212.
7. Renaudet questions her knowledge of Greek, *Révue*, 276.
8. W. G. Moore, *La Réforme*, Appendix I.
9. Imbart, 191 and Renaudet, 286.
10. Lenfranc, 28.
11. See the bibliography under *Letters*.
12. Sckommodau, *Arbeitsgemeinschaft*, 33-45.
13. Lenfranc, *Dernières Poésies*, 212 and Lenfranc, *Bibliothèque*, 282.
14. *Dernières Poésies*, 250.
15. *Ibid.*, 390.
16. Imbart, 111 ff., 163-164, 179.
17. Herminjard, I, No. 115, p. 265.
18. Imbart, 121.
19. *Ibid.*, 118.
20. *Ibid.*, 119.
21. Becker, *BSHPF*, XLIX, 411.
22. *Ibid.*, Herminjard, I, No. 48, p. 85 note.
23. Becker, 448. Herminjard, I, Nos. 93 and 94.

24. Allen, *Erasmi Epistolae,* VI, 362.
25. Herminjard, I, No. 36, p. 67, note 4.
26. See note 8 above.
27. Frank, II, 40.
28. *Ibid.,* 222.
29. *Ibid.,* III, 16-17.
30. Imbart, 229.
31. *Ibid.,* 210.
32. *Ibid.,* 244-245 and Herminjard, I. No. 130, p. 309; No. 132, p. 314, note 3; No. 136 and No. 162.
33. Imbart, 249.
34. Herminjard, I, No. 159.
35. *Ibid.,* No. 165.
36. Imbart, 270.
37. *Ibid.,* 505.
38. Frank, I, 37.
39. *Ibid.,* 55.
40. Jourda, I, 179, 186.
41. Saulnier, *Théatre Profane,* 48-81.
42. Herminjard, IV, No. 566, p. 71 and VI, No. 833, p. 119.
43. Renaudet, 286 and Jourda, I, 212.
44. Jourda, I, 220 and 303.
45. *Ibid.,* 236.
46. *Ibid.,* 236 and the bibliography above.
47. Henry M. Baird, *History of the Rise of the Huguenots,* I (London, 1880), 234-254. On the laugh of Francis and the tears of Marguerite, cf. Farel to Calvin, *Cal.Op.,* XII, No. 643, p. 80. Herminjard, IX, No. 1149, p. 328 note says that Francis better informed ordered an investigation with regard to the alleged rebellion and the damage done. He sees here the hand of Marguerite.
48. Herminjard, III, No. 544, p. 400.
49. Calvin's attack on the Nicodemites in *Cal.Op.,* VI. Letter to Marguerite, *Cal.Op.,* XII, No. 634, fuller reply *Cal.Op.,* VI, 575.
50. Eugénie Droz, *Chemins de l'Hérésie* (Geneva, 1970), pp. 154-157.
51. Schmidt, *Roussel,* 161 says that he died almost immediately in 1550, but Alphonse de Ruble, *Antoine de Bourbon et Jeanne d'Albret* (Paris, 1881), 217 shows that he died on August 10, 1555. He did not function as bishop in the interim.
52. *Cal.Op.,* VII, 153-248.
53. *Ibid.,* XII, 65.
54. Genin, *Nouvelles Lettres,* CXXXV, 243 and Frank, III, 211.
55. See the discussion in *Théatre Profane.*
56. *Dernières Poésies,* Introduction, xvii.
57. Frank, IV, 203-260.
58. *Dernières Poésies,* Introduction, xi-xv.
59. *Dernières Poésies,* 389-439.
60. *Ibid.,* 152.
61. Frank, III, 131-133.

Jeanne d'Albret

2.

Jeanne d'Albret
(1528-1572)

Jeanne d'Albret was the only daughter of Marguerite of Navarre. The daughter is said to have been the only sovereign of the sixteenth century who put no one to death for religion. The same could be said of her son Henry IV and of Philip of Hesse, but her tolerance impressed her generation. Of her childhood we know but little. She was of course given a tutor and, as an only child, a playmate. Jeanne, early aware of her station, thought it quite proper to chastise her friend, who nevertheless, when they had to part, said the more her hand struck the more was it beloved. As pets she had a squirrel, a parrot, and six cocks and hens from India.[1] Jeanne must have had some acquaintances with the Reformed ministers in her mother's entourage but was more inclined to a dance than a sermon and when in later life she published her mother's work the choice fell on the *Heptameron* rather than on the *Chansons Spirituelles*.[2] Jeanne's religion was never marked by the complexities and ambiguities of her mother's. There were no flights of Neoplatonic rhapsody. When Jeanne came to embrace the Reform it was Calvinism undiluted.

Yet her life was marked by complexities and ambiguities because of the merging of politics and religion. Politics affected her marriages. The first was imposed upon her when she was only fourteen. Her uncle, Francis I, desired an alliance with the north. The duke of Clèves, whose relative Anne of Clèves had just been set aside by Henry VIII, desired an alliance with the south. Francis offered him Jeanne in marriage. She stoutly protested. Her parents may have been secretly pleased but her mother was not willing to go counter to her brother and king, and the father was fearful of forfeiting help from the crown with respect to the recovery of Spanish Navarre. Despite repeated protestations from Jeanne the marriage was carried through. At the very ceremony she had to be picked up and carried bodily to the altar by the constable of France. After the ceremony the duke of Clèves fulfilled the ritual by placing his foot in the presence of the king and notables into the bed of his wife. That was as far as it ever got. Jeanne was not old enough for consummation and, when nubile, the political relations had so far shifted that neither the king nor the duke any longer desired the alliance. A papal annulment was easily obtained for a union contracted under constraint.[3]

She was then free for another marriage. A native Frenchman was proposed, Antoine de Bourbon. The union would consolidate territories in the north and the south of France. He was the duke of Vendôme, a little principality north of Orleans. She would become the duchess. She was the queen of Navarre. He would become the king. Although politically contrived the marriage was an affair of affection. Antoine was a dashing cavalier, handsome, courageous, affable, gracious, altogether charming, though, as the sequel proved, irresolute and vacillating. They were rapturous.

His letters, evidently in response to hers, which are lost, breathe tenderness, affection and utter loneliness in absence. He sighs continually *"ma mie, ma mie,* my darling, my darling." She sends him a lock of the hair of their first baby. He finds it lovelier than any bouquet. When she is disconsolate over the loss of this child he promises to be to her father, mother, brother and husband, "the very kindest and most affectionate husband there ever was in the world." After the coming of Henry he writes, "We have one child, *beau et jolly,* who gives us as much delight as a dozen to someone else." There is just one little note of dissonance after fifteen years. "My dear, you know how often I have told you that it is just your nature to torment your hus-

band and those who love you." Yet after eighteen years he tells
her that he never loved her more.[4]

A breach was to come over religion. He was indeed guilty of
marital infidelity, but that was more readily condoned than apostasy from the true faith. The rift widened when she publically
espoused the Reformed faith on Christmas day of 1560. The view
has long been current that Antoine took the lead over Jeanne
in introducing the Reformed ministers, but evidence lately come
to light reveals an earlier clandestine activity on her part.[5]
How, why and by whom she was lead to the decisive step cannot
be ascertained. Theodore Beza, Calvin's lieutenant and successor,
modestly gave himself no credit,[6] but he preached at her court
for three months and became her life long mentor. He was the
kind to put iron into the blood because it was in his own.

After he had become a pastor at Geneva his aged father in
France besought him for an interview in the hope of reclaiming
him for the church he had abandoned. Beza confided that nothing did he so dread as the tears and embraces of the old man.[7]
Later Beza dramatized the story of Abraham sacrificing Isaac and
poignantly described the grief and frightful struggle of the father
called upon to lift the knife against the son of his age.[8] Beza
felt in reverse that he was now lifting the knife to the throat of
his aged sire. He who had survived that ordeal set Jeanne aflame
with an undeviating resolve.

Her conversion may have been sudden. It would appear not
to have taken the form of release from great anguish of spirit
but rather of the conviction that Calvin's teaching was God's
teaching as set forth in the Bible. One wonders whether there
may not be hints as to her own turning in a little poem sung at
her court in the dialect of Béarn.[9] She may have composed it,
for she spoke the native idiom, wrote verse like her mother,
though not so copiously, and the style is reminiscent of her
mother's skit on the inquisition. Here is a free translation.

> He who would trap is the one who is trapped.
> He who would trap is the one who is trapped.
>
> Three lovely girls went walking one morn.
> One sang, one clapped, one plucked flowers to adorn.

A monk, taking a nap, awoke with a start.
The sound of sweet voices went straight to his heart.

Straining to hear what they might sing,
He gasped to hear praises of God their king.

"I thought you dear girls were without blot.
But now I perceive you are Huguenot.

"And you so young, going straight to damnation,
Unless you turn and seek your salvation!

"Pray to the saints and take the veil.
Nothing else can be of avail."

The startled girls, after consternation,
Told him he was on the way to damnation.

One expounded to him the holy creed
To which the reverend paid good heed.

"But without my habit how shall I eat?
I have never worked with my hands and feet."

"Give no thought," said they, "to what you shall eat.
God will give you bread and meat.

"We'll do for you all we can,
Whatever girls can do for a man."

Thereupon he hung his cowl on a bush
And went after salvation with a great rush.

He who would trap is the one who is trapped.
He who would trap is the one who is trapped.

One observes that the exposition of the Huguenot doctrine produced this sudden *volte face* for the monk and very likely also for Jeanne, enabling her to say, "A reform seems so right and so necessary that, for my part, I consider that it would be disloyalty and cowardice to God, my conscience and my people to remain any longer in a state of suspense and indecision." [10]

Antoine's Calvinism had no such grounding. His motives were political and his policy variable. To understand all this, one is plunged into the vortex of a highly complicated piece of history involving two religions, four families and, in the end, six wars.

The religions were, of course, Catholicism and Calvinism. Among the families, two were identified at opposite poles with the religions. The house of Guise was Catholic, the house of Chatillon, Calvinist.

Prominent members of the house of Guise were the duke Francis, his brother the cardinal of Lorraine and their sister Mary, married to the king of Scotland and mother of Mary, first the queen of France and then of Scots.

The house of Chatillon included Gaspard Coligny, the admiral of France, the iron man of the Huguenot resistance, his brother Andelot, who seconded him throughout, and their brother Odet, the cardinal of Chatillon, who, while still a cardinal, married, then resigned and became the ambassador of his brothers to the court of Queen Elizabeth.

The other two families were the royalty of France. The house of Valois at the outset was in power. Its leaders were Francis I and his sister Marguerite, Henry II his son, who by Catherine de Medici fathered three successive kings of France: Francis II, Charles IX and Henry III. The policy of this house as to religion fluctuated. Henry II and Francis II strenuously opposed the reform. During the minority of Charles IX Catherine de Medici took the lead. Her concern was for the security and stability of France and the house of Valois. To these ends she sought to balance the parties, throwing her strength always to the weakest. If one party was not amenable to her machinations she would shift from conciliation to extermination. Witness Saint Bartholomew!

The fourth house was that of Bourbon, next in line for the throne if the house of Valois became extinct in the male line, as indeed it did. The members of this house were Cardinal Bourbon, who remained with the Church of Rome, Prince Condé. who save for one brief lapse was a commander on the Huguenot side and a staunch colleague of Coligny. The third was Antoine, Jeanne's husband. After his marriage he became heir to her father's efforts to recover Spanish Navarre. To this end he would ally himself with whichever party offered him the greatest help. Jeanne abetted his pretensions, except when the kingdom of God conflicted with the kingdom of Navarre.

During the reign of Francis II, Antoine was in the shade. The leadership fell to the Guises, whose niece was the queen. The duke of Guise controlled military affairs and the cardinal of Lorraine the political. Antoine to recoup his strength capitalized on the growing strength of the Calvinist minority. The Huguenots were hoping that he would bestir himself and oust the Guises. A contemporary cartoon displays Huguenot feeling during the last years of Francis II.[11] The minor characters will be explained in a footnote. Among the major 'he central figure is Antoine asleep under a tree. His brother, the cardinal, is piping into his ear. Coligny's hand is reaching round a tree and twigging his hat, Condé, just to the right of Coligny's hand, is holding a candle to enlighten his brother and is pulling on his own nose so vigorously as to sever his head from his body, to intimate how Antoine is being pulled about by the Guises. The masked

Caricature of the Parties in France, ca. 1560

figure to the right of Condé is Cardinal Bourbon. His face is
covered because he wishes to alienate neither his brothers nor
the Catholic party. Just below him, with an arquebus pointed
at Antoine, is the constable, Montmorency. He was the one who
carried Jeanne to the altar at the time of her marriage to the
duke of Clèves. The constable sided with the Catholics but did
not wish to see the Guises supplant the Bourbons. Directly below
Antoine is the duke of Guise, a pilgrim with a staff and the shell
of Compostella, but with no head because he does not know
where he is going. Moving over to the far left we have the cardinal of Lorraine with a crown on his head and a ladder around
his neck for his vaulting ambition. In front of him is King
Francis in a bag. Moving to the right we have a figure with two
heads. This is Catherine de Medici. One head is that of a sub-
missive maid turned toward the cardinal. The other has an
ingratiating smile directed toward Antoine, who had he bestirred
himself, might have set off the wars.

There was an armed conspiracy of the Huguenots, strongly dis-
avowed by Calvin.[12] The plot was betrayed to the Guises, the
leader was killed on the spot and the captured were hanged in
batches. The duchess of Guise, the daughter of Renée of Ferrara,
made an impassioned protest against such indiscriminate slaughter.[13] Condé was accused of complicity in the plot and Antoine
was not above suspicion. They were summoned to court. To
come meant liquidation either by judicial process or assassination. To refuse would be rebellion.

They chose to go. The tactic for the elimination of Condé
was a judicial process. He was promptly imprisoned awaiting
trial for treason. The strategy in the case of Antoine was assassination. He was given surreptitiously the information that he
would be invited by the king to an interview and would be
loaded with recriminations. He would draw his sword. The
Guises would then dispatch him. He went into the conference
telling his lackey if he were killed to take his blood stained
shirt to Jeanne that she might avenge him.[14] Antoine during
the exchange refused to be nettled and came out alive. One wonders how then he could be sure that there ever had been a plot.

Beza in his history admitted that this sounded like a tall tale but credited it because Jeanne later related it in print and was never refuted.[15] To Antoine then the whisper came that he would be invited to a hunt and would be accidently shot. Condé was condemned to death and his execution set for December tenth. On the fifth the king suddenly died.[16] On the twenty-fifth Jeanne publically proclaimed her adherence to the reformed faith.[17] Congratulations came from Calvin and Queen Elizabeth.[18] Had Jeanne waited so long in order not to compromise her husband while the Guises were still in power?

Now they were out. With the king's death their niece was no longer the queen. The new king, Charles IX, was a minor. Antoine, the first prince of the blood, in line for the throne after the Valois, ought now to have been the regent. But Catherine de Medici outflanked him, made herself the regent and compensated him with the office of lieutenant general. He acquiesced. Was it because of timidity or for fear that a feud with Catherine would injure his prospects for the recovery of Navarre?

In the meantime the Guises and the Catholic party were not quiescent. If Antoine could not be assassinated he might be neutralized by pulling him away from the Calvinist phalanx. Let him be brought back to unequivocal adherence to the Church of Rome. The Cardinal d'Armagnac was commissioned to work on him.[19] The bait was that if Antoine would return to the fold the king of Spain would let him have Navarre. King Philip was sufficiently inclined to be willing to dicker. Would not Antoine be even better satisfied with Milan, long the object of French ambition? Yes, Antoine would be willing to accept Milan, but the Milanese would not be willing to accept Antoine. Very well then, how about Sardinia, worth more than four Navarres? Yes, "Sardinia is worth a mass." [20] Jeanne commented, "He planted a thorn not in my foot, but in my heart." [21] Beza ever after called him Julian the Apostate.[22]

Antoine's reversal shifted the balance. Had he, the first prince of the blood, made himself at that juncture the head of the Huguenot party Calvinism might have become the religion of France. His transfer restored Catholic strength to the point that Catherine reverted to the policy of accommodation. She affected at least an outward reconciliation between Condé and the duke of Guise and thought to compose the religious difference by a church council. The pope would have none of that. He had just closed down the Council of Trent and did not wish another. Very well then, a national council. No indeed, was Rome's answer. A Gallican council would derogate from Roman authority. A conference was summoned under secular auspices and called a colloquy. It was held at Poissy.

Jeanne was in attendance. On the way she had visited the court where she was received with fireworks as if she were the

The Colloquy at Poissy

A. The king.
B. The Queen Mother (Catherine de Medici).
C. Monsieur.
D. Madame.
E. The king of Navarre, (Antoine de Bourbon).
F. The queen of Navarre, (Jeanne d'Albret).
G. Princes of the blood.
H. Gentlemen.
I. The table of the abbess.
K. The cardinal of Lorraine.
L. The cardinal of Tournon.
M. The cardinal of Chatillon.
N. The chancellor (Michel de l'Hopital).
O. Bishops and doctors.
P. The cardinal of Armagnac.
Q. Bishops and doctors.
R. Cardinal of Guise.
S. Beza.
T. Ministers with him.
V. Table of the nuns.
X. The King's Guard.
Y. Swiss Guard.
Z. Secretaries.

Messiah. Never had Huguenot strength been so great. Beza preached in Paris to 6000. There are reports even of assemblies of 25,000.[23] A contemporary woodcut of the colloquy shows Jeanne seated on the right of the row in the rear facing the reader. At the other end of the row sits Antoine. Was this separation dictated by symmetry or symbolism? In the center sits Catherine and next to her the young king. On the sides facing each other are the cardinals. The cardinal of Lorraine is in a chair all by himself on our left. Behind him sits Cardinal Tournon. On the other side are the cardinals of Armagnac, Chatillon and Guise. Beza is preaching in the center foreground. The bottom corners show the Swiss guards.

On the Huguenot side the main speaker was Beza, on the Catholic side the cardinal of Lorraine. Beza's allocution was respectfully received till he came to the question of the presence of Christ's body in the mass. He did not in the least temper the Calvinist position and said flatly that the body of Christ is as remote from the altar as earth from heaven, since Christ sits at the right hand of God the Father. Cardinal Tournon shouted "Blasphemy!" But the cardinal of Lorraine was more suave. He thought to play on the difference between the Lutherans and the Calvinists on this point and had arranged for a group of Lutheran divines to attend. They came too late. The Lutherans did believe in a real physical presence of the body of Christ, though they differed from the Catholics as to the manner. The cardinal directed Beza to the Augsburg Confession. "And do you believe it?" asked Beza. "By no means, except on this point." [24] Cardinal Tournon was not at all happy over this measure of accommodation. Jeanne took careful note of these differences in the Catholic camp.

The colloquy settled nothing. Nevertheless Catherine pushed her policy of accommodation and succeeded in bringing out the Edict of January (1562), which conceded to the Huguenots the right of worship in houses or barns beyond the city walls. Yet this edict of comparative tolerance set off the wars of religion. On the first of March the duke of Guise, with his wife, the daughter of Renée of Ferrara and some soldiers, came on the Sabbath upon a congregation of twelve hundred worshipping in a barn within the city limits and therefore in contravention of the edict. The duke's men broke in. A fracas ensued. The duke appeared and was hit with stones. His men began a general massacre of men, women and children. Those who tried to scale the roof were brought down like pigeons. Anne, herself pregnant, besought her husband to spare at least the pregnant women. Sixty persons were killed and a hundred wounded. The Huguenots were violating the law and might have been prosecuted in court. The Massacre at Vassy was a crime and a blunder destined to inundate France.[25]

Hearing of the massacre Beza promptly protested to the king in the presence of Antoine who justified the duke on the ground

The Massacre at Vassy

A. The barn in which 1200 people were worshipping.
B. The duke of Guise.
C. The minister praying in the pulpit.
D. The minister trying to escape. He was wounded and would have been killed if a sword had not broken in two.
E. The cardinal of Guise leaning on a wall of the cemetery.
F. The roof broken for an escape.
G. Several scaled the city wall and were saved.
H. Several on the roof were shot down.
I. The box for the poor was saved.
K. The trumpets.

that the Huguenots threw stones. "I agree," said Beza, "that the
Church should rather suffer than inflict blows but I would re-
mind you that she is an anvil on which many hammers have
been broken." [26] The duke shortly thereafter arrived in Paris
with a large body of soldiery. He was received with great acclaim.
His contingent in the streets passed that of Condé. The generals
saluted. Then moved their troops to advantageous positions.
Condé with inferior support took his stand on Jeanne's advice
at Orleans. Her own position was now precarious. Antoine made
her a prisoner in her quarters, while threatening divorce and
permanent incarceration. Catherine urged her to submit to
her husband on the point of religion. Jeanne answered that were
she in possession of her son and her kingdom she would plunge
them both to the bottom of the sea rather than go to mass. [27]
Antoine took their son, Henry, into custody. Jeanne enjoined
the boy never to go to mass on pain of being disowned. The
father placed him under the tutelage of Catholic tutors who

"The Anvil on which Hammers are Broken,"
Printer's mark on Beza's *Histoire Ecclésiastique* (Toulouse, 1882)

drubbed into him doctrine, bullied and bludgeoned him until after four months he gave in. He was only eight.[28] Then Antoine committed him to Renée who would surely give him a Huguenot upbringing.[29] Was the father's point simply to vindicate his authority and demonstrate his constancy and after that was he willing to make a concession to Jeanne? Only after some years was she able to reclaim her son and she did not disown him.

Antoine talked of deporting her to Béarn. There was no need. Of her own accord she left Paris on March 6, 1562 going by way of Vendôme where she was the duchess. The Huguenot garrison there rioted, sacked the church, melted down the ornaments and desecrated the Bourbon tombs. Antoine was all the more inclined to incarcerate his wife.[30] The Catholics were appalled by the dispersal of relics. They managed to salvage a tear which Jesus wept over the grave of Lazarus [31] but lost forever an arm of St. George.[32] Jeanne evidently sent an account to Beza, who stigmatized the iconoclasm as deplorable and the desecration as unpardonable. His tone implied that she was of the same mind.[33] We know only that she gave the church a receipt for the valuables melted down which indicates that she acknowledged a debt to be repaid.[34] The same letter replies to her query whether in the Reformed churches of her lands public prayers should continue to be said for her apostate husband. The answer was that prayers should be offered only for rulers in general without mention of names.

After this episode Jeanne, already suffering from tuberculosis, made her way to Béarn. She had reason to fear kidnapping until met half way by a contingent from her own jurisdiction. After arrival she maintained her neutrality during the first two wars, keeping the lines open with both Condé and Catherine. This was especially important because the Huguenots claimed that they were not in rebellion against the king and his mother but were bent on liberating them from the dominance of the Guises. Such a claim would have been manifestly hollow if Jeanne had declined to communicate with the Queen Mother who was to be liberated.

Jeanne devoted herself primarily to local administration and to fostering the Reformed faith in her domain. But the war did not leave her unaffected. At the battle of Dreux the Protestants suffered a reverse and Condé was taken captive by the duke of Guise, who received him with courtesy. Since the baggage was scattered and beds rare the victor offered his own to the vanquished, who would accept only one half and they slept under the same blanket.[35] For these gentlemen war was something of a game. Today one wins, tomorrow the other. Finally both were assassinated. The duke's turn came first. He was advancing, swearing that he would sow Orleans with salt, when a young Huguenot sprang out from a wood and brought him down with a pistol shot. Under torture the assassin implicated Beza and Coligny as confederates. Then repudiated the confession, saying that he had involved the chiefs in the hope of prolonging his life. They both strenuously denied participation,[36] but the

The Battle of Dreux and the Capture of Condé

A. The advance guard under Guise and St. André.
B. The Swiss battalions broken and pursued by Condé.
C. The battalions of Condé broken and pursued by Guise.
D. Battalions and mercenaries of Condé fleeing and taking refuge in the city.
E. Knights retiring in order to reform in the wood.
F. The cavalry of Condé coming to their support.
G. Condé captured.
H. The cavalry of Condé rallied by the Admiral (Coligny).

duchess of Guise, the daughter of Renée, could never be dis-
abused of the conviction that Coligny murdered her husband.

The war continued in the north as the Catholic forces laid
siege to Rouen. Among the besiegers was Antoine. He had the
indiscretion to relieve himself within range of the walls and was
caught in the arm by a musket shot. To beguile his convalescence
he sent for his mistress. Were Jeanne to come he could expect
to be berated. But when the news reached her she promptly
packed to nurse him. Having difficulty to secure a pass through
the Catholic lines she demeaned herself to enlist the good offices
of the king of Spain. If he responded the permit came too late.
Antoine avowed in dying that were he to live he would subscribe
to the Augsburg Confession.[37] Jeanne throughout her remaining
years never doffed widow's weeds.[38]

The Assassination of the Duke of Guise

A. Orleans.
B. The duke of Guise shot by Poltrot.
C. Captain Rostain.
D. Poltrot, having tied up his horse, is praying for the success of his enter-
prise.
E. The pistol shot.
F. (far left): Poltrot in flight.
G. Lodge of the duke of Guise.

Jeanne must now face the problems of Navarre alone without even the company of young Henry who was retained as a hostage at court. Her reorganization of the economic and judicial system was so sound that it remained in force well into the eighteenth century. The religious problem was her main and most difficult concern. Already in 1561 she had promulgated an edict which put the two confessions on a par. Huguenot ministers should not be molested. The preaching of idolatry was interdicted and the mass suppressed at Lescar, but with the consent of the bishop. An oath might be sworn on the Bible and not on the Missal.[39]

This last proviso reveals how closely religious and political matters were conjoined. The introduction of the Reform amounted indeed to a social revolution. Baptisms and marriages together with their records, the problems of consanguity and divorce, ecclesiastical properties and the rights of patronage, all of these were under the jurisdiction of the Catholic church. Changes initiated by royal edict inflamed the populace already heated. There were Catholics who declared themselves ready to die rather than see the two confessions on an equal footing.[40]

As for the reformers, their opponents said they talked as if like Moses they had conversed with God.[41] They certainly believed that Moses had conversed with God and that he had delivered the commandment not to make any graven images. In consequence they felt warranted in smashing images even to the point of dragging a head of Christ in the mud.[42] They attacked processions carrying images and despoiled cemeteries with funeral sculptures. The leaders of the Reform deprecated the violence. Calvin and Beza besought the congregations in France to abide by the law to the letter,[43] but the "rascal multitude," as Knox called them in Scotland, were not to be restrained. When the Catholics reproached the Reformed for their outbreaks Beza replied that at any rate "We break only statues, you burn men." [44] That was largely true. The local parlements sent the Reformed to the stake. The Huguenots did not treat the Catholics as heretics, but some perished in the riots.

Rome did not pass over in silence Jeanne's very mild edict. The Cardinal d'Armagnac, who had been used to break down her husband, was made a papal legate to recall her to orthodoxy. He had been a protegé of her mother. In brief here is his letter to Jeanne.[45]

I hope you will not take it amiss if an old and affectionate friend and faithful subject of your parents and yourself addresses himself to your conscience. I have been truly shaken by the report that in your presence and by your command the church at Lescar has been pillaged, the altars broken, the baptismal font mired, the jewels and ornaments stolen and the accustomed services forbidden. You are being misled by evil counsellors who seek to plant a new religion in Béarn and Basse Navarre. You will never succeed because your subjects will not stand for it. You will forfeit their allegiance if you try to force consciences. Your neighbors will intervene. Spain will not tolerate a different religion beyond her borders, nor France within. You have not an ocean to protect you like Queen Elizabeth.

I know you will tell me you would rather lose all your territories than slacken your zeal for the honor of God but you have no right to deprive your children of their heritage. The fruit of the gospel is not an infinitude of murders, robberies, sacrileges, rebellions, apostasies and all the barbarous cruelties perpetrated by those who call themselves evangelicals. I always excuse the poor people beguiled by the wolf in sheep's clothing, but when the wolf comes in his own hide how can you be seduced? How can you incite subjects to take up arms against kings and princes? The apostles, martyrs and saints preferred death to rebellion even though their rulers were infidels and idolators. I do not want to enter into a doctrinal discussion with you but your leaders are full of errors because they do not read the Church Fathers.

You will say we must follow Scripture. Certainly, but Scripture is amenable to diverse interpretations and the Prince of Darkness makes even the plain obscure. Take the words "This is my body." Look at the disputes. To determine the meaning shall we turn from the Fathers to Calvin, Beza, Viret, and Farel? If they want to dispute in a general council why do they not first agree among themselves? They disparage the mercy of God when they say that no one has been saved for centuries because all were idolators. I am shaken that you, Madame, should abet such persons to the ruin of your conscience, your goods and your grandeur. Join the great lords, momentarily seduced, but now striving to exterminate these seditious heretics. Join them and save Navarre for your son. I write as an old friend and also as a legate of the Pope. I implore you with tears to return to the true fold. Restore the churches at Lescar and Pau. Forgive my prolixity. I speak from the heart.

Your very loyal and obedient servant Cardinal d'Armagnac.

Jeanne replied:

My cousin, I am not unmindful of your services to my parents. As for Pau and Lescar I am following the example of Josiah who destroyed the high places. I am not planting a new religion but restoring an old one. My subjects are not in rebellion against me. I have forced no one with death, imprisonment or condemnation. As for Spain, we differ indeed, but that does not prevent us from being neighbors. And when it comes to France the Edict allows both religions.

Your feeble arguments do not dent my tough skull. I am serving God and He knows how to sustain His cause. On the human level I am ringed about by small principalities providing more security than does the channel for England. I do not believe that I am despoiling my son of his heritage. How much good did it do my husband to defect to Rome? You know the fine crowns that were offered to him and what became of them all when he went against his conscience, as his final confession proves.

I am ashamed of your throwing up to us the excesses on our side. Take the beam out of your own eye. You know who are the seditious through their violation of the Edict of January. I do not condone outrages committed in the name of religion and I would punish the offenders. Our ministers preach nothing but obedience, patience and humility. I, too, will refrain from doctrinal discussion, not because I think we are wrong but because you will not be brought to Mount Zion. As for the works of the Fathers, I recommend them to my ministers. You have abandoned the holy milk of my mother for the honors of Rome and have blinded your understanding.

I know that Scripture is sometimes obscure, but when it comes to the Prince of Darkness you are an example. With regard to the words, "This is my body," you should compare the twenty-second chapter of Luke. If I err I may be excused as a woman for my ignorance, but yours, as a cardinal, is shameful. I follow Beza, Calvin and others only in so far as they follow Scripture. You say they are divided among themselves. So are you. I saw this at Poissy [Where the cardinals of Tournon and Lorraine differed]. You charge that we think Christ has been hidden for twelve or thirteen hundred years. No indeed! We pass no judgment on the dead. I am amazed that you endorse idolatry to the ruin of your conscience and for your own advancement in the Church.

If you have not committed the sin against the Holy Ghost you have not missed it far. You say our preachers are disturbers. That is just what Ahab said to Elijah. Read 1 Kings chapter 18. You appeal to your authority as the pope's legate. The authority of the pope's legate is not recognized in Béarn. Keep your tears for yourself. Out of charity I might contribute a few. I pray as I have never prayed from the bottom of my heart that you may be brought back to the true fold and the true shepherd and not to a hireling. I pity your human prudence which, with the apostle, I regard as folly before God. I do not know how to sign myself. After you have repented I will sign as your *cousine et amye.*

The threats of the cardinal were quickly fulfilled. Philip of Spain conspired to kidnap Jeanne and bring her before the Inquisition.[46] The plot was foiled but the pope on September 28, 1563, summoned her to appear within six months on pain of excommunication, confiscation of her goods, and interdict upon her domain and permission to any who would and could invade her lands.[47] This was an egregious blunder on the part of the pope. Philip of Spain did not wish just anyone to take over Navarre and Catherine de Medici would not tolerate interference with her jurisdiction.

Undeterred by threats, and spitting blood, Jeanne the next year (1564) issued an edict on religious liberty. Heads of households should not constrain children or servants as to religion and Huguenot marriages should be valid before the law.[48] At the same time, for all her confidence in God, Jeanne was not oblivious to the human menace nor disdainful of human aid. She realized that she would have to rely on Catherine de Medici unless the Huguenots were to take over the realm of France, which did not appear likely. From December of 1565 to March of 1566 she was at the court. There was this advantage that she was thereby reunited with young Henry.

Responsibility for her own lands during her absence was not diminished or neglected. Progressive edicts on the subject of religion moved toward the establishment of the Reformed confession. In 1566 she suppressed Catholic processions with crosses, banners and batons because these invited attack. Reformed preaching was not subject to interference. She would like to see all idolatry disappear but nothing should be done in her absence. Where Roman services had ceased priests were not to ring the bells. If a priest retired he was not to be replaced and his income should go to the poor, except that lay patrons could invest whom they would, not excluding the Reformed.[49]

In July of 1566 this decree set off rebellions in lower Navarre, the Basque country. Jeanne is said to have disseminated Reformed teaching in Béarnese, Basque, and Spanish, though no example of such literature in print is discoverable until after her death.[50] But there was enough provocation without that. In all there were three revolts. Her procedure was to suppress an insurrection and then issue a general amnesty. She grew harder when some who had been twice pardoned rebelled a third time.

These wars were exceptionally brutal because war is more

humane when God is left out of it. Some on both sides were crusaders. Others, like Condé and Guise treated war as a game of chivalry, but only in the case of noblemen. The duke said that war is necessary to keep down the population.[51] Others regarded war more as a business. Their troops were often mercenaries. An example from each confession will serve by way of illustration. The Catholic was Monluc, the Huguenot was Des Adrets. Neither cared much about religion. Monluc thought of transferring to the Huguenots when their tide was at full in 1561 and Des Adrets deserted to the Catholics at the ebb. Monluc said he would be a Turk if the king said so. He did believe in the system of *une foi, une lois, un roi,* one faith, one law, one king, and thought the way to deal with rebellion was by ruthlessness. "One man seen hanging is more impressive than a hundred dead." His course, said he, could be followed by noticing the traces hanging from the trees.[52] Des Adrets said, "In war only the first acts are cruelty. Everything after that is justice." [53]

One must add, of course, that many of the outrages were committed by undisciplined mercenaries who counted it a part of their reward to rob, rape and butcher. Monluc was not without a feeling for the tragedy. "The groans of the famished and the plaints of those we daily make widows and orphans are upon our heads." [54] But for him, as for Oliver Cromwell, present cruelties were thought to be the preventative of future cruelties. Jeanne felt that severe discipline was the curb and when one of her commanders failed in his duty to protect girls from the soldiery she had him hanged.[55]

In the meantime, while her territories were being ravaged, the wars were continuing throughout France. At the close of the second war the Huguenot leaders perceived that they would be picked off one by one unless they could unite in some secure bastion. The choice was for La Rochelle, open to the sea. Coligny and Condé lead one contingent. Moving down from the north they hastened to cross the Loire before being intercepted. Travel was slow because wives and children were included and the weather was insufferably hot. When they reached the Loire would they be able to cross? Every bridge was guarded and every

boat commandeered. On arrival they discovered that the inordi-
nate heat had so far dried the river that the horses were able
to wade. Having crossed, the company sang in Marot's translation the Psalm 114: "When Israel went forth from Egypt . . .
the sea looked and fled. Jordan turned back." [56]

Other contingents converged on La Rochelle. Jeanne and
Henry were now together in Navarre. Jeanne was torn to decide
whether to abandon her subjects or seek security for her son.
"I had a war in my bowels. I was beset by the wiles of Satan." [57]
Her responsibility for Henry was not merely that of a mother,
but also that of a queen, the guardian of the prince of the blood.
Having decided to leave would she be able to go? Monluc, she
assumed, would cut her off at the Garonne. She was gleeful to
have slipped past within three fingers of his nose.[58] She need
not have worried. Catherine de Medici wanted her in custody,
not in captivity. A messenger was sent to induce her to return
to court. "I would not listen to his bird calls," [59] said Jeanne.
The emissary turned to Henry, now fifteen, and asked why he
wanted to go to La Rochelle. "Because," he said, "if all the
Huguenot leaders are to be plucked I think it better that we all
go together so that we shall not have to go in mourning for
each other." [60] Jeanne effected a union with Condé and arrived
at La Rochelle on September 28, 1568.[61]

On the way and after her arrival she despatched a number
of letters and drafted a *Mémoire*.[62] Three points were reiterated,
that she was loyal to God, the king and the blood, that is the
blood of the house of Bourbon. The entire Huguenot party
claimed to be fighting a war of liberation to free the king and
his mother from the damnable machinations of the cardinal of
Lorraine. Catherine and the king reversed the charge and
claimed that they were waging a war of liberation to deliver
the queen of Navarre and her son from the clutches of Condé
and Coligny. Jeanne was at pains to insist that her action was
voluntary.

Her *Mémoire* ends with an apostrophe to her critics:

> Wake up. Read the signs of the times. Be not as a man
> of twenty wearing the glasses of a man of sixty. In the just

judgment of God your consciences will be your everlasting executioners. Your edict may banish us from the realm of France but what about the realm of heaven? In God's service every country is home. I have been reproached for leaving my lands open to invasion by Philip of Spain. I put my confidence in God who will not suffer a hair of our heads to perish. How could I stay while my fellow believers were being massacred? To let a man drown is to commit murder.[63]

The letters to Catherine and the king add nothing. Those to Cardinal Bourbon, her brother-in-law and to Queen Elizabeth are more personal. To the cardinal she wrote:

If you are separated from us by religion are you also separated by blood? Have the love and duty of nature ceased for this occasion? Monsieur, my brother, women and clergymen like you, who do not bear arms, should be assiduous in the pursuit of peace.

To Queen Elizabeth:

I address you as one of the royal nurses of our church. I left my kingdom for three reasons, any one of them quite sufficient. The first is that our France is afflicted by the inveterate and more than barbarous tyranny of the cardinal of Lorraine. I would be ashamed if I did not join myself to the princes and lords, who all as I and I as they are resolved under the Lord God of hosts to spare neither blood, life nor goods to resist this horror. The second is to support the king, seeing that the ruin of the church is the ruin of the realm. My son and I are opposing those who, trading on the goodness of the king, have violated the Edict of Pacification and plunged us into a pitiless war. The third reason is to save our house. There has been a plot to kidnap my son. We are not guilty of *lèse majesté*. We are faithful to our king and our God.

This letter addressed to the English queen is signed not Jeanne but Jane.

She was to spend three years at La Rochelle, momentous years for French Protestantism. Her direct participation in the events is often only conjectural. For example we can only infer her attitude to the structure of the Reformed church.[64] Should be it congregational with the local congregations autonomous or presbyterian with presbyteries, synods and a general assembly? The favorite tutor of her son favored decentralization, but this might spell the disintegration of the movement under such pressures. The proponent of centralization was her mentor, Beza, but a general assembly might head up a state within the state and give color to the charge of disrupting the constitution. At any rate Jeanne favored the great synod which met at La Rochelle. She was probably responsible for securing Beza as the moderator. She signed all of the decisions and posed a question to the synod: Might she employ Catholics in the civil administration of Navarre? The answer was to prefer the Reformed, to reject the obdurate Catholics, to employ those amenable to instruction.

There is no question that at La Rochelle she exercised the functions of a queen. She levied taxes, issued letters of mark to privateers to capture vessels with rich cargoes for the prosecution of the war. She assumed the burden of sixty thousand refugees who poured into the city.[65] When the commander, La Noue, suffered the shattering of his left arm she held it during the amputation. A smith fashioned for him an iron arm which enabled him to manage his horse. He was called thereafter *Bras de Fer* (Arm of Iron).[66] Jeanne herself worked on the fortifications.[67]

Then came a frightful blow. At the battle of Jarnac, Condé was captured and treacherously shot. His death meant more than the death of a general. It imperilled the theory of the Huguenot resistance that a private citizen should not take arms against the state but a lower magistrate might resist a higher. In this case the princes of the blood could restrain the king. Condé was a prince of the blood. What now? Jeanne had the answer. She rushed at once to the dispirited troops and rallied their courage by presenting to them two princes of the blood, her own son, Henry, and his cousin, the son of Condé. Of the two the higher was Henry of Navarre.[68]

But Jeanne did not want this ghastly struggle to continue. She addressed pleas to the king and his mother. To the king she wrote:

> It is not true that we do not trust your virtue, magnanim-ity and integrity. Prompted by the sincerity of my heart and confidence in your natural goodness and fatherly love for your people I beg you take to heart the misery which this war has inflicted. If you will give to one religion as to the other a general repose your renown will be celebrated by all nations and you will enjoy the fruit of an immortal glory.

And to Catherine:

> You have not replied to our demands for liberty of con-science, with the free exercise of our religion, restitution of goods, honor and dignities. I cannot believe that you would reduce us to the point of having no religion. I implore you with tears and utter affection to make peace. Have pity on so much blood already shed which you can staunch with a word. Do not suspect us of seeking goods and honor. The affairs of the soul are not like those of the body.[69]

The answer was that the Huguenots must lay down absolutely all of their arms. Their answer was that to give up La Rochelle and Angoulême was to pronounce on themselves a sentence of death. The war went on.

Coligny was dispirited with respect to continuance. The two princes of the blood were only boys. The morale of the troops had been wrecked by the late disaster. All reverses were charged to him and he was sick. Upheld by only one woman he resolved to carry on.[70] With the princes he went south to recoup his forces. Jeanne stayed for a time to administer La Rochelle, then in August of 1571 she was back in her own land.[71]

In November of that year she issued her final *Ordonnance* on the subject of religion. She had long been troubled by the desire to constrain the conscience of none and her obligation as a

Christian ruler to forestall the horrible fury of the judgment of God on idolators. Now that the better part of the land had already embraced the Reform she wished to invest it with a formal establishment. Her edict was actually milder than the recent practice of her lieutenants. She expected her subjects to subscribe to the confession of La Rochelle but did not prosecute those who declined. The mass continued to be celebrated in the villages. The most serious problem was the disposal of ecclesiastical revenues. She argued that the benefactions had been given for the glory of God. Since only the Reformed faith ministered to the glory of God a transfer was in accord with the intent of the donors. The money should not go into the pockets of the nobles or the coffers of the state but should be used for the Reformed ministers, schools—she established a university— and the relief of the poor. But she did allow some funds to be used for the expenses of the war.[72]

Hostilities were terminated by the Peace of St. Germain in August 1571 partly as a result of Huguenot victories and partly through general exhaustion. Neither side was satisfied with the peace. Catherine embarked, therefore, again on her policy of reconciliation. This time she employed the ancient but ineffective device of a marriage between representatives of the rival factions. Henry of Navarre, a Bourbon and a Huguenot should marry Marguerite, a Valois, the daughter of Catherine de Medici and a Catholic. Jeanne was in agony. She feared Henry would be debauched by the license of a dissolute court and seduced into defection from the Reformed faith. "To be sure," she told him, "Marguerite is beautiful, discreet and graceful but she has been brought up in a vicious environment and she is Catholic." [73] Quite right! Marguerite told her mother, "I am entirely at your disposal but you must bear in mind that I am very Catholic." [74] What would happen if she became the queen of Navarre and undertook to restore the mass? The Huguenot leaders favored the match. Jeanne submitted but insisted that the ceremony should be celebrated by the cardinal of Bourbon not as a cardinal but as an uncle, and clad not in vestments but in civil attire.

When Jeanne at last gave her consent she outdid herself to

make the marriage a gala event. Anne wrote to her mother Renée, "Jeanne is amazingly courageous. She is bedecking herself with pearls." Jewels for Henry, widow's weeds for Antoine and herself spitting blood! Her husband was right that she was not easy to live with and the little girl was right that the more she spanked the more her hand was loved. The comment of Anne is an example. Jeanne had been stingingly critical of her because after the assassination of her husband she had taken the duke of Nemours away from the girl he had made pregnant. Jeanne took the girl and the babe under her roof. Then there was the duchess of Nevers who strongly resented Jeanne's charge against her mother of having plagarized the *Heptameron*. Now as Jeanne's body lay in state in her chamber the young duchess came, three times made obeisance and kissed her hand.[75]

Jeanne did not live to see the massacre of St. Bartholomew, which the wedding made possible because all of the Huguenots leaders were assembled for the event. The Guises sought vengeance on Coligny, still held responsible for the assassination of the duke. A shot wounded but did not kill. Catherine perceived that this would set off the wars again and resolved to forestall the possibility by liquidating the Huguenot leadership on the eve of St. Bartholomew. Henry saved himself by abjuration. Then, when safe, repudiated his forced conversion and rallied the Huguenot remnant. Charles IX was succeeded by Henry III. When he was assassinated Henry of Navarre became Henry IV of France, but found after three more wars that he could govern France only as a Catholic. Therefore he said, "Paris is worth a mass," and having submitted, promulgated the Edict of Nantes in the spirit of Jeanne d'Albret.

CHRONOLOGY

1528   Jeanne's birth, Jan. 17

1541   Marriage to duke of Cleves, June 14

1547   Death of Francis I, March 31

1548   Marriage to Antoine, Oct. 20

1549   Death of Marguerite, Dec. 21

1551   Birth of Henry (Died as infant)

1553   Birth of Henry (Later king)

1555   Death of Henri d'Albret

1557   Antoine encourages Huguenots

1558   Jeanne at Paris

1559   Birth of Catherine, Feb. 7
        Return to south
        Death of Henry II, July 10

1560   Conspiracy of Amboise suppressed
        Death of Francis II, Dec. 5
        Jeanne announces her conversion, Dec. 20

1561   Edict on equality of confessions
        Jeanne goes to Paris
        Colloquy of Poissy, Sept.-Oct.

1562   Edict of January
        Massacre of Vassy, March 1
        Jeanne leaves Paris, March 6; Iconoclasm at Vendome
        Antoine's defection, March 22
        Jeanne in the south
        Battle of Dreux, Condé captured, Dec. 19

1563   Duke of Guise assassinated, Feb. 18
        Interchange with Cardinal d'Armagnac, Aug.
        Excommunication by the pope, Sept. 28

1564   Edict on religious liberty

1565/6 At court, Dec.-Mar.

1566   Edict restricting Catholicism; Rebellions

1567   Jeanne at Pau, Jan. 4

1568   Jeanne at Nerac, Aug. 8
        Arrival at La Rochelle, Sept. 28

1569   Battle of Jarnac, Condé killed, March 13

1571   Jeanne in the south
        Reform established, Nov.

1572   In Paris for the wedding, May 16
        Death, June 9

BIBLIOGRAPHY

Biographies:

Roelker, Nancy Lyman, *Queen of Navarre Jeanne d'Albret* (Cambridge, Mass., 1968). The standard life.

Ruble, Alphonse de, *Antoine de Bourbon et Jeanne d'Albret,* 4 vols., (Paris, 1881-1886), well documented.

——— *Le Mariage de Jeanne d'Albret* (Paris, 1877).

——— *Jeanne d'Albret et la Guerre Civile* (Paris, 1897).

Background:

Romier, Lucien, *Catholiques et Huguenots à la Cour de Charles IX,* (Paris, 1924).

Thompson, James Westfall, *The Wars of Religion in France* (Chicago, 1909).

Léonard, Émile G., *Histoire Générale du Protestantisme* (Paris, 1961). Admirable on recent bibliography.

Kingdon, Robert, *Geneva and the Coming of the Wars of Religion* (Paris, 1956).

——— *The Consolidation of the French Protestant Movement 1564-72* (University of Wisconsin, Madison, 1967).

Delaborde, Jules, *Gaspard de Coligny* (Paris, 1882).

Writings of Jeanne d'Albret:

Mémoires et Poésies, ed. Alphonse de Ruble (Paris, 1893).

Lettres d'Antoine de Bourbon et de Jeanne d'Albret, ed. Rochambeau (Paris, 1877).

Mémoires de Condé, ed. Secousse (London, 1743), contains the interchange between the Cardinal d'Armagnac and Jeanne, pp. 594-606.

Edicts of Jeanne d'Albret:

Salefranque, Pierre de, edited in *Histoire de l'Hérésie de Béarn,* by V. Dubarat.

Dubarat, V., *La Réforme en Béarn Procès-Verbal* (Toulouse, 1901) Bibliothèque Meridionale, 2 Sér. Tom. VI.

Dartigue-Peyrou, *Jeanne d'Albret et le Béarn* (Mont-de-Marsan, 1934), The edict of 1571.

Contemporary Sources:

D'Aubigné, Théodore Agrippa, *Histoire Universelle,* 10 vol. (1888-1909), Volume III.

Beza, Théodore (in French Bèze), *Histoire Ecclésiastique des Églises Reformées* (Toulouse, 1882). Abbr. *H.E.*

Correspondance de Théodore de Bèze, ed. Aubert, Meyland, Dufour and others.

Five volumes in *Travaux d'Humanisme et Renaissance.* For our purpose volumes III, IV, V (Geneva, 1953-1968).

Bordenave, Nicolas de, *Histoire de Béarn et Navarre,* ed. Paul Raymond, (Paris, 1873). This was written at Jeanne's behest.

Calvin's letters. *Calvini Opera,* vols. XVII-XX.

Monluc, Blaise de, *Commentaires,* ed. Paul Courteault (Bruges, 1965). Courteault has a detailed evaluation of Monluc's history over against others of his time in *Blaise de Monluc Historien, Bibliothèque Mondionale* 2 Sér. XII (Toulouse, 1908).

Noue, Francois de la, *Mémoires* in *Collection Complète des Mémoires,* ed. Petitot (Paris, 1823).

Articles in the *Bulletin de la Société de l'Histoire du Protestantisme Français.* Abbr. *BSHPF.*

NOTES

1. Ruble, *Mariage,* 6-10.
2. Roelker, *Queen,* 124 and 248. Ruble, *Antoine et Jeanne,* I, 314.
3. Ruble, *Mariage* entire.
4. Rochambeau, *Lettres,* nos. xxviii, lxxxii, xlviii.
5. Roelker, 124-130.
6. Beza *H.E.,* I, 180 left col.
7. *Cal Op.,* XCI, No. 2541, p. 305.
8. Beza, *Abraham Sacrifiant.*
9. "Chanson en Langue Béarnaise," *BSHPF* XVII (1868), 477-480.
10. Roelker, 127, from a ms. of Aug. 22, 1555.
11. The cartoon is reproduced from the original in the *Bibliothéque Nationale* in *Correspondance de Théodore de Bèze,* III, 78. The minor figures are these: In front of the duke of Guise is the very young duke of Lorraine emerging from a shell. On the far right at the top the camel bisected by a column represents a man whose fate was in doubt. The knight on a parrot is Maligny who led a revolt at Lyons. Below him with the wooden leg is Marshall Brissac, a commander on the Catholic side. The little old man behind the duke of Guise is the bishop of Amiens.
12. *Cal.Op.,* XVIII, No. 3374.
13. Ruble, *Antoine et Jeanne,* II, 180.
14. Ruble, *Mémoires et Poésies,* 7-11.
15. Beza, *H.E.,* I, 214-216.
16. Ruble, *Antoine et Jeanne,* II, 429 and 438.
17. Ruble, *Antoine et Jeanne,* III, 128 Roelker, 151; Bordenave, 108, incorrectly gives 1561.
18. *Cal.Op.,* XVIII, No. 3315. Ruble, *Antoine et Jeanne,* III, 128.
19. Romier, *Catholiques et Huguenots,* 136, 308-309. Ruble, *Antoine et Jeanne,* III, 268 ff., Roelker, 174 ff.
20. Beza, *H.E.,* I, 371. The words are in the margin.
21. Ruble, *Mémoires et Poésies,* 3.
22. Antoine announced his submission on March 22, 1562, Léonard, *Histoire Générale,* II, 112. Calvin on Dec. 24, 1561 had already exhorted Jeanne to apply pressure lest he defect. *Cal.Op.* XIX, No. 3663. Beza calls him Julian the Apostate Feb. 26, 1562. *Corr.* No. 240 = *Cal.Op.* XIX, No. 3723. and March 4, 1562. *Corr.* No. 243 = *Cal.Op.* XIX, 3732.
23. Ruble, *Antoine et Jeanne,* III, 138. Roelker, 165-167. Romier, *Cath. et Hug.,* 255 and 315.
24. Beza *H.E.,* I, 272 ff.
25. Geisendorf, *Beza,* 191-3. Ruble, *Antoine et Jeanne,* IV, 111.
26. Beza *H.E.,* I, 272 ff.
27. *Ibid.,* 372.
28. Ruble, *Antoine et Jeanne,* IV, 90-91.
29. Roelker, 202.
30. *Ibid.,* 192.
31. Ruble, *Antoine et Jeanne,* IV, 94-95.
32. Abbé Charles Metais, "Jeanne d'Albret et la Spoliation de l'Eglise Saint-Georges de Vendôme 19 Mai 1562," *Société Archéologique Scientifique et Littéraire du Vendomois,* XII, 1 Jan. 1882, 28-46.
33. Beza, *Corr.* No. 252 and note 2. and *H.E.,* II, 105.
34. Ruble, *Antoine et Jeanne,* IV, 96.
35. *Mémoires du Sieur François de la Noue* in *Collection Complète des Mémoires,* ed. Petitot (Paris, 1823), 597.
36. Beza, *Corr.* IV, App. IX.
37. Ruble, *Antoine et Jeanne,* IV, 358, 369, 373. Beza *H.E.,* II, 165.

38. Roelker, 229.
39. Salefranque, *Hérésie*, No. 33, p. 73.
40. Romier, 281.
41. Ruble, *Antoine et Jeanne*, III, 203.
42. Ruble, *Guerre Civile*, 73.
43. *Cal.Op.*, Nos. 3461, 3670, 3374, 3927.
44. Beza *H.E.*, I, 434.
45. Secousse, *Mémoires de Condé*, IV, 594-606.
46. Roelker, 222.
47. Bordenave, *Histoire de Béarn et Navarre*, 120-122.
48. Salefranque, No. 46, pp. 81-82. On her spitting blood Roelker, 231.
49. Salefranque, No. 54, pp. 76-88.
50. Beza, *Corr*. No. 299, note 9 and a brief entry by Schaeffer in *BSHPF*, LI (1902), 606.
51. Beza, *H.E.*, II, 126.
52. *Ibid.*, I, 464. Ruble, *Guerre Civile*, 153.
53. On Des Adrets see Haag, *France Protestante*, (1874, 2d. ed.) under François de Beaumont.
54. Ruble, *Guerre Civile* 208. Monluc's rueful comment in Courteault, *Blaise de Monluc Historien*, 618. In the introduction to the *Commentaires* Courteault shows that Monluc was no worse than the Huguenot commander Duras.
55. Monluc, *Commentaires*, ed. Courteault, 625, 1287; Ruble, *Antoine et Jeanne*, III, 156.
56. Ruble, *Mémoires et Poésies*, 103.
57. *Ibid.*, 90.
58. Roelker, 300.
59. Ruble, *Mémoires et Poésies*, 55.
60. *Ibid.*, 114.
61. *Ibid.*, 119.
62. *Ibid.*, 80-88.
63. *Ibid.*, 204 ff. The apostrophy, 80-88.
64. Kingdon, *Consolidation*.
65. Roelker, 318.
66. H. Hausser, *François de la Noue*, (Paris, 1892), 22.
67. Abel Desjardins, *Negotiations diplomatiques de la France, Collection de documents inédits sur l'histoire de France* I. ser. *Histoire Politique*, III, 605. Nov. 24, 1569.
68. Roelker, 308-309, 314.
69. *Lettres*, To Charles IX, April 17, 1570, 298-301. To Catherine, Dec. 17, 1570, 365-368.
70. D'Aubigné, *Hist. Univ.*, III, 130-131.
71. Roelker, 335.
72. Text in Dartigue, *Jeanne d'Albret*, 147-164. Summary in Roelker, 272. On her dilemma in as early as 1566, see Bordenave, 134-137. On her tolerance, see Nathanael Weiss, "L'Intolerance de Jeanne d'Albret," *BSHPF*, XL (1891), 261-296.
73. Roelker, p. 373.
74. *Mémoires à l'Histoire de France* I sér. X (Paris, 1838), ed. Michaud et Poujoulat, 407 under 1571.
75. *Ibid.*, under 1572 and Roelker, 390.

3.

Minor Sketches

The brevity of the three vignettes in this chapter is dictated not by the relative importance of these women, but by the lack of information about them. Thus it is necessary to sketch their portraits with irritatingly faint strokes. Yet the detail which is present should be sufficient to make their courage and heroism apparent to even the casual glance.

That religion was both an individual and a political matter caused considerable anguish among those who attempted to be faithful to their convictions and at the same time loyal subjects of the French sovereign. Not everyone was able to resolve the tension as easily as Henry of Navarre, who became a Catholic for political reasons and then furthered the cause of toleration by promulgating the Edict of Nantes. The Catholic-Reformed problem was not so easily resolved when it affected husband and wife, as the marriage of Henry's sister, Catherine de Bourbon, poignantly demonstrates.

The religious question affected Éléonore de Roye in a different way. Her husband was also of the Reformed faith, but of royal blood. He was a Bourbon. Together they had to face the peril and sword of the Catholic house of Guise.

Idelette de Bure is of interest here because of her marriage to the most famous of French Protestant ministers, John Calvin.

Catherine de Bourbon
(1559-1604)

Catherine de Bourbon was the daughter of Jeanne d'Albret and the sister of Henry of Navarre. For a decade she was the governor of an area to which she gave an excellent administration. Loyalty to her mother's religion was to embroil her in a ghastly tangle when her brother for political reasons decided that Paris was worth a mass and sought to use his sister in his matrimonial chess game in order to cement an alliance with his former enemies, the house of Lorraine to which belonged the family of Guise, the most ardently Catholic house of France. Catherine was eighteen, a charming young lady with a pretty figure, a fine singing voice, skilled on the lute and versed in Latin. She and her cousin, the son of Condé by his second marriage, were both madly in love. He was, of course a Bourbon, and Henry had no need to conciliate the Bourbons, his own family. One suggestion was that his sister be married to James of Scotland, the son of Mary Queen of Scots, herself a Guise. But Scotland was far away. Much nearer and more important was Lorraine and the choice fell on the duc de Bar, son of the count of Lorraine.

But Catherine and her cousin had already signed a secret agreement of marriage, as binding in the eyes of the church as a public marriage. Henry had that torn up. The cousin slipped away from Henry's side and went to Pau to claim his bride. Henry then instructed his lieutenants to castigate her and bounce him. Catherine submitted, for she was as devoted to her brother as her grandmother had been to Francis I. But there were two impediments to the marriage. The first was consanguinity. They were cousins in the eighth or ninth degree. Pope Clement VIII let it be known that this difficulty could easily have been surmounted had it not been for the second. She was a heretic. He knew of no precedent for granting a dispensation to marry a heretic. Henry told the pope that the best way to convert his sister would be to get her married to a Catholic and told Cath-

Catherine de Bourbon

erine that the best way to obtain a dispensation from the pope would be to confront him with a *fait accompli.* Henry would then see to it that the pope did his part.

But Henry did not have as much leverage, with the pope as he supposed. He had not reinstated the Jesuits and had not promulgated the edicts of the Council of Trent in France. And who would be willing to officiate? No Huguenot minister was ready to marry her to a Catholic and no priest to marry him to a Huguenot. Henry solved that problem by co-opting his illegitimate brother, the archbishop of Rouen. The marriage was celebrated on January 9th, 1599. The couple then went separately, he to mass and she to a Reformed service.

The pope thereupon declared the marriage void and denied Easter communion to the duke. Henry protested to the pope that the dispensation was necessary for his conscience since he had promised it. The duke went in person to Rome to plead either for a dispensation or a divorce. "What a double dealer!" exclaim the historians, seeing that all this time he was writing amorous letters to his wife. But he need not have been insincere. He did love her. To lose her would be devastating for life. To live with her in sin would entail damnation for eternity. He was not as chivalrous as Milton's Adam who ate the proffered apple in order to go to hell with Eve rather than to heaven alone. The duke really believed that the pope could damn him. Catherine did not. She felt his plight but could not compromise to save not his soul but his feelings. The only solution would be her death and that might well come shortly, seeing that like her mother she suffered from tuberculosis. She and her husband lived apart for a time.

We have none of the letters of Catherine to her husband. We have a number to her brother, one to the pope and some to Theodore Beza, who had been such a tower of strength to her mother, and also to Du Plessis Mornay. The latter was a staunch Huguenot who had long and well served William of Orange in the Netherlands and then Henry IV in France. But after Henry's return to the Church of Rome, Mornay was in difficulties.

Here are a few excerpts from the correspondence arranged in chronological order. The first is to the ministers at Nerac, September 21st, 1598 prior to her marriage.

> Messieurs: Do not believe the rumors that I have abandoned the Reformed religion. I will attend the Reformed services in Lorraine itself where I must live because of the marriage arranged by my brother. I know this will not be easy but I will not lose courage. I am sure that the God who gave me the grace to praise him at Paris [she had caused services to be held at the Louvre] will enable me to do the same at Nancy. Join me in prayers that I may be able to surmount the difficulties and temptations which may beset me.

March, 1599, after her marriage in January, she tells Henry that a fever has delayed her journey to Bar.

> I am sure you don't mind that your little sister brings herself to your attention and assures you of her undying affection and humble obedience. O my dear king, how I miss you! I am sure my cruel pain results from having to part from you. I pray God I may have before long the honor of seeing you. Let me close this letter which I have not the strength to finish, by sending you a million kisses, my dear, wonderful king.

Again in March 1599.

> I have received word that you have given an order to dismiss from my service the women of the Reformed faith. I cannot believe that this order comes from you in view of your assurance. I cannot believe that you would be so cruel after I have obediently married the husband you gave me of another faith. I may have to seek help from the Huguenot leaders.

That last remark nettled Henry and he evidently told her so. She mollified him, adding, "I am on good terms with my husband and his family. I look to you to give me the remedy you deem best and that right speedily."

June 1599. To Henry:

The country here is delightful. I have the best husband in the world. The height of my joy would be to see you. My husband has gone hunting. If he fells a deer—he usually doesn't—you shall have the head. I'd like to bring it myself, but not wearing just horns. For like my mother I am of a jealous disposition. . . . I am grateful to you for a good husband. He loves me passionately. There never was a happier marriage. My father-in-law has a painting of you which I cannot view without tears. My husband is nearly dying to come and kiss your hands and renew his vow of fealty. The change of my condition makes me no less subject to your commands. I'm sure there will be no difficulty in fulfilling them. You are my advocate and judge. I took the husband you gave me. Let me know that this obedience pleases you. You are able to make me happy or miserable.

July 23, 1599. To Theodore Beza:

My health is good and so is my conscience. I am loyal to the religion in which I was reared. Though I do not have as much liberty as at Paris, I am resolved to live and die by the grace of God in this faith. I am very happy among these princes who do me extreme honor, despite my constancy in religion. Uphold me by your prayers and I pray the Creator to give you a happy and long life. Your affectionate friend.

August 9, 1599. To Henry:

I had hoped to give you the news you desire, but I am not pregnant. I'm too weak to finish this letter.

November 1599. To Henry:

I hope you will marry again. I think you are more likely to have a child than I.

November 1599. To Du Plessis Mornay:

I hear you are in trouble because of your defense of the Reformed religion. I can offer you a place of security in my quarters. I have to endure sore trials not only because of the constant pressures to make me give up my religion but because my husband cannot get a dispensation for the marriage from the pope. This affects me deeply because I feel his pain, but I can do nothing about it save to lament. The tenderness with which he treats me makes me wonder whether it is only my life which can relieve him of his fear of damnation.

He has been refused Easter communion. This grieves me frightfully, but it does not make me love him any the less. He expresses his distress with such words of love that I can only weep. I am resolved to live and die in the fear of God. Don't show this to any one. If only I can be delivered from all this I shall be the happiest wife in the world.

August 7, 1600. Her husband had gone to Rome and had written her from Florence. She writes to Henry:

My husband awaits word from the pope. He is tormented because he is constantly told that he is damned because of his marriage to a relative. He still loves me passionately. Have pity, have pity, my dear, wonderful king on your very humble servant who has received at your hand a good husband whom she so loves that she cannot live without him. You promised before we were married to clear the matter and you thought it would be easier if we were married. Won't you send a messenger to the pope? You are the only one who can do it. For God's sake deliver me from this Gehenna. I swear before God that I wish for death a thousand times a day.

The duke came home and they lived apart. He thought of becoming a Capuchin. Catherine lived with her Huguenot household. Henry thought he might be able to do more with her if she were close at hand and invited her to Paris. She came with intense joy and quite fell in love with his new wife, Marie de Medici. But Catherine instituted Reformed services in Paris. She was driven to accept instruction in the Catholic faith, but the most persuasive theologians could not shake her resolve.

Henry turned to force, telling her that if she were expelled from Lorraine she would find no refuge in his domains. She answered, "If you desert me, God will not desert me. I would rather be the most miserable creature on earth than to desert God for the sake of men." Henry wept and declared he would never again try to coerce her. She returned to Lorraine, then came again to Paris this time with her husband. There was no more talk of constraint. Marital relations were resumed. The duke fell into a profound despair and besought his wife on his knees and wringing his hands to have mercy on his soul.

Henry was active at Rome. The pope said the matter of con-sanguinity could easily be handled but there was no precedent for allowing marriage to a heretic. A precedent was found. He was still unwilling to assume responsibility and appointed a committee to give judgment. They ruled that a dispensation validating the marriage would be granted if Catherine would accept further instruction and agree that any children would be brought up as Catholics. She was relieved of that decision. A tumor developed. She thought she was pregnant and would accept no medical help lest the fetus be injured. Her last words were, "Save my child." And there was no child. Henry wept but was not present at the service when she was interred beside their mother.

BIBLIOGRAPHY

Ritter, Raymond, *Lettres et Poésies de Catherine de Bourbon* (Paris, 1927). The full correspondence with a biographical introduction.

Davillé, Louis, "Le Mariage de Catherine de Bourbon," *Annales de l'Est* XV (1901), 386-436.

Éléonore de Roye

Éleonore de Roye
(1535-1564)

The career of Éléonore de Roye illustrates once more the intricate crossing of religious confessions and family ties. This little genealogy carries the point.

The Montmorencies

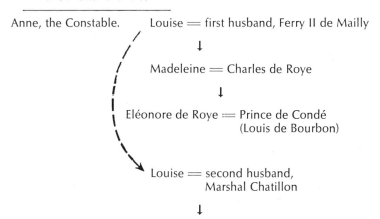

Anne, the Constable.   Louise = first husband, Ferry II de Mailly

Madeleine = Charles de Roye

Eléonore de Roye = Prince de Condé
(Louis de Bourbon)

Louise = second husband,
Marshal Chatillon

*The Chatillon brothers: Gaspard (Coligny), and Odet (Cardinal),
Andelot.*

From this one sees that Éléonore was the grand niece of the Constable Montmorency, the one who picked up Jeanne d'Albret and carried her to the altar for her first marriage. He was on the Catholic side. And she was the niece of her mother's half brothers, the Chatillon trio. And they were on the Huguenot side. By marriage to Condé she became a Bourbon and sister-in-law to his brother Antoine, the husband of Jeanne d'Albret.

Éléonore was married at the age of sixteen in 1551. One would not have expected her to be too greatly involved in political affairs seeing that in thirteen years she bore eight children, including twin boys. But she could not stand aloof from the crises of the age seeing that by marriage she was of the royal blood and by conviction, along with her husband, of the Reformed faith. Her involvement began when he was accused of treason through complicity in the conspiracy of Amboise and together with his brother Antoine was summoned to court, then under the dominance of the Guises, resolved to wipe out the Bourbons. Éléonore and Jeanne advised their husbands not to go. Said Éléonore, "Better to die by the sword than by the rope." But they went rather than prove rebellious intent through refusal.

We recall the failure of the plot to assassinate Antoine. Condé was promptly confined in a room with grilled windows and with artillery planted in three approaching streets. Éléonore was denied any communication whether in person or by letter. Her quarters were ransacked in the search for incriminating papers and she was placed with her children under surveillance in a chateau. But she contrived to get to Orleans. Friends rallied. There was the duchess of Montpensier, who, though a Catholic, was unwilling to see the Guises crush the Bourbons, since her husband, too, was a Bourbon. She was the mother of Charlotte de Bourbon, whom we shall meet shortly. Renée of Ferrara came to court to intercede with her son-in-law, the duke of Guise. He was inexorable. Queen Elizabeth and Frederick III of the Palatinate expressed their sympathy.

Apart from the guard the only person given access to Condé was a priest who came to say mass. Condé said he had done with that long ago. The Guises sent an agent to bribe him into acquiescence to their rule. He replied that the king had no greater enemies than the house of Lorraine (the Guises). A committee came to pass judgment on him. He appealed to the king meeting with the estates, and added that he was not so much a prisoner as were those enslaved by their vices. He wrote letters to his brothers and to Éléonore. She was not permitted to reply. Sentence of death was passed with December 10th set as the date of execution. Éléonore in tears pleaded with the king that she might be allowed a farewell. The cardinal of Guise told her that if she did not dry up he would throw her to the bottom of a ditch. Word reached her that the Guises were plotting to dispose of her also. On the fifth of December the king was dead.

The Guises fell from power. Condé achieved not merely a royal pardon but complete vindication. Then came the defection of Antoine, the Colloquy of Poissy, the massacre at Vassy and the outbreak of the first war of religion. The duke of Guise entered Paris with a large force. Condé withdrew. He was reproached for dallying because he held back from a swift military coup in order to be with Éléonore at her delivery. Then he assembled his forces at Orleans. In a very few days, after giving birth to twins, she set out to join him by coach in the company of servants and children including young Henry, then eight or nine, on horseback. On the way they were pelted with stones by a mob incited to fury when the men of the party refused to doff their bonnets before a crucifix carried in procession. But the party reached Orleans.

Then followed frightful months with ravages of the plague. Éléonore and the wife of Coligny ministered to the suffering. The latter lost her own son. When not engaged in nursing, the women along with the men worked on the fortifications. Condé, Coligny and Andelot brought together their forces and met the Catholic army at Dreux. Condé was captured. We recall that the duke of Guise, who had refused to lift a finger to save him from execution, now shared his bed with him. Another commander was taken prisoner from the opposite side, the Constable Montmorency, the grand uncle of Éléonore. With a smashed lower jaw and other wounds he was taken to Orleans and lodged in the apartment of Éléonore who nursed him with the tenderest solicitude. He testified to Catherine de Medici that Éléonore had saved his life.

Throughout this time her concern was intense, alike for the cause and for the release of her husband. For the sake of the cause she made a journey with her mother and five children to Strasbourg to enlist the aid of the German Protestants that they might supply funds for the payment of the soldiers. Appeals were addressed to Philip of Hesse, Duke Christoph of Württemberg and Frederick III of the Palatinate. Éléonore shortly left her mother to conduct further negotiations and with the children returned to France to exert herself for the release of her husband.

The proposal was that Montmorency and Condé be exchanged. Catherine de Medici agreed but stalled because her position was more maneuverable with Condé in her hands and she could also the better lure him to the Catholic side, as she had done his brother Antoine through the promise of Sardinia. The snare for Condé was to beguile his loneliness with the company of one of the young ladies of the Queen Mother's "flying squadron." Condé, cut off so long from wife and family, rose to the bait, and then moved to an affair with the wife of one of the Catholic commanders. Calvin and Beza reproached him sternly for his *amour des dames,* the more so because he was growing lukewarm as to the Reform. One can imagine that his wife could use the words of Jeanne d'Albret, "He has planted a thorn not in my foot but in my heart."

When at length he was released he did not at once join Éléonore but went off on a military expedition for the taking of Havre from the English. His success brought a warm letter of congratulation from Catherine but she did not reward him by making him lieutenant general in place of his brother, lately killed at Rouen. Then came word that Éléonore was dying. He rushed to her side. When she was gone he exclaimed, "She lives. I am dead." She was only twenty-eight. Consoling his children he enjoined daughters to emulate their mother, but to his son Henry he said, "Ordinarily boys are expected to try to grow up to be like their fathers. I would urge you to try to be like your mother." And Condé went out to join Coligny in the leadership of the forces of the Reformed.

BIBLIOGRAPHY

Delaborde, Jules, *Éléonore de Roye* (Paris, 1876), 1-340. An extensive and well documented account on which this sketch is based. Note in the appendix, 332, Conde's exclamation on the death of his wife. This author did not have access to the *Correspondance* of Beza (listed in the bibliography for Jeanne d'Albret). The following letters are valuable not only for the text but also for the notes, numbers 249, 256, 263, 267, 287. See also *Calvini Opera,* XIX, no. 3927, col. 188.

Idelette de Bure

As remarked in the preface we have but scant information about the wives of the French Protestant ministers. Even in the case of Calvin, whose correspondence is so voluminous, the references are sparse. He married while in Strasbourg under pressure from that indefatigable matchmaker, Martin Bucer. One could say with greater justice of Calvin than of Luther that he might as well have married a plank, for his main concern would appear to have been to show that he approved of marriage. But still not any plank would have done. It must have conformed to exact specifications. Calvin enlisted the help of his friend Farel to find for him someone suitable and outlined for him the requisite qualifications. "As for marriage," he said, "I am not one of those infatuated lovers who captivated by a pretty face kiss even her vices. The only beauty which interests me is that she should be modest, obliging, not haughty, not extravagant, patient and solicitous for my health."

While Calvin was at Strasbourg a friend proposed his sister as a mate, but she did not know French and was much richer than Calvin deemed appropriate to his state. He did marry the widow of a converted Anabaptist, Idelette de Bure, who brought with her a son and a daughter. The son remained in Strasbourg, the daughter accompanied the mother to Geneva. The marriage took place in May of 1539. In 1542 she bore Calvin a son who died after two weeks. Her health was never good thereafter and Calvin was constantly solicitous. Despite her own illness she cared for the sick. When she died in 1549 Calvin wrote an account of her passing to his two friends Farel and Viret. Passages from these letters may be combined as follows.

You will perhaps have heard of the death of my wife. The ministers came together to pray and when one spoke to her words of faith and comfort she betokened very briefly her assent. I added a word. Since she never spoke of her children I was afraid she was suffering less from the sickness than from worry about them and fear of troubling me. So I said in the presence of all that I would take care of them. She said she had commended them to the Lord. I said that was no reason why I should not help, too. She said she knew I would do whatever the Lord laid on me. "The main point," said she, "is that they should be godfearing and upright." As her voice began to fail she whispered, "Pray, pray, all of you pray for me." I spoke to her of the grace of Christ, of the hope of eternal life, of this life's pilgrim tent and of the homecoming. Then I broke into prayer. She passed quietly so that one scarcely marked the difference between life and death.

I struggle as best I can to overcome my grief. Friends do everything in their power. Nothing altogether avails but I can't tell you how grateful I am for everything. You know how sensitive I am or rather how weak. If I did not take myself severely in hand I could not stand up. The cause of my grief is nothing trivial. I have lost the best companion of my life. Had it been our lot she would not have shrunk from exile, poverty and death. While she lived she was a faithful helper in my ministry. Never did she in any respect ever stand in the way. During her illness she never spoke about herself and never troubled me about her children. Her greatness of spirit means more to me than a thousand commendations. Now I am plunging into work to drown my sorrow. Goodbye my dear, dear brother. May the Lord Jesus strengthen you in the spirit and me in my affliction, which would certainly have broken me had not that hand from heaven been extended which lifts the fallen, confirms the weak and refreshes the weary. My best to the brothers and to your house.

BIBLIOGRAPHY

See Émile Doumergue, *Jean Calvin,* II (Lausanne, 1902), index under Bure.

Calvini Opera, X, No. 172; XIII. Nos. 1171, 1173. An excellent sketch in Richard Stauffer, *The Humanness of John Calvin* (Abingdon, Nashville, 1971).

4.

Charlotte de Bourbon
(1546/7-1582)

Charlotte de Bourbon, in her teens a nun and an abbess, ended her life as the wife of a Calvinist, the architect of the Dutch Republic, William the Silent. Charlotte's father was the duke of Montpensier. The title is necessary to distinguish him from Condé, since both were Louis de Bourbon. The duke was a commander on the Catholic side in the wars of religion. The duchess was no less Catholic. We encountered her trying to save Condé, not because he was a Huguenot, but because he was a Bourbon. The father and mother desired that Charlotte be a nun to intercede for their souls and an abbess to enhance the prestige of their house. The mother's sister, the present abbess, agreed to stay on till Charlotte should succeed.

The succession was pushed precipitantly. Between the ages of twelve and thirteen Charlotte was called upon to take the vows. This was on the 17th of March, 1559. She was mature enough to make a witnessed deposition of protest. When after four or five years she was made the abbess there was another protest. At the installation she was so choked with tears that she could not respond audibly. The sisters later testified that they heard nothing audible. They told the bishop they did not want her for abbess if that was the way she felt. He told them not to worry. She could not alienate their property because the consecration was irregular, below the canonical age, by constraint and at the hands of a relative without authority. One wonders why he did not quash the proceedings. She was consecrated and for a dozen or so years faithfully discharged the duties of the office which seems to imply that her objection to the monastic life must have arisen from indisposition rather than from theological considerations. All along she let the sisters know that she would be glad to leave.

Why, then, did she wait so long? What in the end precipitated her flight as late as 1571? One suggestion is that she was affected by the *volte face* of her mother who for the two years until her death in 1561 befriended Protestants and in her last hours was attended by a Huguenot minister. But if this example was determinative why did Catherine wait ten years to make the decision? Another suggestion is that she was prompted to leave out of revulsion against her father's behavior. He is alleged to have forced the baptism of Huguenot babies by the Catholic rite. Then, after the death of his wife, he married a girl of nineteen years when he was fifty-nine and she came from the most Catholic house in France. She was the daughter of Duke Francis of Guise who started the wars of religion and was assassinated. Was Charlotte outraged by having a mother younger than herself and of such connections? There is no indication that any of these factors was influential. More plausible is the suggestion, made several times in the depositions of the sisters that she had received frequent visits from a young man of Huguenot persuasion. Whether he was chiefly interested in her soul or her person is not clear. At any rate when she left with two of the sisters they were escorted by this young man and his brother.[1]

That she was moved by religious considerations is evidenced by the character of those whom she consulted as to where to go. She did not consult her father. She did consult her sister, married to the Huguenot duc de Bouillon. By the way he had not been Huguenot when her parents consented to the wedding. His capital city was Sedan and to Sedan she went. The other person consulted was Jeanne d'Albret, at the time at La Rochelle inspiring the Huguenot resistance. She suggested that Charlotte were better out of France altogether for a time. Let her go to Germany. Most of Protestant Germany was Lutheran and the Lutherans had few dealings with the Calvinists. Charlotte was Calvinist. But one section of Germany had hearkened to Calvin. It was the Palatinate with its capital at Heidelberg. The ruler was the Elector Frederick III, staunch in his Calvinism. Let Charlotte seek an asylum with him and, when the father had cooled from his predictable rage, Jeanne would try to persuade him that a more congenial residence would be in France in Jeanne's own kingdom of Navarre. In accord with this advice Charlotte went by way of Sedan to Heidelberg. The remainder of the plan was never realized for Jeanne's efforts were utterly unavailing in mollifying the father.[2]

Charlotte arrived in February 1572. The elector received her with honor and wrote on her behalf to her father, addressing him as cousin. Most of the ruling class were cousins in some degree. He wrote:

> *Monsieur mon cousin,* since she has left out of conscience, principally for the cause of religion, I trust that as a father, *très débonnaire,* you will take this in good part and so arrange matters that she may worship God in liberty of conscience, obeying you and enjoying the revenues due her according to the royal edicts. May you have health and a happy life.[3] Heidelberg, 15 March, 1572.

The duke replied:

> *Monsieur mon cousin,* just as the virtue of a dutiful child is a great consolation to fathers and mothers, so, as I can testify, their disobedience causes the most extreme distress that can afflict old age. I say this because I had expected to derive the greatest satisfaction from the Christian upbringing of the daughter who is now under your roof. I am simply crushed. I have loved her, cared for her, assisted her in all her affairs as becomes a very affectionate father and now she is so beside herself that, paying no regard to her station and profession and the honor due to those to whom she belongs, she has left this country and gone to a place where she can falsely lament that of which she never complained while she was here. Moreover, my cousin, I am not so cruel toward my own flesh that if she had let me know directly or indirectly that she did not want to stay in the nunnery, I would not have tried to find an honorable way

of retirement with the least possible scandal in order to bring her to a position more conformable to her affections.

Who would have thought that when she had been an abbess for thirteen or fourteen years, when she had worn the habit, when she had professed several initiates and in my presence had satisfied ordinarily all of the exercises of piety pertaining to her office, who would have thought that she was dissatisfied?

I am not sure that she was out to defend the honor of God, as you wrote, but rather to seek the world and the flesh. This is evident because she was accompanied on this journey by two or three dissolute escorts, though I don't find this so strange because such conduct befits vagabonds like these.

I do not believe that she acted for the glory of God and to give me obedient service. I have never heard that the glory of God was advanced by breaking a vow voluntarily taken. The kings, queens, princes and princesses of this crown never acquired the name of good Christians by such extraordinary and damnable means. She is the first of her race to despise her honor and the holy religion of our forebears, to wear the habit of a religious for a span of eighteen years or more, to bear the title of an abbess for thirteen or fourteen years and then all of a sudden, without consulting father, brother, sister or relatives, to abandon all, including her king, and to betake herself to Germany.

As for the claim that she was forced to make her profession, I can assure you that I was not present to make her take the vows. Neither was my wife, the duchess of Montpensier. . . . Besides, she then continued in the abbey without complaining to me or to any of her superiors. Consequently this force of which she prates is just a pretence to cover her audacity. And now she has had the indiscretion to go so far away as to suggest that her life was at stake. Her godliness takes the form of disobedience and rebellion.

I think that a prince of your name and of the parentage of our houses will not be willing to have your territories serve as a retreat for children running away from their parents and especially one who cannot cite a single act of harshness that I have ever done her. She is the most un- grateful child in the world. . . . And now at this hour, de- spite the grievous wrong she has committed, I would gladly embrace her and have her back and treat her as my daugh- ter, if I knew that God would give her the grace to follow His desire.

I am asking of you nothing that you would not ask of me in like case. . . . When it comes to liberty of religion, I venture to say that there is no province of Europe that gives more liberty to all sorts of people or where the religion we carry in our hearts is less impeded. . . . I know there are those who demand of the king a liberty which they do not accord in the lands over which they have control. They have the arrogance to demand what they do not grant. As for me, I will follow the religion of my predecessors. Now that they are dead I propose to continue in their steps, being assured that this religion is the religion taught by Jesus Christ and transmitted by the church. I am so per- suaded of this that I will not recognize as my children those who renounce it.

I will not leave her anything. She has unjustly taken with her some of the goods of the abbey. After the pain she has caused me in my old age she shall not reap a profit from my labors. If you will search your conscience I am sure you will see that you would do the same if your daugh- ter were with me. I hope God will so move the heart of my daughter that she will recognize her fault and submit to her duty. Put your hand to this and do not give me just reason to reproach you for affording her an asylum in her folly, which is and will be recognized as such by all the potentates of Europe, who will not receive her in their lands. I am sure you will act as a relative and friend. I end this long and tiresome letter with my humble recommen- dation of myself to your good graces and I pray God, my cousin, that He will give you the contentment you desire.

Your humble and obedient cousin,
Loys de Bourbon [4]

The duke was, of course, perfectly right that in view of all of the uncanonical features of her admission to the nunnery he might indeed have procured her release. But in that case he would have expected her to be a lay adherent of the church. By this time, however, she had plainly come to adopt Huguenot opinions and preferred exile to a mere release from the convent. She settled in Heidelberg where she was much occupied in the care of refugees. The young man who had escorted her disappears. Another suitor appeared in the person of William of Orange. His fortunes were at so low an ebb as to make marriage to him an act of courage.

William of Nassau, Prince of Orange

We must briefly review his career up to this point. He may be regarded as the father of the Dutch Republic. The Netherlands consisted at that time of fifteen united provinces, later to be divided into Belgium and Holland. The prevailing religion was Catholic. Only later was there to be a division into the Catholic south and the Protestant north. By the 1570s, however, the Protestant minorities were formidable. Lutheranism began to infiltrate from the north in the 1520s. Anabaptism gained strength in the thirties but never attained military power. Calvinism came in force only in the sixties and at that by way of the French speaking southern provinces later to be Catholic Belgium. William himself passed through three stages in his religious development. He was first Catholic, then Lutheran and finally Calvinist, but at no point would he persecute the others. His father was a Lutheran with estates in Germany, whose religion sat so lightly that he was willing to have his son William brought up as a Catholic in the Netherlands in order to secure the family possessions.

William became the favorite of the ruler, Charles V, king of Spain, lord of the Netherlands and Holy Roman Emperor. The arm on which he leaned, when in 1555 he abdicated in the great hall at Brussels in favor of his son Philip, was that of William and this same William was to become the most implacable foe of his son. The reason was that Charles, reared in the Netherlands, sometimes abetted the provinces even against the empire, but Philip reared in Spain tried to exploit the dependencies and coerce them at the point of religion. Whereas the father, though ready enough at times to coerce, would bow to political exigencies, the son, imbued with the spirit of the Counter-Reformation, was resolved to wipe out heresy in Spain and the Low Countries. His exploitation alienated all of the Netherlanders. His religious policy infuriated the "heretics." Feelings became so inflamed that fanatical outbursts of violence erupted on both sides.

William moved slowly both as to his religious affiliations and as to his political policy. He tried to be loyal to his new sovereign and to Philip's deputy in the Netherlands, Margaret of Parma. As an officer in Philip's army, William fought the French and contributed to the victory at St. Quentin, where Coligny

was taken captive. But the sequel to the battle began to under-
mine William's loyalty. Hostages were exchanged to ensure the
keeping of the peace in accord with the treaty of Cateau-Cam-
brésis in 1559. William was one of the hostages delivered to
France. Henry II, the French king, supposing that William was
aware of the interpretation placed upon the treaty by the respective powers, disclosed their intent to wipe out heresy in
their domains. In the case of Spain this meant also the Netherlands. William listened in silence and thereby received the so-
briquet of William the Silent, though actually he was fluent in
six languages. Years later he affirmed that at this moment he
resolved "to drive the Spanish vermin from the land." [5]

He was certainly not precipitant about it. On his release he
undertook as an officer serving under the regent to suppress a
Calvinist riot at Antwerp. This he did by combining Catholic
and Lutheran troops and by promising the Calvinists freedom
from molestation as to religion. Such a promise could scarcely
be kept in view of the sovereign's determination. Philip intro-

Abdication of Charles V, 1555

Riot at Antwerp, March 1567

duced the Inquisition and appointed Cardinal Granvelle as counsellor, but really as director of the regent Margaret. William, thereupon, gave a tacit approval to his brother Louis and a group of nobles to present her with a "Request" that she dismiss the cardinal and discontinue the Inquisition. One of her council said to her, "Will you be intimidated by these beggars?" The slur became a slogan and the cry went up, "Long live the Beggars!" The regent yielded. The cardinal was dismissed. The Inquisition was to be discontinued. But Philip retaliated by demanding of the leaders in the Netherlands an oath of absolute obedience. William refused and left the country.

Philip sent from Spain the duke of Alba, a great general with seasoned Spanish troops, to reintroduce the Inquisition and to establish in addition a secular tribunal to deal with heresy, popularly dubbed "The Council of Blood." Some of the leaders who had presented the Request went to the block. William's son, named Philip for his king, was kidnapped while a student at Louvain and taken as a hostage to Spain, where he was to be held for twenty-eight years. William's brother Louis headed an armed revolt but was crushed and saved his life only by swimming the Ems. Alba said, referring to himself, that "the man of iron had melted the man of butter."

William sought help from abroad and first of all from France, where Coligny, long since released from captivity, was now in high favor. The first aid was advice. Let William create a navy by giving letters of mark to Dutch privateers that they might prey on Spanish shipping. Appropriating the slogan, they called themselves "The Beggars of the Sea," and on April 1, 1572, they captured the island of Brill. Since in Dutch the word Brill means spectacles the ditty was coined, "On April Fool's day Duke Alba's specs were snatched away." The beginning was propitious but insufficient.

Coligny offered more than advice. He would invade the Low Countries and thus strike at the belly of Spain. But French help was not enough. William turned to Germany. He realized that Lutheran Germany would not help Calvinist France, but one

The "Request" presented to the Regent in 1566

section of Germany was Calvinist. As we have noticed the center was Heidelberg. Here William arrived seeking aid and here he met Charlotte. This was in April of the year 1572. In the meantime Coligny was preparing to bring military aid from France. But in August came the news that his mangled body lay on a Paris street after the night of St. Bartholomew. Again William was melted butter. Before his fortunes could be retrieved Charlotte agreed to marry him. This was for her scarcely an advantageous match, and he could not reap a political advantage from a union with a refugee. Three years elapsed before the wedding. He was too involved in the wars at home to come to Heidelberg for the ceremony. She made the journey and they were joined at Antwerp.

She undertook first of all to make the home as tranquil a spot as love could devise and invited under her roof all those close to William by blood. This meant first of all William's children by previous marriages. His first union was with the daughter of the local nobility, who during the three years of marriage

The Capture of Brill, April, 1572

bore him two children, the son Philip and a daughter Marie. The second wife was Anne of Saxony, a German Lutheran, the daughter of the Elector Moritz and the granddaughter of Philip of Hesse, who did not relish her marriage to a Catholic, which William then was. He promised that her religion would be respected and they were married by Lutheran rites. She proved to be an encumbrance, constantly complaining that she was not accorded the honor due to a daughter of an elector of the Holy Roman Empire. She deserted William and lived on his resources in Cologne with the father of the painter Rubens. Divorce was granted. She was returned to her family and died at the age of thirty-three, stark mad. Before the desertion she bore William three children, Anne, Emilie and Moritz, who was to succeed his father. In English works he is called Maurice.

Those gathered under the new roof also included William's brother John and the children Marie, Emily and Maurice. Marie wrote affectionately to her father and became very devoted to Charlotte. In addition to all of these relatives the home was peopled with the six daughters borne in seven years to William by Charlotte.

She was not in a position to bring in her own relatives but kept in continual touch save in the case of her father who repulsed every gesture of reconciliation, even though she came as close as she could to giving his name Louis to her first daughter Louise. In 1579, hearing that he had been ill but was now recovered, she ventured to write:

> My dear father, I am as happy to learn that you are well as I was grieved to hear that you were sick. I have refrained from writing you as often as my heart dictates lest I annoy you. There is nothing in all the world for which I so long as for a token from you. I have enlisted the aid of the King of Navarre to see if you cannot be persuaded to let me explain some things which you may not have understood in the hope that you will forget the past and not be angry with me any more. I do so grieve over this long loss of your affection. The Prince of Orange is writing you, too.[6]

No reply.

In addition to all her household cares Charlotte was her husband's assistant in administration. He instructed the estates of Flanders to address all communications to his wife.[7] During his absence on the field she kept constantly in touch, apologizing for bothering him with decisions about the household. But she did not hesitate to lay before him the claims of the oppressed. Some villagers had appealed to her for redress because more horses were quartered upon them than they could feed.[8] She rejoiced over the capture of Breda by the forces of her husband but nearly split her head lest the settlement should not establish religious liberty.[9] Even the naming of her children was given a political turn. One daughter was called Flandrine [10] to soothe Flanders and another Brabantine to curry favor with Brabant.[11] Queen Elizabeth, when she was being wooed as a political ally, was invited to stand godmother to another daughter and complied.[12]

Charlotte sustained her husband's morale. When his cause appeared hopeless she wrote him, "Humanely speaking it will be very difficult for you, receiving no support, to resist such a formidable adversary, but do not forget that the Almighty has until now delivered you from great perils and with Him everything is possible." [13] Brother John said that "William held up amazingly under his frustrations and it was chiefly because God had given him such a wonderful wife." [14]

William's most severe trials were still ahead. Don Fredericq, the son of the duke of Alba, undertook to conquer the towns to the north captured by the Sea Beggars. He thought to take Haarlem in seven days. It took him seven months. When a fleet of the Sea Beggars was caught in the ice he ordered seven thousand skates. On another occasion three thousand of his veterans in the dead of night traversed ten miles at low tide, though at the end the water reached their lips. William was told that his case was hopeless unless he secured help from the outside. He answered, "When I took in hand the defense of these poor Christians I made an alliance with the mightiest of potentates, the God of Hosts who is able to save us if He chooses." [15] But William did not on that account cease negotiations with the French and the English. There was a plan that the duke of Anjou

Sea Fight

Protestant Iconoclasm

should marry Elizabeth and both would aid the Low Countries. He was made protector of the Netherlands, but to no avail. Louis and his army were trapped and letter after letter to him remained unanswered.

Then came a succession of deputies of the Spanish crown. All were feeble and hampered by lack of funds. When the Spanish troops were not paid they would mutiny and pillage. Resources were not available for carrying through the draconian policy of an Alba, and occasional outbursts of fanaticism served only to inflame, not to subdue the populace. William throughout was coincidentally engaged in armed resistance and negotiation. Yet despite the weakness of the deputies of Philip, the siege of Leyden bade fare to end in capitulation for the insurgents. William from his sickbed ordered the cutting of the dykes. The waters at first seeped but slowly through the breach. Then for three days came a heavy wind which sent the waves surging over the fields, driving back the Spaniards and floating the vessels of the Sea Beggars to the very walls with supplies of bread. Leyden for her valor was rewarded by the founding of a university, at a time when education might have seemed irrelevant.

The excesses to which the populace were subject had driven the provinces to accept the Pacification of Ghent in November 1567, by which Catholicism was to be tolerated in the north and Protestantism in the south. In September of the next year William entered Brussels as the acknowledged leader of the land. But the union did not last. The Catholics formed the League of Arras and the Protestants the League of Utrecht. The division into the Catholic south and the Protestant north had been brought about partly by geography.

A new deputy arrived, a very able military commander, Alexander Farnese, who overran the south. William came to the realization that only the north with its rivers and islands was defensible. Farnese's policy as to religion accentuated the division between the two areas, for he permitted migration without prejudice. Thousands of Calvinists from the south transferred to the north, leaving Ghent almost depopulated.

But if the generals of Philip could not dislodge William from the north by assault there was another weapon at the king's disposal, assassination. On the fifteenth of June, 1580, Farnese, the general, addressed the estates in the name of King Philip telling them that William was guilty of ingratitude, dissimulation, iconoclasm, profanation of the sacred, and abetting heretics. He had married an abbess in shameful contravention of the Christian religion, the Roman law, and all decency. He had subverted Holland and Zealand and had introduced religious liberty. Wherefore as a pest of the Christian republic, as a traitor and enemy of the land, he is banished from all our dominions. No one is to harbor him or give him to eat or drink. That this matter may be handled the more promptly we promise in the name of the king and as a minister of God that if any one of generous heart wishes to do a service to the state by killing this pest he shall be rewarded by the sum of 25,000 *écus d'or*. If he has committed a previous crime it shall be pardoned and if he is a commoner he shall be ennobled. Any who aid him will also be recompensed.[16]

This was just too much for Charlotte's father. The honor of the house of Bourbon had been assailed. He came out with this proclamation on June 25, 1581.

> Louis de Bourbon, Duke of Montpensier, vassal of France and lord of Dombes, to all whom this may reach, greetings: As is well known my dearly beloved daughter, Charlotte de Bourbon, under the authority of the late puissant prince and my very dear cousin, M. Friedrich, Count Palatine of the Rhine and Elector of the Empire, acting in *loco parentis,* and with the consent of the most Christian King, our sovereign the Duke of Anjou, was united in marriage with our very beloved son-in-law William of Nassau, Prince of Orange, etc., and in as much as God has blessed this marriage and made it fruitful, all must recognize it as legitimate. But since there are detractors, let me say that this marriage is useful, profitable and honorable for our daughter and the grandeur of our house.

Let it then be known that we approve and embrace this marriage as much as if we had been present and had signed the contract and that we recognize the children born and to be born of this union as our grandchildren, born in legitimate wedlock, as much as the children born to our other daughters. Therefore we beg his imperial Majesty and all kings, princes and potentates that if any question or dispute arises about this marriage to the prejudice of our children born or to be born that they should take them under their protection, granting them aid and favor such as princes show to each other and we would show to them in like case. Signed and sealed with our own hand.[17]

Charlotte signified her joy by inducing her five year old Louise to embroider a girdle for grandfather Louis. He sent this letter of thanks:

My dear granddaughter: You have done just wonderfully at your tender age to have embroidered for me this sash of beautiful violet silk bordered with a fringe of silver. This is the greatest joy that I could possibly have that you have sent me your first work. You couldn't have sent it to any one who would love it more. I'll use it as a girdle around my nightgown every night when I go to bed to make me think of you. Of course I'll think of you all the time, but then especially. I send you now my thanks and later a present in return for yours. But love me always. And I pray God, my dear little girl, to give you all goodness with His holy grace.

From Champigny the eighth day of January, 1582.

Your very good Grandpa
Loys de Bourbon.[18]

William naturally did not neglect his defense against the ban and first addressed the estates:

December 13, 1580. In as much as the king of Spain and
the prince of Parma have accused me of atrocious crimes
I feel bound to defend myself. I am ready to give my life
for you. I am ready to withdraw to some other land if this
is your wish.

The Estates answered by giving him a guard. Again he wrote:

Feb. 4, 1581. The king of Spain has detained my son and
my properties. He has placed a price upon my head and
has promised to ennoble the homicide. He has called me
a public pest, an enemy of the world, ungrateful, faithless,
traitorous, villanous—insults which no man can take. Therefore I am impelled to write. Since I am a subject of the
emperor and not of the king of Spain I am the more free
to defend myself.

Then came the public Apology, which is here briefly digested.
It, too, was addressed to the Estates. William began:

The children have a ditty that he should not find fault
who is not free from fault. By this token King Philip, with
his irregularities, has no ground for reproaching me about
my marriage, which is godly, honest, legitimate, according
to God and solemnized by the rites of the church. Even if
Philip were not so sullied he could not reproach me. My
previous wife was pronounced guilty by the most learned
men and doctors. As for my present wife, her father the
duke of Montpensier, after reading the judgment of the
lawyers and ecclesiastics, has declared that she was not
bound by a monastic vow. In any case the rules of conscience set up by men do not constitute an obligation
before God.

And now my son has been kidnapped from the University
of Louvain and is held in dire imprisonment. I am reproached with promoting religious liberty. If by liberty
you mean the license practised by the house of the prince
of Parma or the atheism and vice of Rome, this is not what
I mean. I will say that the smoke of the fires which have

tormented so many poor Christians have never been agree-
able to me as they are to the duke of Alba and the Spaniards. I am of the opinion that the persecutions in the
Netherlands should stop. When the king, on leaving Zeeland called on me to execute certain men suspected of
heresy, I refused, knowing that I must obey God rather
than men. I know I do not need to convince you on this
point.

I do not know of any impudence equal to that of the
Spaniards who put a free prince under the ban and offer
to ennoble one who dispatches him. If the assassin were a
nobleman do you think any gentleman in the world would
eat with a scoundrel who killed for money? If this is the
way to gain nobility in Castille I can understand why people say that most of the Spaniards are Moors and Jews.
The ban goes on to offer pardon for any crime committed
by the assassin. Even if he has wiped out Christianity in
his domain? Even if he has committed rape? Even if he has
maligned the Inquisition, the greatest crime in Spain?

They seek my life. How gladly would I welcome death
could I thereby save you from the scourge of these Spaniards. Why have I sacrificed my goods, lost my brothers,
seen my son kidnapped, if not for the sake of your liberty?
If you think sirs, that my absence or my death will aid
you, here is my head. I am responsible only to you. If the
little that I have can serve, let us go on with the defense
of this people. By the help which you have always given
me, by the grace through which God has hitherto sustained
me in grievous trials, in order to maintain you, your wives,
your children and all things holy and sacred, I will hold
fast.[19]

Charlotte was apprehensive and besought her husband when
away from home not to eat in public places, but the home was
no more secure. While William was dining a young man of
sinister appearance entered and persuaded the guards that he
wished to present a petition. As he stepped forward William
arose. A pistol shot went through the upper palate and came

out above the right ear. William, still able to speak, called out to spare the assassin, but he was cut down. Maurice searched his body and found prayers in Spanish to the Virgin, Christ and the angel Gabriel to aid him in the accomplishment of the assassination.[20]

Charlotte, not yet recovered from her sixth childbirth, nursed her husband. For three weeks the outcome was in doubt. On the 18th of April she was able to report that by the grace of God he was recovered.[21]

But her strength was depleted and only three weeks later she was taken on the fifth of May, 1582. The grandfather then wrote to little Louise:

> My dear granddaughter: I am so sorry for you and your sisters that you have lost my daughter and your mother. I wish God had been willing to let her live longer to help you to grow up to be fine, good girls as you have already begun to be and you will, if you follow your good mother and obey your father. I will never forget you and your sisters and I pray our Lord to keep you in his grace. From Champigny June 16th, 1582. Your very good grandpa, Loys de Bourbon.

At the same time a letter was sent also by the duke's young wife, Catherine of Lorraine:

> My dear girl, I'm so sorry to hear that you have lost your mother, not only because I know what this means for you and your sisters, but because of the love she showed me. I trust, my dear, that you will love me, too. Believe me, I will do everything I possibly can to help and I'll put in a good word for you with your grandfather. I pray our Lord that He may give you, my dear, good health and a long and happy life.
>
> Your more than affectionate grandmother,
> Catherine of Lorraine.[22]

Perhaps the good word with the grandfather was responsible for the invitation, now lost, to which William responded in September, 1582:

Monsieur, I have received the letters which you sent me from Paris disclosing your kind intent which pleases me more than any news I could ever receive and all the more when I am given to understand that you will take charge of my little daughter. I'll have her ready to leave on the fourteenth of this month. She should be at Calais in four days if the wind is favorable. I hope that you can have a coach or litter to carry her. As for my other daughters, about whom I have not yet made any decision, I hope you won't mind that this time I send you only one. [She was Louise.] You don't need to assure me that she will receive excellent care. . . . Antwerp, September 5.

Guillaume de Nassau.²³

William must have assumed that the excellent care would include a Catholic upbringing. In his eyes the mass was not such an abomination as intolerance. But grandfather did respect the faith of his ward.

CHRONOLOGY
WILLIAM AND CHARLOTTE

1533 William's birth.
1546/7 Charlotte's birth.
1555 Abdication of Charles V. Peace of Augsburg.
1559 Treaty: Cateau Cambrésis. William a hostage. Charlotte a nun.
1566 The Request.
1567 William suppresses a Calvinist riot.
    Alba arrives. Philip, William's son, kidnapped.
1568 Egmont and Hoorn executed. William outlawed. Louis barely escapes.
1569 Alba's tax.
1571 Anne of Saxony divorced.
1572 March. Louis de Bourbon's outraged letter.
    April 1, Brill captured.
    William at Heidelberg.
    December to July, siege of Haarlem.
    August 23, Massacre of St. Bartholomew.
1573 December. Alba retired. Requesens governor general.
1574 April, Death of Louis. October, Leiden delivered.
1575 June 12, William and Charlotte married.
1576 Death of Requesens. March, Pacification of Ghent.
1577-8 Spanish deputies: Don Juan, Mathias, Farnese.
1579 Leagues of Arras (Catholic) and Utrecht (Protestant).
    Charlotte writes to her father.
1580 June, William put under the ban. His *Apology*.
1581 June, Louis de Bourbon acknowledges Charlotte's wedding.
1582 January, He writes to little Louise.
    March 18, Attempted assassination of William.
    May 5, Charlotte's death.

BIBLIOGRAPHY

Biographies of Charlotte and William:

Delaborde, Jules, *Charlotte de Bourbon* . . . (Paris, 1888), an excellent study replete with the text of documents. The following notes refer to this work by pages without repeating the title.

Putnam, Ruth, *William the Silent*, 2 vols. (New York, 1898), with source references.

Harrison, Frederick, *William the Silent* (New York, 1924), without notes.

Wedgewood, C. V., *William the Silent* (London, 1944), documented, vivid.

Background:

Geyl, P., *The Revolt in the Netherlands* (London, 1932), for the total story.

Halkin, Leon-E., *La Réforme en Belgique sous Charles-Quint* (Brussels, 1957). An excellent summary for the southern provinces.

Kühler, W. J., *Geschiedenis der Nederlandsche Doopsgezinden in de zestiende Eeuw*, 2d ed. (Haarlem, 1961), on the Anabaptists.

Knappert, L., *Het Ontstaan en de Vestiging van het Protestantisme in de Nederlanden* (Utrecht, 1924). On the Lutherans and others.

Moreau, Gérard, *Histoire du Protestantisme à Tournai jusqu'à la veille de la Revolution des Pays-Bas* (Paris, 1962). Shows the introduction of Calvinism by way of the southern French speaking provinces.

De Vries de Heekelingen, Hermann de, *Genève Pepinière du Calvinisme hollandais* (Fribourg en Suisse, 1918-24), 2 vols. Volumes I, p. 194 f. shows that the first students from the Low Countries to study at Geneva were from the French area.

Güldner, Gerhard, *Das Toleranz-Problem in den Niederlanden im Ausgang des 16. Jahrhunderts* (Liebeck, 1968) gives a graph (opp. p. 34) of the number of executions for heresy between 1530-1580. The Lutherans have a low percentage throughout and nothing after the Peace of Augsburg in 1555. The Anabaptists have the largest number with two peaks in 1560 and 1573. The Calvinists exceed all others between 1565-1575.

Documents in G. Groen van Prinsterer, *Archives de Correspondance Inédite de la Maison d'Orange-Nassau*, 14 volumes (Leiden, 1835-61).

William's Apology in Dutch: *Apologie ofte Verantwoordinge van den Prince van Orangien*, ed. Mees-Verwey (preface 1923), 2d printing 1942.

NOTES

1. pp. 7-10, the depositions of the sisters, 37-45, the mother's *volte face*, 12-15. The bishop's name was Ruzé. The young man was George d'Averly.
2. Rochambeau, *Lettres d'Antoine de Bourbon et de Jeanne d'Albret,* (Paris, 1877). Nos. 216, 238 and 239.
3. p. 33.
4. Appendix, 320-326.
5. *Apology* (Dutch text, 61).
6. pp. 187-188.
7. p. 209.
8. p. 144.
9. pp. 151-152.
10. p. 201.
11. p. 219.
12. p. 136.
13. p. 108.
14. p. 211.
15. Harrison, *William the Silent,* 144, without documentation. There is a similar passage in Groen, *Archives,* V, 380.
16. pp. 222-224.
17. pp. 256-257.
18. p. 291.
19. pp. 233-244, The *Apology* in French.
20. Eating in private, 147; prayer to Virgin, 300.
21. pp. 268-269.
22. pp. 315-316.
23. Groen, *Archives,* VIII, 126.

Louise de Coligny

5.

Louise de Coligny
(1555-1620)

Louise de Coligny was a widow at seventeen. Until her marriage a year earlier in March of 1571 we know almost nothing about her, but her upbringing can be reconstructed from what we know of her family. The father was Gaspard de Coligny, the admiral of France and the most outstanding leader of the Huguenot party. The mother, Charlotte Laval was her husband's spine. Both were of the nobility. The father belonged to the house of Chatillon. He and his brother Andelot were men at arms. A third brother, Odet, entered the church and became a cardinal. All three became staunch Huguenots. The cardinal resigned and married. All were born Catholics. Why and when they changed is not clear. The admiral's wife may well have taken the lead.

Gaspard's youth was filled with the usual sports and military exercises of the nobility destined for the camp. His closest chum was Francis, later the duke of Guise. The lads were so devoted to each other as to wear the same costumes.[1] Gaspard had never persecuted the Huguenots, but the manner of his joining them is shrouded in legend. The common version is that he was converted by reading Calvin's *Institutes* while a prisoner following the battle of St. Quentin. His earliest biographer says simply that he read the Scriptures. That would have been enough without Calvin, but Calvin did write to him saying that God had brought upon him the affliction of imprisonment in order

that he might be withdrawn from the distractions of the world
and able to listen with undivided attention to God's voice
speaking through the Scriptures.[2] Release came in 1559.
Returning to France he announced his adherence to the Reformed faith.[3] But before taking the public step he asked his
wife whether she was ready to share with him the risks. He reminded her that under the previous sovereigns the Reformed
had been condemned to be burned and their estates confiscated.
She replied that so had it been always in the church of Christ
and pledged her faith.[4] In their household the children and
the servants were gathered for morning and evening prayers
with the singing of Psalms and sometimes a sermonette.[5]

The trials predicted by Coligny to his wife soon became actual. Some of the Huguenot leaders in order to break the power
of the Catholic house of Guise had recourse to arms in the
conspiracy of Amboise which utterly failed. Condé of the house
of Bourbon was implicated and escaped execution only by reason
of the sudden death of King Francis II. Coligny disclaimed involvement. Then came in 1562 the massacre of Huguenots at
Vassy at the hands of the duke of Guise. Should the persecuted
now unsheathe the sword? Condé hesitated this time. Coligny's
brothers, Andelot and Odet, came to urge him to take the lead.[6]
He pointed out the dubiousness of rebellion against the crown
and the hopelessness of the struggle. They left. That night Coligny was awakened by the sobs of his wife.

"I am sorry," she said, "to wake you with my worries, but when
the members of Christ are rent how can one be insensitive? Your
feeling is no less strong than mine but you conceal it better.
Do you take it amiss that your loyal half lets her tears fall on
you with more boldness than respect? Here we are, couched in
comfort while our brothers, bone of our bone and flesh of our
flesh, are some in prison and some dead in the fields at the
mercy of dogs and crows. This bed is to me a tomb because
they have no tombs. These sheets are a reproach because they
have no shrouds. Shall we snore in sleep and not hear their
cries in death? I recall the prudent arguments with which you
shut the mouths of your brothers. Will you take the heart out

of them, too? I tremble because this prudence savors of the world
and not of God, who has given you the skill of a commander.
Can you in conscience refuse? Does not your conscience bite
you? Is it not the voice of God? Don't you fear that He will
hold you guilty? Is the sword which you carry meant to oppress
the afflicted or to pull out the nails of tyrants? You have confessed the rightfulness of taking up arms against them. Can your
heart, then, abandon the love of right for fear of failure? God
takes away the sense of those who resist Him under pretense of
sparing the shedding of blood. He saves the soul that is willing
to be lost and damns the soul that would save itself. Monsieur,
I have on my heart the blood already shed. Their blood and
your wife cry to God in heaven and from this bed I say you will
be a murderer of those you do not save from murder."

He replied: "Look at our weakness, the defection of Anthony
of Navarre and the Constable (Montmorency). Put your hand
to your breast. Sound your constancy. Are you able to face the
debacles, the reproaches of enemies and partisans who measure
justice by success, the treachery of our friends, the exiles in
store in foreign lands, the rebuffs of the English and the Germans, your shame, your nudity, your hunger, and what is worse
those of your children? Can you face your death at the hands of
the butcher after witnessing the body of your husband exposed
to the jeers of the mob and your children enslaved by your enemies? I give you three weeks. If then you are ready to face all
this I will go and die with you and our friends."

She answered: "The three weeks are up right now. You will
never be beaten by the virtues of your enemies. Use your own
and let not the deaths to come in the next three weeks be upon
your head. I beg you in the name of God, don't let us down.
If you do, I will testify against you in the judgment day." [7]

Woe to the man whose wife joins the prosecution at the judgment day! Coligny took to horse. We have the account only from
the pen of Agrippa d'Aubigné, who presumably did not overhear the conversation. Some of the details suggest composition
in the light of the outcome but the gist may have been communicated by one of the participants.

Charlotte did not leave her husband to bear the cross alone.[8] With the children, including Louise, she went to the Huguenots at Orleans. During the protracted siege she succored the dying. Her own son died. The duke of Guise was descending with troops upon the city swearing that he would sow it with salt. As he approached, a Huguenot youth, imbued with the conviction that the best way to serve the Lord was to fell his enemy, brought down the duke. Under torture the perpetrator incriminated Coligny, who disclaimed any complicity. But denial did not allay suspicion and to the clashes of religion and of the nobles with the crown was added a family vendetta between the Guises and the Chatillons. The admiral moved his family to the safer Huguenot center of La Rochelle, open to the sea.

All of this would not have turned the queen mother against Coligny, for the policy of Catherine de Medici was to keep the peace by balancing the parties. Coligny was often invited to court where he aroused the mother's jealousy by gaining ascendency over the mind of her son and by enlisting his support for a program of which the mother disapproved, namely military assistance to the Netherlands in order to cut the lines of Spain. The dowager was of no mind to incite a war with Spain. She was willing, therefore, to join a plot of the Guises to eliminate Coligny.

Conceivably it might have failed had it not been for the guileless trust of the emissary employed by Coligny to communicate between La Rochelle and Paris. He was a young man named Teligny in whom the admiral had the utmost confidence to the point of sending him on diplomatic missions to England and even Constantinople, presumably to induce the Turks not to aid Spain. Between such commissions Teligny was frequently in the household of the admiral and thus came to know his daughter Louise. The admiral desired their marriage.[9] Not unwillingly they complied. Teligny continued his visits to the court and came to trust the integrity of the king.

Yet at this very time the queen mother and the Guises were drawing the king into the plot of assassination. A mercenary fired, wounded but did not kill. The admiral was brought to bed. Catherine and the king called solicitously. Yet, perceiving that the whole Huguenot party would now clamor for revenge, resolved to wipe them all out, all that were in Paris and there were many. They had assembled for the marriage of their representative, Henry of Navarre, with the daughter of Catharine. The object of the match had been to cement the parties. Now it was the occasion of the extermination of one. Teligny and Louise were by the bedside of the father. So also were Huguenot leaders who proposed that he be moved to a place of greater safety. The king had given assurance of security and Teligny insisted that he be trusted. At midnight the bells rang for carnage. The mangled body of Coligny was thrown through a window and fell at the feet of the duke of Guise. Two thousand are claimed to have fallen in Paris on this day of St. Bartholomew, August 22, 1572. Among them was Teligny. How Louise escaped we do not know, certainly not because she was a woman. Neither age nor sex was spared. She fled to Geneva, Berne and Basel.

For the next decade from 1573-1583 we know next to nothing about Louise, save that a shift in the political situation in 1576 made possible her return to France. At the end of the ten years, Henry II, the new king of France, received a letter from the widower, William of Orange, requesting the royal consent to a marriage with the king's subject, Louise de Coligny. The king consented and so did she. William was so involved in the affairs of the Netherlands that he could not come to France for the wedding. She made the journey to Antwerp where they were married on April 2, 1583.

For a time she lived at Middleburg in Zeeland where there was a large French colony, then moved to Delft in Holland. Commenting on these journeys she related that travel in the Netherlands was not as commodious as in France where one was carried in a litter. Here one sat on a plank in a coach and, though the distance from Rotterdam to Delft was only three leagues, one arrived congealed and done in. She did not add that on this occasion she was in an advanced stage of pregnancy. On January 29, 1584 she bore William a son, named Henry Frederick for his two godparents,[10] Henry of Navarre and Frederick, the king of Denmark. Settled in Delft, Louise tucked under her capacious wings most of William's numerous brood. Daughter Louise, now seven, having returned following the death of her grandfather, wrote to an uncle: "the new mother loves us all and takes very good care of us."[11]

THE CHILDREN OF WILLIAM OF ORANGE

By Anne of Egmont
  Philip—December 19, 1554
  Marie—February 7, 1556

By Anne of Saxony
  Maurice—September 14, 1567
  Anne
  Emilie the First

By Charlotte de Bourbon
  Louise—March 31, 1576
  Elisabeth—March 26, 1577
  Catherine—July 31, 1578
  Flandrine—August 18, 1579
  Brabantine—September 17, 1580
  Emilie the Second—December 19, 1581

By Louise de Coligny
  Henry Frederick—January 29, 1584

The ban pronounced by King Philip was still at work. The monetary reward on William's head did not induce anyone to risk his life to accomplish the assassination. For that, one needed the readiness to be enrolled in the company of the martyrs in order to remove a rebel against the king, a perverter of the faith and an enemy of God. Balthazar Gerard, the assassin, declared that he would have been willing to traverse a thousand leagues over rivers and mountains to render this glorious service to the king, the church and the Lord. From the duke of Parma he received a blessing, coupled with the injunction not to incriminate him if tortured. The conspirator purloined the seal of the duke of Mansfield, whom he served as a secretary, and with false papers insinuated himself under an assumed name into the entourage of William. To feign adherence to the Reformed faith he carried, a Bible, for which guile let God forgive him. Out of pity for his shoeless feet William gave him some money with which he bought pistols. As the prince was coming down to dine with his wife, his sister the countess of Schwartzburg and three of the girls (they are not named), Gerard, the pistols concealed beneath his cloak, stepped forward requesting a passport and unloaded his shots into William's stomach. *"Mon Dieu,"* he cried, "Have pity on my soul. I am sorely wounded. *Mon Dieu,* have pity on my soul and on this poor people."

Louise de Coligny with "a withered heart" [12] assumed now heavier responsibilities, domestic and political. Maurice, only eighteen, succeeded to his father's position as prince [13] and leaned upon his stepmother whose many connections with important people stood him in good stead. Her own son, Henry Frederick, was now the heir apparent. His education in consequence assumed greater relevance. Training in language and literature was entrusted to the distinguished scholar, Scaliger. Religious instruction fell to Louise's pastor, John Wtenbogaert. For three years he was very close to the boy. When the lad was old enough to throw a leg over a horse, his half brother Maurice made him an

Assassination of William of Orange

apprentice in matters military. The mother, as a result, was not able to see as much of him as she would have liked.

The question was raised whether she should keep all of the children. If they were to be distributed religion was a consideration. Little Louise, now eight, wrote to uncle John:

> Please don't let us be brought up in any religion other than that of our late father and Madame, our mother. You have more influence than any one else. I leave it entirely in your hand.[14]

The Duchess of Bouillon was ready to take one. She was Protestant. Her brother François, now the duke of Montpensier, would take one. He was Catholic. Mother Louise reported the whole matter to Queen Elizabeth in England. She was willing to take her namesake and made suggestions for placing all of the others in good Protestant hands. But there was nothing to be done about Flandrine. She was already under the tutelage of her relative, the abbess of the Paraclete in France. At the age of fifteen she insisted on taking the vows. All of her Huguenot relatives sought vehemently to dissuade her, but she was as adamant about taking the veil as her mother had been in casting it off. Queen Elizabeth's suggestions were disregarded because mother Louise kept five herself. The youngest was three. The allowance for their support granted by the estates was pitiful and she had to draw on her resources in France.[15]

The little brood was a blessing in assuaging her loneliness in this alien land, but not altogether. At times she was desperately homesick for France and for visits from French friends. We have a batch of letters sent to Turenne in the 1590s. He was later her son-in-law, a dashing young chap, engaging and persuasive. Henry IV sent him on missions to England and Germany. Louise begged him to pay her a visit on his way to or from England. On successive occasions she wrote:

> My cousin, I do hope you will come to see me. We have not seen each other for over nine years. Nobody comes to see me and people here think I am in disrepute with my family. In my miserable privation nothing gives me such intense

joy as the thought of seeing you. I am sure you will be welcomed by the Estates and by my son-in-law (Maurice). Your little cousin is dying to see you. Pardon this scribbled and incoherent letter. I am so afraid that you will take another route that I have dashed it off. P.S. I have a particular matter touching the service of the king which I do not want to trust to paper. This is an especial reason why I want to see you.[16]

Again after a visit from Mlle. D'Andelot she wrote:

She is gone. What a joy to have had her here for two months and for a week Monsieur, my cousin, as well! I have had nothing like this in seven years and now not anything under heaven will be so religiously guarded by your miserable cousin all her life as the affection and friendship which she bears to you. I kiss your hands legions of times.[17]

The advancing ages of her little flock soon brought contacts with France and beyond. The girls became eligible for marriage at sixteen. Louise, the eldest, was married to Frederick IV of the Palatinate, the son of that Frederick III who had given asylum to her mother. Louise became the mother of Frederick V, who married Elizabeth, the daughter of James I of England and the sister of Charles I. Frederick was the most rigorous exponent of Calvinism during the Thirty Years War.

Daughter Elizabeth, when seventeen, was courted by Turenne. Since he had lately become the duke of Bouillon, she became the duchess. She wanted to have her sister Brabantine close at hand and the suggestion was made that she marry a not too distant Frenchman. But she was already practically promised to the staunch Huguenot, Rohan. He was deliberately dropped in favor of Tremouille and mother Louise did a little soothing. On the death of Tremouille, Brabantine was left with six children. Louise took over one.

Some of the marriages presented more serious problems. Contrary to the wishes of Prince Maurice, Emily married the dethroned king of Portugal.[18] His Catholicism might have been overlooked but not his dethronement. Louise did some more soothing. The problem with Henry Frederick was to get him married at all.[19] His sisters Brabantine and Elizabeth conspired with mama to lure him to Paris for a baptism which would be attended by the Huguenot, Anne de Rohan. He was too busy to come. He finally married the daughter of the landgrave of Hesse.

Mother Louise followed all of her step daughters with maternal solicitude. She was quite put out when Tremouille did not invite her to help at Brabantine's lying in. To her daughter she wrote:

> It is no good for you to tell me you wish I could be with you. The only reason I shall not is your husband. I am angry with him and I won't write. I will never forgive him or at any rate not for a long time. My heart tells me it will be a boy, because every time I mention the child I say *le petit* and not *la petite*. Be delivered soon. I am always your mother who loves you as herself and is praying now and always that God will give you a safe delivery.[20]

Then came the news:

> My girl, it is a boy. I weep for joy. I cannot tell you how happy I am. . . . . God be praised that you have come through so well. I wish I could have been with you, to hear what you said, and to see how you have fared since. I am just dying to have a look at this tiny grandson and to see how you manage him with your little hands. Your small brother is delighted to have a little nephew. The duc de Bouillon is consumed with envy that his wife has not given him a boy.[21]

Little glimpses of her own life are disclosed in the letters. While in France for a period she wrote to Brabantine:

> You'd have to laugh if you saw how I'm tangled up in my present quarters. I'm going on Monday to make some purchases. I love my garden like the one you saw at the Hague. But whatever I do I can't make this place attractive. I have neither wood nor water. If I can get my money I'd rather have another place.[22]

Again from France she wrote to a celebrated botanist at Leyden saying that she wished to obtain for the king's physician some of the many bulbs available in Holland. She knew of no one better able to supply her need than the professor.[23]

At the same time Louise was never devoid of involvement in political matters. Her letters from Holland to Turenne in the 1590s are sufficient witness. She discusses with him the aspects of his missions to England and Germany and relates particulars. France had engaged some vessels for three months to keep the coast of Brittany clear of the Spaniards but these ships had never left Dieppe. She suspected that Dieppe and Rouen were holding them to protect their own trade, whereas the king would like to have them at La Rochelle. Let Turenne use his influence. She is fully aware of the problem of communication on all matters of political delicacy. She had entrusted a packet of letters to a merchant seaman to be delivered at Dieppe, but he had run aground in the mouth of the Somme and had been captured. She hoped

Prince Maurice

he had had the presence of mind to throw the packet over-
board.[24] She reports all the news and rumors. "The duke of
Parma works in great secrecy. He will assemble his forces to be-
siege a town and then all of them vanish. It is said now that he is
starting for Guelders with 1500 horses and 4000 men." [25]

Her political influence was even greater in the years 1598-1603
when she was permitted to reside in France. The main reason
was that Henry IV by returning to Catholicism had been able to
enter Paris without a battle in 1594. His defection from the faith
troubled her but she still held him in esteem. Louise remained
in France partly to be closer to her daughters, partly to secure
the vindication of the name of her father by the rescinding of all
the acts against him. She succeeded. She was with Henry IV at
Nantes during the drafting of the famous Edict of Toleration.
Whether she had a hand in the drafting we do not know. She
was in close touch with all of the members of the royal house
and with such advisers as Du Plessis Mornay, who in earlier years
had been a trusted adviser to her late husband in the Netherlands.

After 1603 Louise, back in Holland and in residence at the
Hague was embroiled in the tensions and controversies by which
the northern provinces were rent. There were class divisions. The
governing group was the old aristocracy represented by the advocate of the estates, Oldenbarnevelt. The lower classes looked
for their defense to the military forces under the command of
Prince Maurice. The rising commercial aristocracy, centered in
the great port of Amsterdam, was sometimes able to swing the
balance. In addition there were religious divisions not only between Catholics versus Protestants, and Lutherans versus Calvinists, but also within the ranks of the Calvinists acrimonious
dissensions emerged.

Holland had long been the home of a religious attitude which
assumed no institutional form. Some of its roots lay in the anti-
dogmatic piety of the Brethren of the Common Life and of their
disciple Erasmus. Very influential was Castellio, whose impassioned denunciation of the burning of Servetus, passed from
Basel to the Low Countries where his views were further dis-

seminated by Coornhaert. Assigned to refute him, Arminius was converted and he it was who gave his name to the party called Arminians. Because of their remonstrance against the views of the ultra-Calvinists they were also called Remonstrants.

The differences between the two parties appear incredibly small. Both were agreed as to predestination, but the rigorists insisted on double predestination both as to salvation and damnation. If one accepts predestination at all one will find it difficult to regard it as anything other than double. The main concern of the Remonstrants was to exculpate God from the charge of arbitrariness and they, therefore, explained predestination to damnation as due to God's foreknowledge of what the unborn would turn out to be. The Counter-Remonstrants maintained that God's decision was absolutely unconditioned by any consideration of what would follow.

Both parties were agreed that man can do nothing good save through the assistance of divine grace, but the Remonstrants said that man does not have to accept it. Grace is resistable, the Counter-Remonstrants said it is irresistable. But if grace is resistable there is the possibility that a person, having once been accepted, may subsequently be rejected. One cannot be certain of perseverance and consequently cannot be assured of salvation. To say this was to sever the very nerve of Calvinism, for the great drive of the saints came from their utter certitude of election. A further point with the Remonstrants was the tentativeness of creeds. The Belgic Confession and the Heidelberg Catechism were subject to revision. The above tenets were subsumed in the Five Articles of the Remonstrants.

There was another consideration which some of them advanced in private, that Catholics might be saved. One would have supposed that even the rigorists would not have limited God's omnipotence by denying the possibility, but to admit the conceivable salvation of a Catholic was to suggest toleration and toleration might enable Catholics to seize power in the northern provinces and reintroduce the Inquisition. Consequently he who asserted the possible salvation of a Catholic was presumably a secret agent of the king of Spain. The Counter-Remonstrants blasted the Roman anti-Christ with his Spanish minions. War was preached from the pulpits, war, which inspires courage, expels the vices of peace and ushers the fallen into eternal bliss.[26]

Obviously the religious dispute had political implications. The crusading mood of the extreme Calvinists coalesced with other motives for war. Maurice, a skillful general, having already pushed back the duke of Parma, desired to fulfill in toto the word of William of Orange that he was resolved "to drive these Spanish vermin from the land." The northern provinces would then be consolidated into a national state. The commoners gave him support. So also did the merchants because Spain demanded as the price of peace that the Dutch yield to her a monopoly of the Indian trade east and west. Thus religious, nationalist, and commercial interests coincided. The feeling was such that he who would admit a Catholic to heaven was regarded as traitor on earth.

The leader of the moderate party recruited largely from the old aristocracy was the advocate of the estates, Oldenbarnevelt. He had come to feel that further resistance to Spain was hopeless. No help could be expected from England because after the defeat of the Armada she no longer feared Spain. And no help could be expected from France, because after Henry IV returned to the church of Rome the religious division was diminished, and in any case Henry was assassinated in 1610. Therefore, argued Oldenbarnevelt, the Netherlands should make a negotiated peace, even at the price of losing the Indian trade.

In his religious views Oldenbarnevelt inclined to the Remonstrants. He would not go so far as to say that a heathen might be saved—a book with that tenet had been suppressed—but any good Christian might be saved, presumably even a Catholic. At any rate he treated Catholics leniently[27] and testified that among them were many good patriots.[28] As advocate of the estates he represented the civil and Maurice the military arm of the government. Tension developed which Louise sought to allay. She counselled Oldenbarnevelt to pass over scurrilous attacks in silence.[29] But any thwarting of his ambition irked Maurice. Nevertheless Louise at length prevailed and is believed to have had much to do with bringing to pass the Peace of Antwerp which in 1609 established a truce of twelve years between the Netherlands and Spain.[30] Political dissension was temporarily quieted.

But religious dissension stirred it up again. The leader of the Remonstrants and the drafter of their Five Articles was the one time tutor of Prince Henry Frederick[31] and the pastor of Louise, John Wtenbogaert. After serving as a chaplain to the troops of Maurice, he had become the pastor to two churches in the Hague, one using French, the other Dutch. Louise and her son attended the French service. Wtenbogaert held that religion is more a matter of the heart than of the head. A devout attitude is better

John Wtenbogaert

than speculation about predestination. There is no need for creeds and synods. There is no one true church. Any church is true which is sincere, devout and scriptural.[32] On that last count he might have seen fit to exclude the Catholics, but apparently he did not. He would accord them toleration.[33]

Wtenbogaert began to feel that he was in disfavor with Maurice and was ready to leave rather than cause him embarrassment.[34] Louise assured him that she had talked with Maurice, who was well disposed, as evidenced by attendance at his church.[35] The situation became more tense and when the Counter-Remonstrants took over the cloister church, Maurice transferred his attendance. Wtenbogaert again contemplated leaving. Louise besought him to stay. Let him go into hiding for a time and if the situation became really worse he could count on help from France. She had the assurance from the ambassadors.[36]

Her own position had become definitely uncomfortable. In 1595 Philip, the oldest son of William of Orange, was allowed to return from his captivity in Spain which had lasted twenty-eight years.[37] During so long a disuse he must almost have forgotten his native Dutch. At the time of the kidnapping he had been a Catholic and was not likely to have become a Calvinist in Spain. On his return he simply did not fit. Louise welcomed him as a human being. For that she might have been forgiven, had she not suggested that as the eldest son he had a better claim to the succession than did his half brother. Maurice was *faché*.[38]

A sharper difference arose when Maurice asked Louise to support him in taking the title of king which after him would pass to her son. And would she kindly enlist Oldenbarnevelt for the plan? That staunch old republican declined and she took his side.[39] Maurice was even more *faché*.

Louise turned to Du Plessis Mornay in France for counsel:

> I do wish you could be here. We are in the gravest need of your wise and sagacious advice. It is not just a matter of religion. The whole state is involved and may fall apart. If the deceased [William of Orange] knows what is going on down here I think his ashes will swear. I know how busy you are, but I do hope you can manage to come.[40]

A provincial synod condemned the teaching of Wtenbogaert and excommunicated him from the sacraments. He fled from the Hague and became an exile at Antwerp. In the meantime there was widespread agitation on the part of the Counter-Remonstrants for the calling of a national synod which would then make his deposition in Holland valid for all of the provinces and would also impose a uniform creed upon the entire land. The assumption was not fatuous that the opponents of Wtenbogaert would dominate the synod. The commercial interests, desirous of war with Spain, pushed for it vigorously and the more moderate older aristocrats were losing power because Maurice was in the process of displacing them from local government. The Remonstrants, perceiving what was in store, opposed the calling of the national synod. Their spokesman was the great international jurist Hugo Grotius who employed a delaying tactic, pleading that prior to the national assembly many local synods should thoroughly air the points in debate. His counsel was rejected.

Everything depended on the attitude of Maurice. The religious question did not concern him. When the Remonstrants and Counter-Remonstrants would not celebrate communion together his comment was, "Very well. Let them celebrate separately, but let them not separate." A divided church would impede his effort to establish a united state. Besides the Counter-Remonstrants were bellowing for his cherished project of a war with Spain. Maurice lined up with the ultra-Calvinists.

During these developments Louise corresponded with Wtenbogaert in hiding and besought him to make every concession compatible with conscience. This was before the meeting of the national synod. He replied in February, 1610:[41]

> I am sorry not to have written you sooner. For a year I have been confined to my room with palpitation of the heart and acute depressions. I am greatly disturbed for the ship of the church and the ship of the state. I cry unto my God: "My flesh faints for Thee as in a dry and weary land where no water is" (Psalm 63:1). It is a great comfort to me to have your prayers. How I long to be released from

this earthly tabernacle and to be with Christ. I could depart
this life with greater peace could I look upon the fruit of
my labors, but I must remember that our Lord was rewarded
with a crown of thorns and I must have fellowship with
his death.

My deposition from the ministry was hastened to dis-
qualify me from attendance at the national synod. The Roman Consistory adheres better to the rules of order. You ask
me what I think will be the outcome of the synod. I don't
think any good will come of it. The ostensible purpose is to
avoid schism but the actual is to condemn the Remonstrants
and to bring them into disrepute throughout Europe.

You tell me that there are godly men who will attend the
synod and I must assume that they will be fair. But godly
men can be mislead by misunderstanding, passion, and too
great respect for authority. Were there not godly men at the
Council of Trent? You tell me to wait and see what the
synod will do and you say that my party is obstinate and
will not submit. Yes, but we cannot give up the very core
of the Reformation that decisions must rest on God's Word.
You ask how then differences are to be resolved. That's just
the question the Catholics put to us. The synod will be
dominated by the Counter-Remonstrants who are parties to
the dispute and should not be judges. This gathering will
be no conference when the Remonstrants are treated as
rebels against the government and criminals. You are
troubled because the Remonstrants will be taxed with
schism. Shall we then condemn all separation? What of the
Protestant departure from Rome or the separation of the
Calvinists from the Lutherans? Why should not the Counter-
Remonstrants submit?

A month later he reported to Louise:

My house was assaulted with torches, arms and ladders in
the middle of the night. My wife was there and some friends.
The intruders searched the premises and would not believe
I was not there. My wife, who was half dead, was threatened
with imprisonment if she did not disclose my whereabouts.

Oldenbarnevelt has been accused of *crimen laesae Majestatis* on the ground that he hatched a conspiracy to oust the prince with Spanish help.

This last statement was quite correct. There had been outbreaks of violence in Holland. The house of a Remonstrant at Antwerp had been sacked. Maurice began to throw a ring of troops around Holland. His move was countered when Holland engaged a corps of guards. Today they would be called an auxiliary police force, but in that day there were no police other than soldiers. These guards were to be subject to the civil administration and not answerable to the officers in the army of Maurice. He interpreted the move as treason and taxed Oldenbarnevelt with responsibility. Charges were lodged against two others of whom one was Hugo Grotius. The trial was before an improvised and packed tribunal. Oldenbarnevelt was condemned to death as "a disturber of the peace" and as "an abettor of Spain." "This," he said to his judges "is the reward of thirty years of service to the state." The other two accused were given life sentences of imprisonment.

Louise could not at first believe the news. She sought an audience with Maurice and was denied. The French ambassador sought to address the estates and was denied. A friend of the accused suggested to Louise that she enlist the children of Oldenbarnevelt to petition the estates for a pardon. Her first reaction was: "Does Maurice know this? He will be upset if he doesn't." "Madame," answered the friend, "You should do it anyway." She did, but the children were too paralyzed by fright to comply. The execution took place on May 16, 1619.[42]

The imprisonment of Grotius was terminated by a ruse. His wife was allowed to live with him and books were sent to him on loan. They came in a chest used also for fetching and returning his linen. In time the guards no longer examined the chest prior to removal. Grotius' wife substituted her husband for the books to be returned. Two guards with great effort brought this load of hefty tomes down a ladder and conveyed it to the lender. Grotius fled to France.

Wtenbogaert continued to hide in Antwerp. Again Louise

besought him to make any honorable concession which would terminate his "miserable exile." He replied:

> You have advised me to submit in all that I can in good conscience for it is hard to live in exile. But can I say that I was rightfully deposed? Shall I make myself a laughing stock and return to slavery? Having begun in the spirit shall I end in the flesh? Where else can I go than here? You fear that if I stay here I may become a papist. O come now! I don't want to go where I can never see my family. I will hide here as a beggar till my friends at home work out something. 25 June, 1619.[43]

Louise decided to return to France together with Henry Frederick. Passing through Antwerp on the 28th of March, 1620 they called upon the exile. In his autobiography he recorded:

> The prince and the princess called on me. She wept. They thanked me for the instruction I had given and spoke to me in the most Christian manner, promising all grace and friendship should I come to France. Then we discussed many things. I never saw her again, for by the time I was released she had died in France.[44]

Louise de Coligny had lived through the assassinations of her father, of her first husband, of her second husband and of her great friend Henry IV of France, the execution of Oldenbarnevelt and the exile of her beloved pastor. Could she have lived half a decade longer she would have witnessed the accession of her son after the death of Maurice in 1625, the return of the exiles Wtenbogaert and Grotius, the abandonment of any more national synods and an extension of religious liberty to a degree eventually emulated by all Europe.

BIBLIOGRAPHY

Delaborde, Jule, *Louise de Coligny* (Paris, 1890).
Gaspard de Coligny, 3 vols. (Paris, 1879-1882).

Marchegay, Paul Alexandre, *Correspondance de Louise de Coligny....* (Paris, 1887, Slatkine Reprints, Geneva 1970), with introduction.

Correspondence with Wtenbogaert in *Historische Genootschap Werken*, vols. 15, 17, 19-20 and 22.

General Background:

Evaluation of modern treatments in *Preconditions of Revolution in Early Modern Europe*, ed. Robert Foster and Jack P. Greene (Baltimore and London, 1970).

Geyl, Pieter A., *The Revolt of the Netherlands, 1555-1609*, (London, 1932). For 1609-1648 consult the Dutch version: *Geschiedenis van de Nederlandse Stam* 1 (Amsterdam, 1948).

Religious Background:

Brandt, Geerent, *Historie de Reformatie . . .* tweede Deel (Amsterdam, 1674).

Contemporaries:

Johannis Wtenbogaert, *Leven* (Haarlem, 1647) bound with his *De Kerkelicke Historie* (1647).

Rogge, H. C., *Johannes Wtenbogaert en zijn Tijd*, 3 vols. (Leiden, 1874-76).

Kühn, Johannes, *Toleranz und Offenbarung* (Leipzig, 1923), on his views with respect to tolerance.

Knight, W. S. M., *The Life and Work of Hugo Grotius* (London, 1925), The Grotius Society Publications No. 4.

Tex, Jan den, *Oldenbarnevelt*, 2 vols. (Haarlem, 1960), down to 1609.

Brandt, Geerent, *Historie van de Rechtspleging gehouden en den jaaren 1618-19* (Rotterdam, 1710 second edition).

NOTES

References to Delaborde are to his life of Louise unless that of her father is designated.

1. Francis Hotman, *Gasparis Colinii Castellonii. . . . vita,* (1575 n.p.), 21.
2. *Calvini Opera, Corpus Reformatorum,* XVII, No. 2950.
3. *Bulletin de la Société de l'Histoire du Protestantisme Français,* I, 263. Hereafter abbreviated *BSHPF.*
4. Delaborde, *Gaspard de Coligny,* I, 416.
5. Hotman, 24, 25, 158-166.
6. Théodore Agrippa d'Aubigné, *Histoire Universelle,* ed. Alphonse de Ruble, 10 vols. (1886-1909). II, iii, 2, 11-13.
7. Delaborde, *Gaspard de Coligny,* II, 43 ff. Miss J. Shimizu "Conflict of Loyalties . . . " *Travaux d'Humanisme et Renaissance,* CXIV (Geneva, 1970), who minimizes the religious motivation of Coligny is somewhat skeptical of Agrippa's account.
8. The following account condensed from Delaborde, Hotman, Marchegay.
9. *BSHPF,* I, 263.
10. Delaborde, I, 110.
11. *Ibid.,* 106.
12. Marchegay, Introduction, xxix.
13. Delaborde, I, 145.
14. *Ibid.,* I, 166.
15. *Ibid.,* On Brabantine, I, 315; on Flandrine, I, 326 and 480.
16. Letter XLI, Nov. 12, 1590.
17. Letter LII, May 24, 1591.
18. Delaborde, II, 221 ff.
19. *Ibid.,* 229.
20. Letter LXXXIII, Dec. 6, 1598.
21. Letter LXXXV, Dec. 31, 1598.
22. Letter XCVI, Oct. 11, 1600.
23. Delaborde, II, 68. Aug. 11, 1603, not in Marchegay.
24. Letter XLI, Nov. 12, 1590.
25. Letter LIII, May 31, 1590.
26. Rogge, *Wtenbogaert,* I, 339-340.
27. Rogge, I, 337.
28. Geyl, *Geschiedenis van de Nederlandsche Stam,* 373.
29. Brandt, *Reformatie,* II, 745.
30. Delaborde, II, 144-145.
31. Rogge, I, 234.
32. Kühn, *Toleranz,* 393.

33. Wtenbogaert, *Leven,* 125 right column bottom.

34. Rogge, II, 464.

35. Letter CLXXIX, May 1616.

36. Letter CLXXXII, September 1618.

37. Delaborde, I, 379.

38. *Ibid.,* II, 256-258 and Rogge I, 351.

39. The reliability of this account is discussed in a note in Aubéry du Maurier, *Documents Inédits sur l'Histoire du Protestantismeen France et en Holland 1566-1636* (Paris, 1885), 186-187.

40. Letter CLXXVII, Dec. 28, 1617.

41. Wtenbogaert, *Leven,* 94-119.

42. Brandt, *Histoire van de Rechtspleging,* 166 ff.

43. Wtenbogaert, *Leven,* 116 f. June 25, 1619.

44. *Ibid.,* 119 f., March 26, 1620.

PART II

WOMEN OF THE
REFORMATION
IN ENGLAND

INTRODUCTION

The role of women in the English Reformation differs somewhat from that in France where almost all of the examples chosen are from the nobility, but in England from royalty. Women could rule in England as they could not in France and nearly all of the Tudor queens played a role in the religious movements, sometimes of necessity seeing that religion and politics were so intertwined, sometimes of deliberate and even passionate choice. Only one representative of the English nobility has been given here, the duchess of Suffolk. There were others, who for considerations of space have been omitted. I am contemplating a separate article on four daughters of Anthony Cook, all protagonists of the reform, all of the high nobility—Lady Bacon, the mother of Francis Bacon, Lady Burghley the wife of Elizabeth's great minister, Lady Hoby who was later called Lady Russell, and Lady Killigrew. The material about them is not overly abundant. And for the lower classes we read of assemblies rather than of individuals except in the case of some of the martyrs.

The paucity may be attributed to male chauvinism, and in some respects with justice. Women could be rulers but not members of parliament. Hence we have parliamentary speeches only from queens. And women, whatever the reason, were not theologians. But at this point clerical rather than male chauvinism may be to blame. The material about lay men is also scant. Yet. despite all of the restrictions, women were powerful in the religious movements of the century.

6.

Catherine of Aragon
(1485-1536)

Catherine of Aragon might have saved England for the Church of Rome had she not been made of the same stuff as Martin Luther. Had she allowed Henry VIII to have his way, had she acknowledged that for eighteen years she had lived with him in sin, had she admitted that her daughter Mary was a bastard ineligible for the throne, had she been willing to take the veil or simply to have accepted the title of dowager instead of queen, Henry would not have needed to throw off the "usurped primacy of the bishop of Rome." This is not to say that nothing would have changed. The cry for reform in the church resounded throughout Europe and the nationalizing of the church was going on apace in France and Spain without a formal break with the Holy See. England, too, might have remained within the fold had it not been for the "Spanish stubbornness" of the queen.

Spanish she was, the daughter of Ferdinand of Aragon and Isabella of Castille, who, having united their provinces, sought to unify the Iberian peninsula in league not with Islam beyond the straits but with Christendom beyond the Pyrenees. Isabella was the heiress of the millenial Spanish pattern of militant orthodoxy, royal control of the church and relative independence of Rome. The Moors were conquered, the Inquisition established and the Jews expelled. Catherine inherited alike the fiber and the faith of her forebears. In later life she attended mass three

Catherine of Aragon

times more frequently than her husband and wore the coarse habit of a Franciscan tertiary.[1]

At the age of sixteen Catherine was sent to England to marry Prince Arthur, aged fourteen, the heir to the throne. Since he was the Prince of Wales the honeymoon was spent at Ludlow castle. Here, after six weeks, the lad died of consumption. Catherine never wavered in her assertion that the marrige had never been consummated. What now was to be done with the young widow? Her father did not wish her back because he had already paid half of the dowry and could hardly expect a refund from the penurious English king. Henry VII did not want her returned, in which case the other half of the dowry would never be paid. She remained in England with her considerable retinue of Spanish attendants. The head of her household was the governess, the Dona Elvira. A special favorite was Maria de Salinas.

At first Henry gave an allowance for their maintenance and betrothed Catherine to his second son, later to be Henry VIII. Then came an altercation between Henry and Ferdinand. Young Henry was called upon to renounce the marriage compact[2] and the stipend was cut off. Catherine and the Spanish ambassador sent to Ferdinand unending complaints that the ladies in waiting were in rags and reduced to begging. Catherine herself was all but naked. The servants were unpaid and her conscience deeply troubled. There were no funds for the dowries of her ladies whose hands were sought by Englishmen (though Maria de Salinas did later marry). Catherine was having to dispose of her jewels, not for luxuries but for food and since the jewels were a part of the dowry their value would have to be refunded. When, after five years, Ferdinand did send a sum insufficient to pay her debts she did not know whom first to reimburse. Her Spanish household was grumbling to go home, save for the ever faithful Maria de Salinas.[3] But Catherine said she would die in England rather than give up the marriage.[4]

She did not reproach her father for his niggardliness and sacrificed herself to his interests. They were being prejudiced by the machinations of Henry VII. One recalls that Ferdinand was king by hereditary right only in Aragon. Castille belonged to his wife Isabella. When she died the succession passed to her daughter, Joanna, the beloved sister of Catherine. Joanna was married to Philip of the house of Hapsburg. Henry was negotiating for an alliance with this pair to the disadvantage of Aragon. The scheme was being pushed by the Dona Elvira, who had a brother in the diplomatic service. The sovereigns were to meet in the Netherlands to complete the negotiations. The queen might attend and would have the joy of seeing again her sister. Catherine was exultant, until by an inadvertence she found out that the alliance would be detrimental to her father. She resolved at once to forgo her pleasure and in a frightful hour dismissed the Dona. Catherine had come of age.[5]

Then Henry VII died. And now young Henry, who had been called upon to renounce his betrothal to Catherine, declared that he regarded the compact as binding. His reasons are hard to divine. He said he was attracted to her. She was comely. They were married with all the dazzling pageantry of the age. Catherine had become England's queen. And what a queen she was! When Henry went prancing about France as a knight errant to win another Agincourt with antiquated English bowmen, Catherine was left as regent. So well did she manage the realm that the English inflicted on the Scots a resounding defeat at Flodden Field. Catherine reported to Wolsey, "This matter is so marvelous that it seemeth to be of God's doing alone. I trust the King shal remember to thanke hym for it." [6] The king, plucked of his plumes, straggled home ready to let God thank him for Flodden Field. Better than the famous victory was the magnanimous peace which Catherine offered to the now dowager queen of Scotland, Margaret, the sister of Henry VIII.

Catherine was not only queen in England but also ambassador to England from Spain and as such ever alert to serve her father's interests. This was difficult because he was a fox. When the king of France complained of being twice deceived, "He lies," barked Ferdinand, "Five times!" When deception was practiced on Henry, Catherine could not bring herself to believe in the duplicity of her father and satisfied herself with plausible excuses, until, when the treachery was blatant, she refused to see her husband swindled. She had become not simply queen in England but England's queen.[7]

Yet, for all her devotion, she could not supply England's need for an orderly succession through a legitimate heir to the throne. During eighteen years of marriage she had borne many children of whom only one survived and this one a girl, the princess Mary. England did not relish the prospect of a female sovereign. The experience of Queen Mathilda had not been reassuring. There had been as yet no such queens as Elizabeth and Victoria. Henry believed that a legitimate male succession was necessary to prevent a recurrence of the wars of the Roses. He was the national stallion to supply the imperative need. But he must obviously have a partner and at this point Catherine had failed.

Political expediency required that she be set aside. The king made plain that he esteemed her highly and, even while the divorce proceedings were under way, would sometimes spend an evening with her. His fight was for the tranquility of England, hers for his immortal soul. There is no reason to tax him with having been driven solely by the lust of the flesh. He could satisfy that without benefit of matrimony and did. Catherine, like many another, accepted infidelity, and when a son by him was born to Bessie Blount, the rejoicings at court were attended by Catherine. The king's mistress was an institution, but she could not produce a legitimate heir. That is why Anne Boleyn held Henry off for five years till marriage was assured.

But marriage with Anne could be assured only if the previous marriage with Catherine were annulled. Any marriage could be annulled if some defect were disclosed which rendered it no marriage at all. In this case the defect was that Catherine had been the wife of Henry's brother, and the Book of Leviticus said that "If a man takes his brother's wife, it is impurity. They shall be childless." There was, however, another text in the Book of Deuteronomy which said that if a man died without a son his brother should take his wife and give him issue.[8] Henry sent embassies all over Europe to canvass the opinions of learned men.

Behold the spectacle, today incredible, of all the universities of Europe wrangling over the relative authority of verses in Leviticus and Deuteronomy! Leviticus won. There was, then, a defect in the marriage of Catherine and Arthur. This obstacle had been removed by a dispensation granted at the time by Pope Julius II and since the initial dispensation was not sufficiently explicit another was dispatched. The original of this one was in Spain. England demanded to see it. Spain would supply only a copy.

The next question was whether the pope had authority to dispense from a law of Scripture. Henry himself asked the pope how he had the effrontery to set his authority above that of Moses.[9] But if the pope did have the power to grant a dispensation from Scripture did a subsequent pope have the authority to dispense from the dispensation of a previous pope? On scriptural grounds the simplest solution was bigamy. Luther said that in the Bible divorce was forbidden, bigamy allowed. Erasmus said he would prefer to see Jupiter take two Junos than that he should set one aside. And the pope himself suggested at least provisional bigamy. This whole discussion was predicated on the assumption that Catherine and Arthur had really been married. In Catherine's eyes marriage consisted in consummation and there had been no consummation. She was a virgin when she came to Henry. Let the doctors stop their cavilling. The whole debate was beside the point. From this stand she would never recede.[10]

But others took a different view of what constituted marriage—not consummation but a public contract. Not to honor this would be a violation of public honesty. Plainly there had been a public contract between Catherine and Arthur and from its obligation the pope had granted no dispensation. Consequently the marriage was valid, and Catherine was not free to marry Henry. He did employ this argument but his main plea was that his conscience was troubled as to the past because the failure of his union with Catherine to supply an heir was the manifest proof of the curse of God upon disobedience to his holy Word, and as to the future since, were there no heir, "much blood would be spilt and the kingdom totally destroyed."[11]

Henry might easily have obtained an annulment from Pope Clement VII had the case not been complicated by political factors. Annulments had been granted in like cases but Catherine was the aunt of the Emperor Charles V, the son of her beloved Joanna. The emperor would not lightly see his aunt set aside. The pope feared to incur his ill will because he himself had only recently been released from captivity by the imperial troops. On the other hand the pope was loath to give Henry a flat refusal lest he be driven into schism. The tactic adopted was dilatory obstruction. The case should be heard in England at the hands of the legate Cardinal Wolsey and a special emissary from Rome, Cardinal Campeggio, with instructions to interpose interminable delays.[12]

A court was held at Blackfriars to which the king and queen were summoned as if they had been common citizens. The crier called, " 'King Henry of England.' Whereunto the king answered and said, 'Here.' Then called he, 'Katherine, Queen of England, come into the Court.' " Not answering she crossed the room to the king, "and kneeled down at his feet saying in these words in broken English as followeth":

> Sir, quoth she, I beseech you, do me Justice and Right, and take some pity upon me, for I am a poor Woman, and a Stranger, born out of your Dominions, having here no indifferent Counsel, and less Assurance of Friendship. Alas! Sir, how have I offended you, what Offence have I given you, intending to abridge me of Life in this Sort? I take God to witness, I have been to you a true and loyall Wife, ever conformable to your Will and Pleasure, never did I contrary or gainsay your Mind, but always submitted myself in all Things. Wherein you had any Delight or Dalliance, whether it were little or much, without grudging or any Sign of Discontent: I have loved for your Sake all Men whom you have loved, whether I had Cause or not, were they Friends or Foes; I have been your wife these 20 Years, by whom you have had many Children; And when I first came to your Bed, I take God to witness, I was a Virgin; whether it were true or no, I put it to your Conscience: If there be any Cause that you can alledge either of Dishonesty or of any other Matter, lawfully to put me from you, I am willing to depart with Shame and Rebuke, but if

there be none, then I pray you let me have Justice at your Hands. . . .

She complained of the partiality of the court. "And with that she rose, making a low curtsy to the King, and departed from thence." Summoned to reappear she answered: "It is no indifferent Court for me, therefore I will not tarry." [13] Nor did she ever again appear.

The story is familiar of how the king, receiving no definitive ruling in his favor from the pope, cowed parliament and Convocation, and by successive stages repudiated the "usurped primacy of the Bishop of Rome," and established the Anglican Church with the king as the supreme head. Cranmer as archbishop of Canterbury annulled the marriage with Catherine and married Henry and Anne. Unremitting pressures were applied to Catherine to induce her to accept the title of dowager with all that this implied. Against every threat, even as to her life, she held out with unbroken constancy.

Her greatest trial was enforced separation from her daughter Mary. The king agreed that Mary might be lodged not too far away but yet might not be seen. Catherine wrote to Cromwell:

> Howbeit, you shall say unto his highness that the thing which I desired was to send her where I am; being assured that a little comfort and mirth, which she should take with me, should undoubtedly be half a health unto her. I have proved the like by experience, being diseased of the same infirmity, and know how much good it may do. . . . And since I desired a thing so just and reasonable, and (that) so much touched the honour and conscience of the king my lord, I thought not it should have been denied me.[14]

But it was.

Correspondence was carried on clandestinely. To Mary, Catherine wrote:

> Answer you with few words, obeying the King your father in everything, save only that you will not offend

God and lose your own soul; . . . Speak you few words,
and meddle nothing. . . . And sometimes, for your recrea-
tion, use your virginals, or lute, if you have any. But one
thing specially I desire you, for the love that you do owe
unto God and unto me, to keep your heart with a chaste
mind, and your body from all wanton company, [not] thinking nor desiring any husband, for Christ's Passion; neither
determine yourself to any manner of living until this troublesome time be past; for I dare make sure that you shall
see a very good end. . . . And now you shall begin, and by
likelihood I shall follow [She hints at martyrdom]. I set
not a rush by it; for when they have done the uttermost
they can, then I am sure of amendment. I pray you recommend me unto my good lady of Salisbury, and pray her
to have a good heart, for we never come to the kingdom
of Heaven but by troubles. . . .

By your loving mother,
Katharine the Queen.[15]

To the pope she sent a remonstrance over the delay. Since
all conscientious persons agree that the marriage was indissoluble,

I cannot then do less than complain that my petitions,
both true and just, should have been so long disregarded
by Your Holiness. One thing only comforts me in the midst
of my tribulations, which is to think that God wishes to
punish me for my sins in this world, and that therefore
Your Holiness, His vicar on earth, will not forgive me.
I humbly beg Your Holiness to have pity on me, and accept
as though I had been in purgatory, the penance I have
already suffered for so many years, thus delivering me from
the pains, torments, and sudden fears, to which I am daily
exposed, and which are so great and numerous that I
could not possibly bear up against them had not God
given me strength to endure the same; God, in whom all
my hopes are concentrated, sure as I am that He will not
abandon me in this cause, in which justice is so clearly
with me.[16]

When the pope continued to delay she addressed herself to her nephew the emperor.

> I think I ought, were it for no other purpose than to relieve my conscience, to inform you of the strait in which I find myself, begging your Highness for the service of God with all possible speed to induce His Holiness to decide this cause without delay.[17]

The Spanish ambassador advised the emperor that he should apply "stronger remedies" and that right early. Let him invade England. "The attempt would be easy; for they have no horse, nor men to lead them, nor have they the heart of the people, which is entirely in favor of you, the Queen and the good Princess." The Swiss mercenaries will serve. The Scots will invade. The French will not intervene.[18] Catherine's comment was that she would consider herself "irretrievably damned" were she to countenance war.[19]

As those who refused to take the oath to the royal supremacy were being sent to the block or the stake, Catherine sent a letter of encouragement to Friar Forest who was shortly to suffer by fire. She wrote:

> My revered father,
>
> Since you have ever been wont in dubious cases to give good counsel to others you will necessarily know all the better what is needed for yourself, being called to combat for the love of Christ and the truth of the Catholic faith. If you will bear up under these few and short pains of your torments which are prepared for you, you will receive, as you well know, the eternal reward, which, whoever will basely lose for some tribulation of this present life, I verily esteem him wanting both in sense and reason. But O happy you, my father, to whom it has been graciously granted that you should experience this more fully than other men; and that none otherwise than by these bonds, by this imprisonment, by these torments, and finally by a most cruel death, for Christ's sake, you should happily fulfil the course of your most holy life and fruitful labours.
>
> But woe to me, your poor and wretched daughter, who,

in the time of this my solitude and the extreme anguish of
my soul, shall be deprived of such a corrector and father,
so loved by me in the bowels of Christ. And truly, if it
were lawful for me freely to confess what is my most
ardent desire in reference to this, to your paternity, to whom
I have always hitherto revealed (as was my duty) all the
secrets of my heart and conscience, I confess to you that
I am consumed by a very great desire to be able to die,
either with you or before you; which I should always seek,
and would purchase by any amount of the most heavy
and infinite torments of whatever sort, provided it were
not a thing repugnant to the Divine will, to which I always
willingly submit all my life and my every affection and
desire: so much do I dislike, and so greatly would it dis-
please me, to allow myself any joy in this miserable and
unhappy world, those being removed of whom the world
is not worthy.

But perhaps I have spoken as a foolish woman. Therefore,
since it appears that God has thus ordained, go you, my
father, first with joy and fortitude, and by your prayers
plead with Jesus Christ for me, that I may speedily and
intrepidly follow you through the same wearisome and
difficult journey; and, meanwhile, that I may be able to
share in your holy labours, your torments, punishments
and struggles. I shall have all this by your last blessing in
this life, but when you have fought the battles and obtained the crown, I shall expect to receive more abundant
grace from heaven by your means. . . . Since this is a very
principal and supreme good bestowed by God on mortals,
that for his sake they may endure grievous pains, I shall
always supplicate his Divine Majesty with continual prayers,
with passionate weeping, and with assiduous penitence, that
you may happily end your course, and arrive at the incor-
ruptible crown of eternal life. Farewell, my revered father,
and on earth and in heaven always have me in remembrance before God.

Your very sad and afflicted daughter,
Catherine.[20]

The ultimate attempt to break Catherine's will was to deprive her of all servants who insisted on calling her queen and to remove her to a location which the Spanish ambassador described as the "most insalubrious and pestilential residence in all England." The duke of Suffolk and others were commissioned to remove her. The duke hoped he might have an accident on the way but fortune did not favor him. In his report to the king he said that Catherine with open voice protested "that she was your Queen, and would rather be hewn in pieces than depart from this assertion." She locked herself in her room and said that if they were to remove her they would have to take off the door. She is "the most obstinate woman that may be. There is no other remedy but to remove her by force. . . . Wish for immediate instructions." [21]

She was induced at length to remove to Kimbolton in the north. Here she was closely guarded and none permitted to visit save with a license. But she was able to write and sent this letter to Henry:

> My most dear lord, king, and husband.
>
> The hour of my death now drawing on, the tender love I owe you forceth me, my case being such, to commend myself to you, and to put you in remembrance with a few words of the health and safeguard of your soul which you ought to prefer before all worldly matters, and before the care and pampering of your body, for the which you have cast me into many calamities and yourself into many troubles. For my part, I pardon you everything, and I wish and devoutly pray God that He will pardon you also. For the rest, I commend unto you our daughter Mary, beseeching you to be a good father unto her, as I have heretofore desired. I entreat you also, on behalf of my maids, to give them marriage portions, which is not much, they being but three. For all my other servants I solicit the wages due them, and a year more, lest they be unprovided for. Lastly, I make this vowe, that mine eyes desire you above all things.[22]

Maria de Salinas besought Cromwell for a license to visit.[23]

It did not come in time. Maria did not wait. When word came of the near end she took off for Kimbolton and "came thither on New-year's day about six o'clock at night: with whom these officers [named above] met, and demanded a sight of her licence to repair thither. She said, she would deliver next morning letters sufficient for their discharge. But at present she desired them, being in such a case, (by reason of a fall, as she pretended, from her horse) to repair to the fire; and so was immediately conveyed to the princess. And since that time they never saw her, nor was any letter of licence to repair thither shown them. She appeared in her countenance at her coming to be greatly dismayed, saying she thought never to have seen the princess alive, by reason of such tidings she had heard by the way." [24]

Thomas Cromwell paid Catherine a tribute which would not be relished by the women of our day, for he said that "Nature had done great injury to the said queen in not making her a man." [25] The duke of Suffolk did her greater justice. When he told Henry that Catherine placed two authorities above his own, the king surmised they were the pope and the emperor. "No," said the duke. "God and her conscience." [26]

NOTES

The best study of Catherine is that of Garrett Mattingly, *Catherine of Aragon* (1941). Paperback edition, Vintage Books, New York 1960, with a different pagination is used here.

Abbreviations: *LP, Letters and Papers Foreign and Domestic.*
Spanish, Calendar of State Papers Spanish.
Wood, Mary Anne Wood, *Letters of Royal and Illustrious Ladies,* 3 vols. (London, 1846).

1. Mattingly, 166-167.

2. *Spanish*, 1, No. 435.

3. Mattingly, 85, 105. *Spanish*, 1, Nos. 446, 448, 459, 513, 516, 532, 541.

4. *Spanish*, 1, No. 551.

5. Mattingly, 74.

6. Henry Ellis, *Original Letters,* I (1843), No. XXXIII, 90.

7. Mattingly, 147, 157-158.

8. Lev. 18:16; 20:21. Deut. 25:25.

9. *Spanish*, 4,1, No. 460, p. 759.

10. *Spanish*, 4,2, p. 174.

11. *Spanish*, 4,3, No. 1100, p. 737.

12. A detailed account in J. J. Scarisbrick, *Henry VIII,* (Berkeley, Cal., 1970).

13. George Cavendish, *The Life and Times of Cardinal Wolsey,* ed. J. Grove (1844) IV, 8-9.

14. Wood, II, No. LXXXI, addressed to "Mine especial friend" a form used elsewhere for Cromwell.

15. *LP*, VI, No. 1126.

16. *Spanish*, 4,1, No. 548.

17. *Spanish*, 4,2, No. 994.

18. *LP*, VI, No. 324, pp. 150-151. *Spanish*, 5,1, pp. 153-154.

19. *Spanish*, 4, 3, No. 1063, p. 649.

20. Wood, II, No. LXXXI.

21. *Spanish*, 4,3, pp. 892-893, 896. *LP*, VI, Nos. 1541 and 1542.

22. Mattingly, 410.

23. *LP*, IX, No. 1040 and Wood, 1, No. LXXXIII.

24. John Strype, *Ecclesiastical Memorials* I, 1 (Oxford, 1822), in the whole series X,10, p. 372.

25. *Spanish*, 4,3, No. 1100, p. 739.

26. *Spanish*, 4,2, No. 739, pp. 169-177.

7.

Anne Boleyn
(1507?-1536)

Was Anne Boleyn a sincere Protestant or a brazen hussy supporting with sheer opportunism any man or measure that would bring her to the throne? Did she work for the rejection of the "usurped primacy of the bishop of Rome" simply that Henry might be free to marry her or because of genuine concern for the new teaching? Catholics have branded her, and Protestants claimed her as a Lutheran. In Catholic eyes, heresy amplified the enormity of her guilt. In Protestant eyes, adherence to the word of God was her crown of glory.

On the Catholic side, the Spanish ambassador reported to the emperor that when the king and the Privy Council allowed a preacher to call the pope a heretic, the duke of Norfolk would have burned him save for the intervention of the earl of Wiltshire [Anne's father] and "another whom I would not name" [meaning Anne].[1] At Cambridge, a Protestant hive, a groom at the Horse's Inn had an altercation with the hosteler who asserted that there is no pope but only a bishop of Rome and he who says the contrary is a heretic. "Then is the king a heretic," replied the groom "and this business would never have been had not the king married Anne Bullen." Thereupon the groom "brake the hosteler's hed with a faggot styke,"[2] thus proving that Anne had seduced the king against his real conviction. The cardinal of York, who did support the king on the divorce, and may to that degree be called Protestant, claimed to have known that the Lady Anne was a Lutheran.[3]

Anne Boleyn

Clearly in the Protestant camp was John Foxe, writing under Elizabeth with every reason to exalt the queen's mother and exhort Elizabeth to follow the example of her godliness. According to Foxe, so long as Anne, Cranmer, and Cromwell were the king's counsellors his delight was in the law of the Lord.[4] The annalist Strype declared that Anne induced her husband to lead his people out from the "Egyptian darkness and Babylonian bonds."[5]

What concrete evidence is there in favor of such claims? Agitation for a breach with Rome may have been purely strategic. As evidence of evangelical persuasion Foxe records Anne's extraordinary charities, for she "gave wonderful much privy alms to widows" and money to villagers "to buy kine withal." But this was not Protestant activity. The same was recorded of the Princess Mary. Again Anne her father and her brother "maintained many learned men at Cambridge." Any Maecenas might do that. But some of those appointed at Cambridge were "great professors of the gospel of Christ."[6] This is more to the point. Yet on two occasions Anne supplicated Cromwell not to suppress a nunnery where "the sisters had lived without suspicion of irregularity for sixty years."[7] To do Anne pleasure Henry had vetoed the appointment of an abbess notorious for "levity."[8] All of this proves no more than that Anne was a reforming Catholic.

On the same order is that she bestirred herself to boost absentee Italian bishops out of English sees, Campeggio at Salisbury and Ghinucchi at Worcester.[9] More weight is to be attached to their replacements. The new incumbent at Salisbury was Shaxton, at that time an ardent Protestant.[10] The appointee at Worcester was the later Protestant martyr, Hugh Latimer. Anne had first heard him when, because of his support of the divorce, he was invited to preach by the king. Thereafter she became his patroness, which is significant only because he was Protestant on many more counts than the divorce.

There are two instances in which Anne is credited with having inclined the king to lean to the left. They have to do with books. The first was Simon Fish's *Supplication of Beggars*. The author, having offended Wolsey by a satire, was in refuge on the continent with Tyndale. There Fish composed a violent diatribe against the mendicants and wealthy prelates who left beggars to starve. A copy was sent to Anne who brought it to the attention of the king.[11] He was highly pleased by this indictment of those he intended to despoil. Yet even this tract cannot be called strictly Protestant seeing that protest against clerical extortion was endemic even on the part of those loyal to Rome.

The second instance has to do with Tyndale's *Obedience of the Christian Man*. For fear of Henry's mandates, the author was on the continent working on his translation of the New Testament. The purpose of the tract on obedience was to convince the king that the Protestants were not revolutionaries. A copy was sent to Anne who brought it to the king's attention. It was by no means radical. Obedience was enjoined to rulers unless they transgressed the laws of God and in that case passive resistance alone was allowed to subjects and active resistance only to lower magistrates, a common Protestant position. The strictures on the bishop of Rochester, John Fisher, would please Henry because the bishop was citing Scripture against the divorce. But the jibes at prelates who "juggle their dumb ceremonies with vain words," and against "the belly brotherhood of monks and friars" [12] need not have gone beyond the house cleaning which any serious bishop would introduce. Still, any favor to Tyndale implied a leaning to the left, because he was engaged on a translation of the Scriptures contrary to the royal decree.

More eloquent than all else are two interventions on the part of Anne to save obscure men suffering for radical Protestantism. The first was the case of Patmore, a priest who had blamelessly served his parish for sixteen years. Coming under suspicion he was kept in dire imprisonment in the Lollard's Tower for two years, constantly belabored with charges and harassed by queries on this order. Had he not visited Luther and read Lutheran books? He answered that to do so was not illegal and he would not answer. Had he not advised his maid to marry a priest? He had not advised her but he considered such marriage lawful in the eyes of God. Had he not said that a bundle of hay is of more use than the pope's curse? He might have said it jestingly, but it is true. Had he said that God lays on us commands we cannot keep in order to save us by faith? He had said only what Paul says. Had he taught that it is against God's law to burn heretics? Not adulterers, thieves and murderers but those called heretics. Under pressure he collapsed and abjured. Nevertheless he was deprived of his cure and condemned to perpetual imprisonment. He appealed to the king, was released and restored at the instance of Queen Anne.[13]

The second instance comes to light through a letter of Anne to Cromwell in this summary:

> She is credibly informed that the bearer, Ric. Herman, merchant and citizen of Antwerp, was expelled from his freedom and fellowship in the English house there in the time of the late cardinal, for, as he says, setting forth the New Testament. Desires Cromwell to see him restored to his pristine freedom, liberty, and fellowship.[14]

The indications are strong, then, that she did favor Protestants deemed extremists. Can we say that her striving for the throne was anything more than personal ambition? A letter to Wolsey throws light on the inner spring of her behavior. She reproaches him for having grown lukewarm in her cause and continues:

> For the future I shall rely on nothing but the protection of Heaven and the love of my dear king, which alone will be able to set right again those plans which you have broken and spoiled, . . . and to place me in that happy station which God wills, the king so much wishes, and which will be entirely to the advantage of the kingdom.[15]

"Which God wills!" Is it conceivable, then, that Anne, like Henry, believed that a fresh outbreak of the wars of the Roses could be averted only through a legitimate male heir and, since Catherine could have no more, Anne was commissioned by heaven to supply England's need?

There is a confirmatory legend which found its way into print only in the days of Elizabeth and may have originated with an eye to exalt the queen's mother. The story is that Anne was shown a book with the prophecy that her marriage to Henry would bring certain destruction. Anne showed the book to her maid, Nan, calling attention to a picture of a king and queen wringing their hands and "myself with my head off." Nan responded, "If this is so, though he were the emperor, I would not marry him." "Yes, Nan," was the rejoinder. "I think the book a bauble; yet for the hope that I have that the realm may be happy by my issue, I am resolved to have him whatsoever might become of me." [16]

This tale, were it not for her letter, might be dismissed as tendentious fiction. Do the two together warrant considering Anne not merely a victim but also a martyr?

NOTES

The best life of Anne Boleyn is that of Paul Friedmann, *Anne Boleyn* (London, 1884), but it throws little light on her religious position.

1. *Spanish*, 4, No. 951, p. 445. Carl Meyer, *Elizabeth and the Religious Settlement, 1559* (St. Louis, 1960), 5 note 7.

2. *LP*, VII, No. 754, p. 280.

3. John Foxe, *Acts and Monuments*, V, 52.

4. *Ibid.*, 605 and 135.

5. Strype, *Ecclesiastical Memorials*, I, 170.

6. Foxe, V, 60.

7. Wood, II, No. LXXV, 184.

8. *Ibid.*, II, No. XV, 34.

9. William Hapworth Dixon, *Two Queens*, (London, 1874), 236.

10. Wood, II, LXXVI, 187 and Foxe, V, 136.

11. Foxe, IV, 657.

12. S. L. Greenslade, *The Works of William Tyndale*, (London, 1938), 10. The tract on "Obedience" is in *British Reformers*, (London, n.d.).

13. Foxe, V, 36-37.

14. *LP*, VII, No. 664, p. 255.

15. Wood, II, No. XIX, 48-49.

16. George Wyatt, *Extracts from the Life . . . of Queen Anne Boleyne*, appended to George Cavendish, *The Life of Cardinal Wolsey*, (Chiswick, 1825), II, 190.

8.

Minor Sketches:
The Negligible Wives of Henry VIII

Three wives of Henry VIII are negligible so far as the religious issues are concerned. Catherine Howard was an imprudent minx. Anne of Cleves is described by her fullest biographer as not Catholic minded.[1] That scarcely means that she was ardently Protestant. Her sister was indeed married to that most stalwart Lutheran, John Frederick of Saxony, who would not help Henry unless he signed the Augsburg Confession, but this proves nothing as to the views of Anne. Cromwell, in promoting the match, had less in mind an evangelical confederation than a German counterpoise to Spain and France. In England, Anne was an obliging cypher.

As for Jane Seymour, she was lauded by the Catholics for having brought about a reconciliation between Henry, her husband, and his daughter Mary. This is doubtful. The Protestants exalted her as the mother of Edward VI. This is not doubtful. But neither point has any real bearing on her religious views. After her death masses were said for her soul with crosses, images and censers. During her reign she appears to have been very docile and disinclined to any sort of involvement.[2]

NOTES

1. Karl Wilhelm Bouterweck, "Anna von Cleve," *Zeitschrift des Bergischen Geschichtsvereins*, IV (1867), 337-413; VI (1869), 97-180.
2. Agnes Strickland, *Lives of the Queens of England*, IV (Philadelphia, 1851), 222 ff.

Catherine Parr

9.

Catherine Parr
(1512-1548)

Catherine Parr was the only one of the six wives of Henry VIII to survive him. One reason was that her failure to bear a son was not crucial since Henry already had an heir in Edward; another that she was English and no shift in foreign alliances could require that she be set aside and finally her irreproachable deportment precluded execution for infidelity. But there was one subject that might have meant her undoing and that was religion. Henry was of no mind to renounce the royal supremacy or restore the monasteries, but he was not inclined to doctrinal innovations and, to quiet disturbance occasioned by what he had already done, issued the Six Articles forbidding clerical marriage and visiting with death the denial of transubstantiation.

Among his counsellors was one thoroughly committed to what has been called the Tudor reaction, Stephen Gardiner, the bishop of Winchester, chancellor of the realm and successor to Wolsey's preeminence. Gardiner accepted the royal supremacy on the ground that since the entire population of England belonged both to the church and to the state the same individual might be the head of both. In other words he believed in the nationalizing of the English church, the very point for the rejection of which More and Fisher went to the block. In other respects Gardiner was quite as conservative as they. Henry with an even hand sent Catholics to the block for the repudiation of the royal supremacy and Protestants to the stake for the rejection of transubstantiation. Gardiner feared that he might veer to a more Protestant policy unless delivered from the seductions of Catherine Parr.

John Foxe, the ardent Protestant chronicler gives us this account.[1] The ageing Henry, he tells us, plagued by gout became testy and brooked ill any divergence from his opinions. But with Catherine he was very patient, for "besides the virtues of the mind, she was endowed with very rare gifts of nature, as singular beauty, favor and comely personage, being things wherein the king was greatly delighted." Catherine came often to begile his leisure and contrived to bring the conversation around to the zealous furthering of the reformation of the church. On one such occasion Gardiner was present and Henry was nettled by Catherine's "frowardness." When she went out of the room he remarked, "A good hearing it is when women become such clarks; and a thing much to my comfort to come in my old days to be taught by my wife!"

Winchester (Foxe thus names Gardiner) assured him that it was very "unseemly that any of the king's subjects should argue with him malapertly." Those who so controverted the sovereign in words might seek to overthrow him in deeds. The religion which "the queen so stiffly maintained would dissolve the government of princes" by teaching that all things should be common. Opinions so odious, though spoken by the highest subject in the land, were worthy of death. But far be it from him to say anything against the queen.

"These flattering words so whetted the king to anger" that he gave warrant to certain persons to draw up articles against the queen by which her life might be touched. He pretended to be fully resolved not to spare her if any "color of law gave countenance to the matter." Winchester then proposed to bring charges not at first against the queen but against three of her ladies, whose quarters could be searched and might yield something incriminating with respect to the queen, who might be taken by night in a barge to the Tower. The king consented, being a "politic prince," and desiring to "prove the bishop's malice, how far it would presume, . . . knowing notwithstanding what he would do."

The queen, in the meantime, was innocent of the trap but the Lord "from his eternal throne of wisdom saw the inventions of Ahitophel and rescued his poor handmaid from the pit of ruin." For the warrant signed by the king fell from the bosom of one of the counsellors and was taken to Catherine. She became positively ill but not devoid of the wisdom of the serpent, for she instructed her ladies to remove all books contrary to the law and then sought the presence of the king. He received her courteously and brought the conversation around to religion, desiring, as she perceived, to draw her out. She responded with a "mild and reverent countenance," saying:

"Your Majesty doth right well know, neither I myself am ignorant, what great imperfection and weakness by our first creation is allotted unto us women and to be ordained and appointed as inferior and subject unto man as our head, from which head all our direction ought to proceed. Her womanly weakness and imperfection ought to be tolerated, aided and borne withal so that by his wisdom such things as are lacking in her, ought to be supplied."

"Since therefore God hath appointed such a natural difference between man and woman and your Majesty being so excellent in gifts and ornaments of wisdom, I, a silly, poor, woman, and so much inferior in all respects of nature unto you; how then comes it now to pass, that your Majesty in such diffuse causes of religion, will seem to require my judgment? When I have uttered and said what I can, yet must I, refer my judgment in this and all other cases to your Majesty's wisdom, as my only anchor, supreme head, and governor here in earth next to God, to lean unto."

" 'Not so, by Saint Mary,' quoth the king, 'You are become a doctor, Kate, to instruct us . . . and not to be instructed, or directed by us.' " " 'If your Majesty took it so,' quoth the queen, 'then hath your Majesty much mistaken me, who have ever been of the opinion, to think it very unseemly and preposterous, for the woman to take upon herself the office of an instructor or teacher to her lord and husband; but rather to learn of her husband, and to be taught by him. And whereas I have, with your Majesty's leave, heretofore been bold to hold talk with your Majesty, where sometimes in opinions there hath seemed some difference, I have not done it so much to maintain opinion, as I did it rather to minister talk, not only to the end your Majesty might with less grief pass over this painful time of your infirmity, being attentive to our talk, and hoping that your Majesty should reap some ease thereby; but also that I, hearing your Majesty's learned discourse, might receive to myself some profit thereby: wherein I assure your Majesty, I have not missed any part of my desire in that behalf, always referring myself, in all such matters, unto your Majesty, as by ordinance of nature it is convenient for me to do."

" 'And is it even so, sweetheart!' quoth the king, 'and tended your arguments to no worse end? Then, perfect friends we are now again, as ever at any time heretofore.' And kissing her he added saying, 'that it did him more good at that time to hear those words of her mouth, than if he had heard present news of a hundred thousand pounds in money fallen unto him.' "

Now on the morrow Winchester arrived with forty of the king's guard at his heels to take her to the Tower, whereupon Henry called him an "arrant, beast and fool," and though these words were "uttered somewhat low," yet were they so "vehemently whispered" that all heard and the queen received no little comfort. Perceiving her husband to be "much chafed" she put on a "merry countenance," and besought him not to deal harshly with the bishop who had sinned in ignorance. And thus "by God's only blessing" she "escaped the dangerous snare of her bloody and cruel enemies for the gospel's sake."

Such is the recital of John Foxe. What are we to make of it? Did Henry all along intend to vindicate his wife and was he simply giving the bishop more faggots for the fire of his burning? Did Henry plan to reverse the policy of his last days and push ahead with the reform? The case was so represented by the Edwardians, but a recent historian gives reasons for thinking that if Henry had veered it would not have been for the sake of religion but to keep the balance of the continental powers and their confessions.[2] In that case was Henry amusing himself by playing with his ministers? Would he actually have put Catherine Parr out of the way if she had obstructed his program? Did she in fact mollify him by using as a weapon the myth of female subjection? The question probably admits of no answer, and in any case our purpose is not to fathom the mind of Henry but to bring to light, if we can, the intentions of Catherine.

There are three ways of assessing her religious stance, by her words, her friends and her deeds. Her words include a collection of prayers, which, although belonging to the devotional classics of the Tudor age, are not helpful at this point because they voice the aspirations of the ages and might well have been composed earlier by St. Augustine, St. Bernard and St. Francis or later by Launcelot Andrews, George Herbert or William Law.

Her writings look toward a furthering of the reform. The prayers were rather a compilation than a composition, of which a further word later. *The Lamentation or Complaint of a Sinner*, appeared in 1547 with a preface by William Cecil, who came to be the great Lord Burghley of Elizabeth's reign. He lauds Catherine because "forsaking ignorance wherein she was blind, she has come to knowledge, whereby she may see; removing superstition wherewith she was smothered, to embrace true religion, wherewith she may revive." For him, then, her tract was a manifesto of reform. But it was more than that. This little treatise is one of the gems of Tudor devotional literature[3] and may well be compared with the *Chansons Spirituelles* of Marguerite of Navarre and the *Rime Religiose* of Vittoria Colonna. All are suffused with the rapturous glow of adoration for Christ the crucified.

There are some differences. Catherine does not ascend to the mystical exaltation of Marguerite which caused the baffled Cardinal Pole to say that she was "forever soaring into the bosom of God." There is no trace of the Neoplatonic dualism of flesh and spirit in which the flesh is the corporeal component of man. For Catherine the flesh is whatever wars against the spirit of Christ, such as envy and malice which are not of the body. And although Catherine uses the language of heat and light, her

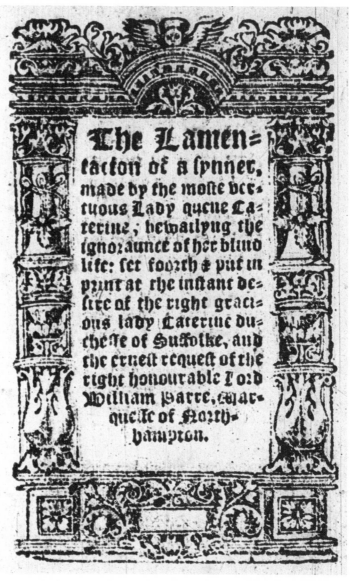

Lamentation of a Sinner by Catherine Parr published at the "instant desire of the right gracious lady Catherine, duchesse of Suffolke"

meditations do not teem with recurrent contrasts of light and dark, sunlight and shade, fire and cold, the dazzling and the tenebrous as in the *Rime* of Vittoria. What Catherine has to say about the contemporary situation is entirely in line with the policy of her late husband, and does not overtly go beyond. She laments her one time error in listening to the pope and rejoices that Henry as the new Moses delivered his people from thralldom under the new Pharaoh, the pope. She would encourage Bible reading—and Henry had cooled on that—undeterred by the fear that it would engender heresy or incite dissension.

The burden of her meditation is the benefit of Christ's death upon the cross. Listen to these passages somewhat condensed:

> Let us consider the great charity of God in sending his Son to suffer death for our redemption. A more noble and rich gift he could not have given. He sent not a servant or a friend, but his only Son, so dearly beloved; not in delights, riches and honors but in poverties and slanders, not as a lord but as a servant, yea, and in most vile and painful sufferings to wash us, not with water, but with his own precious blood; not from mire, but from the puddle and filth of our iniquities. He hath given him not to make us poor, but to enrich us with his divine virtues, merits and graces; yea, and in him he hath given us all things, and finally himself, with such great charity as cannot be expressed. Even in the time when we had done him most injury he first showed his charity to us with such flames of love that greater cannot be showed.
>
> Inwardly to behold Christ upon the cross is the best and goodliest meditation that can be. We may see also in Christ crucified the beauty of the soul better than in all the books of the world. For he that with a lively faith seeth and feeleth in spirit that Christ, the Son of God, is dead for the satisfying and purifying of the soul, shall see that his soul is appointed for the very tabernacle and mansion of the inestimable and incomprehensible majesty and honor of God.
>
> There are those who make not Christ their chief founda-

tion. The fleshly children of Adam are so politic, subtle, crafty, and wise in their kind that the elect should be deceived if possible. But the children of light know the contrary and are not abashed though the world hate them. They are not so foolish as not to give God thanks for their election, which was before the beginning of the world, for they believe most surely they are of the chosen. They are not by this godly faith presumptuously enflamed. Nor are they curious in searching the high mysteries of God, which are not meet for them to know. The crucifix is the book wherein God hath included all things and hath most compendiously written therein all truth profitable and necessary for our salvation. Therefore let us endeavor ourselves to study this book, that we, being enlightened with the spirit of God, may give him thanks for so great a benefit.

Some of this sounds like John Calvin. The mere reference to predestination need not of course have come from him. A devotional work published in Latin in 1498 and in English in 1525 addressed Jesus with reference to "the predestination of all thy chosen souls that should be saved by the merit of thy passion." [4] But there is an Ariadne thread which runs from England to Geneva by way of Italy. The clue is in Catherine's references to "the benefits of Christ's death." Once again the mere word "benefit" calls for no specific source beyond the Psalm, "Bless the Lord, O my soul and forget not all his benefits." But *The Benefit of Christ's Death* was precisely the title of the favorite compendium of the piety of the Italian evangelicals! It appeared in Italy in 1543 with the title *Del Beneficio de Giesu Christo Crucifisso,* and in an English translation in 1548.[5] Catherine may not have seen the English. She could handle the Italian.[6]

How this work was conceived in England appears from the circumstance of the translation. It was the work of Edward Courtenay, who for ten years since the age of twelve had been a prisoner in the Tower for combining Plantagenet blood with possible royalist pretentions. He had spent his time learning Italian and now on the death of Henry dedicated this translation to the duchess of Somerset that she might "set her gracious good will and helping hand, that by the same your godlie and piteful meanes it may please my Lord's grace of his manyfolde and abundaunte goodness, to deliver me out of this miserable captivitie." A copy with an inscription in Courtenay's hand was presented to the Protector, evidently with the thought that this tract would further the reform.

Little did Courtenay know, little did Catherine know that the last three chapters of this "most profitable treatise" were a reworking and sometimes a direct translation from the *Institutes* of John Calvin! [7]

When we look at the religious complexion of Catherine's associates we find that she brought under one roof Mary, Edward and Elizabeth, all ultimately of different persuasions. The *Lamentation* was published by the ardent Protestant, the duchess of Suffolk, with a preface by William Cecil, a moderate Protestant. The queen's chaplain was Parkhurst, an exile under Mary, and a nuisance for abetting non-conformity under Elizabeth. Something can be inferred from the stands of the translators [8] engaged by Catherine for translating the *Paraphrases* of Erasmus, which appeared in two volumes under Edward in 1548. The project began under Henry.

In the first volume the chief contributor was the dramatist Nicolas Udall, the author of the play *Royster Doyster*. His prefaces are staunchly Protestant though he managed later to survive under Mary.[9] Thomas Kay (Caius) proved to be more of a willow than an oak. The third translator was the inflexible Catholic, the Princess Mary. When she was too ill to carry through the rendering of John's gospel Catherine besought her to allow her name to appear along with that of her substitute, Malet, later sent to the Tower for having said mass in Mary's chapel. The inclusion of Mary shows a spirit of catholicity.

We are warned not to infer too much from the character of the translators in the second volume because the lead had passed from Catherine to the duchess of Somerset.[10] To be sure the dedications shift but that was out of deference to the ruling house. The continuing influence of Catherine is indicated by the use in both volumes of a title page border with her coat of arms. This might, of course, have simply been automatically carried over by the intrepid Protestant printer, Whitechurch. But he used the cut also for the first *Prayer Book* of 1549 and if the duchess had been out of favor her arms could have been expunged, as they were when this same woodcut was taken to Mexico and used for a Spanish work. The initial W for Whitechurch was overlooked and retained.

But we need not rest the case on evidence so frail. The chief figure in the second volume was Miles Coverdale who pronounced the oration at Catherine's funeral and of whose Protestantism there was no question. Another in this second volume was John Olde, appointed to a living by the duchess of Somerset at the instance of the undoubted Protestant, Hugh Latimer. Under Mary, Olde was in exile. Edmund Allen proved his Protestantism already under Henry by securing leave to reside on the continent where he begat "eight legitimate children" (legitimate presumably only if he were Protestant). Leonard Coxe was to this extent hospitable to the reform that when Frith, the later martyr was in the stocks he "procured his releasement, refreshed his empty stomach and gave him money."

The composition of this body of translators suggests Protestant leanings with a spirit of catholicity. The tone is that of Erasmus. Why did Catherine sponsor the project and induce the Protector to enjoin that copies be set up in the parish churches? The most obvious answer is that she wished to disseminate the word of God and believed that the simple elucidations of Erasmus would assist "silly souls" to grasp those passages "hard to be understood which the ignorant and unstable twist to their own destruction" (1 Peter 3:16). The appeal to the authority of Erasmus would of itself prove nothing as to the alignment of parties, for all referred to him.

The translators bent him to their own use by the devices of marginal annotations, additions in the text and especially by prefaces. Nicolas Udall, in the preface to Edward VI, called attention to the commentary on Christ's entry into Jerusalem on Palm Sunday.[11] The marginal annotation reads: "The Byshop of Romes pompe is covertly described." There can be no doubt about that. Here is my own translation directly from the Latin of Erasmus:

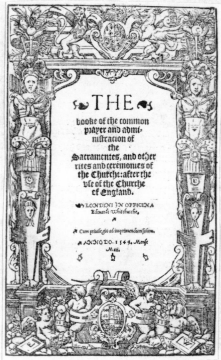

Title pages of the second volume of the *Paraphrases* of Erasmus in English, of the first *Prayer Book* of Edward VI and of a Spanish tract published in Mexico.

Now for a moment, reader, compare with me this scene with the behavior of one of those who hold the chief seats among the Jewish priests. But consider first of all how great is he who rides upon the ass's foal. He is none other than the Son of God, to whom the Father has given all power in heaven and on earth. He is the Savior and Ruler of the whole world, the Author, Lord and King of all things that are created, and King forever after the order of Melchizedek, who with a beck can do whatsoever he will, whose majesty is adored by all the orders of angels, who sits at the right hand of the Father Almighty.

Now with his dignity compare the pontiff of a certain temple, who for the price of a year's income buys a benefice from an impious king. Compare the bare head of Jesus with this man's tiara glittering with gold and gems. Compare the modest gentle face of Jesus with this priest's bloated visage, grim brow, beetling eyebrows, lofty eyes and insolent mouth. Compare the bare hands of Jesus with this man's fingers laden with rings and precious stones.

Look at Jesus clad in the simple garment of a peasant and this man in his theatrical robes, stirrups of silver and gold. Look at the common foal of the ass which carries Jesus and with it compare the many mules caparisoned with silk and cloth of gold, so many lordly coursers, so many palfreys of great price, so many wagons, so many chariots, so many palanquins, all ready to carry this one man. Compare once more the few and lowly followers of Jesus with the throngs before this priest of noble youths, trumpeters, pipers, henchmen and guards with a pomp exceeding that of any prince and among them he is most proud who is nearest and most pleasing to the pontiff. Compare the cries of the throng before and after Jesus, who filled with the Holy Ghost chant the prophecy of the psalm, 'Hosanna, blessed is he that comes in the name of the Lord,' compare this with the profane acclamations with which the chorus of adulators hail the base Jewish High Priest, 'Long live the most holy pontiff.' How greatly Jesus despised such priests is plain since he ordered the destruction of their tinselled, proud priesthood and of their very temple. And such today are those who kill Christ in his members, for he wills to be alone the head of the priesthood.[12]

Now, who ever heard of the Jewish high priest wearing a tiara? Manifestly this is meant for the pope and what is more, Erasmus reworked the description of Pope Julius II in the anonymous satire *Julius Excluded from Heaven,* of which Erasmus himself was in very great likelihood the author. The English translator has added a few embellishments. To the tiara he has added the miter and *pontifex* is translated commonly bishop or prelate to include the whole hierarchy.

But this diatribe, however stinging, is really not radical, even in the last days of Henry VIII, for it could be used to justify nothing more drastic than the demolition of the usurped primacy of the Roman pontiff. There is a much more radical passage which might seem to be utterly innocuous. It is the exposition of Jesus' word in Matthew 6:7,[13] "In praying do not heap up empty phrases as the Gentiles do, for they think they will be heard for their many words." Erasmus expands: "This also must be considered in prayer. It is the affection and hearty desire that moveth God, not the noise of the lips and it skilleth not how long and how loud the prayer be, but how fervent and sincere the affection and desire is. . . . We ought to pray often rather than much, and vehemently rather than long; finally with the heart rather than with the voice. Neither always with prescribed and purposed wordes after the custom of the heathen, but so much as the fervencies of the mind and the ravishment towards God doth stir and provoke." Such a passage might serve to eliminate *The Book of Common Prayer* in favor of free prayers, or private prayers or prayers unuttered, as in a Quaker meeting.

The radicalism of Erasmus consisted in his spiritualizing of religion to the degree that the external aids to worship were regarded as superfluous or even impediments: prayers by rote, telling of beads, reverence for relics, adoration of images, including the crucifix, prayers for physical benefits to the saints and the blessed Virgin, dietary rules, the obligatory celibacy of the clergy—All these might go, but should not be rooted out by

royal fiat. Conversion, not coercion, should be the method. This
was the point over which he had clashed with the reformers at
Basel in 1529. In accord with his assumed principles, they called
for the smashing of the images, the removal of the organs, the
abolition of fast days and distinction of foods, the removal of
the prohibition of clerical marriage, the discontinuance of the
mass in favor of the Lord's Supper as a memorial of Christ's
death. The mass should not be celebrated in any church in the
city. The penalty for non-compliance was banishment. Erasmus
left. Now in England, nearly twenty years later, appeal was again
made to his principles, again to be implemented by methods
which he could not have condoned.

But our concern for the moment is not with what he thought
but with what they thought he thought, and more especially
what they thought, and then as to whether Catherine was of their
mind. Their prefaces are more revealing than the translations.
The preface to Mark by Thomas Kay [14] is addressed "To the
most excellent and vertuous princesse quene Catherine, wyfe to
our moste gracious soueraigne Lorde Henry eight," obviously
during the lifetime of her husband, who is extolled as the new
Josiah, the demolisher of the shrines of Baal on the hilltops of
Israel. Whereas in time past

> many a thousand putte more confidence of soule healthe in
> workes that were but of mennes phantasying, as in pardons,
> in pilgrymages, in kyssing of reliques, of offerying to saintes,
> in halowed beades, in numberying of prayers, in mumblyng
> up of psalmes not understand [understood] in the merytes of
> those that called themselfes relygious, and in other lyke
> thynges. . . . Nowe hathe England cleane forsaken Antichrist
> of Rome.

This enumeration was programatic rather than descriptive.
Henry VIII had by no means gone so far.

The prefaces of Udall are more realistic and afford an interesting contrast to each other.[15] The first was addressed to Catherine while her husband was alive, the second to Edward after
the death of his father. The one to Catherine begins by calling

attention to the praises bestowed on women in the Bible. For
Udall to extol her virtues would be like bringing out a smoking
firebrand on a sunny day.

> Your manifold unestimable giftes of grace and among
> them most principally your studious seekyng to promote the
> glory of God and of his most holy ghospell, haue been the
> thynges that haue moued the most noble, the most re-
> nounned, and the moste godly Prince of the universall
> worlde, our most gracious soueraigne Lord kyng Henry the
> eight, to iudge and esteme your grace a mete spouse for his
> maiestie.
>
> [Your] contemplative meditations [show that] women are
> no lesse apt, no lesse wittie, no lesse able, no lesse indus-
> trious, no lesse active, no lesse frutefull and pithy in the ac-
> quirying or handlying of all kyndes of disciplines then men
> are. All your delite, all your studie, and all your endeuour
> is by all possible meanes emploied to the publique com-
> moditie of all good English people, the kynges moste louyng
> and obedient subiectes, to bee nourished and trayned in the
> readyng of Gods woorde.
>
> This is the grayne of mustard sede . . . [which now]
> spredeth the braunches in suche a coumpace, that all Eng-
> lishe readers may therein fynd many places where to lyght
> and to bylde them nestes, in whiche their soules and con-
> sciences may to theyr ghostely comfort quietly repose them-
> selves. Where the texte of the gospel afore was in sum
> partes . . . to the complexcion of grosse, rude and grene
> stomaked Englishmen disagreeyng and harde of digestion
> [yet through the *Paraphrases* of Erasmus you have] minced
> it and made it euery English mans meate.

Then begins praise of Henry, the new David who with the
stone of God's word and the sling of the divine spirit put down
the idol of the Roman Antichrist. Henry is the new Hezekiah
commissioned to put down false religion and root out superstit-
tion and idolatry. When then God shall bestow on our most
gracious sovereign the "croune of immortality and he shall sur-

render this emperiall croune to the most regal Impe his sonne, our noble prince Edwarde . . . may he without any let of stumblyng blockes to be layed in his way by papistrie . . . continue the godly trade nowe at this daye well begonne." David laid the foundation. Let Solomon build the temple.

Now compare the preface to Edward VI. "During the reign of your most noble father all hoped that you would be equal to your sire. But now you have shown such towardness of godly zeal that we have conceived no less than an undoubted hope that you will by God's gouernance surpass your sayd father." Far be it from me to engage in flattery but all who speak of your Majesty extol your "incomparable virtues." This is not "clawing adulation," but rather an exhortation that you should not degenerate from the godly trade of religion. Your noble father, having begotten the two daughters, Mary and Elizabeth, yet for the tranquility of England provided a son in your person. Your father was another Cyrus to deliver us from the bondage to the Romish Nebuchadnezzar, who with "develish inventions" cast the "mist of ignorance" over God's most holy Word, perplexed the grace of the gospel with false, feigned merits and works of supererrogation, mangled the Christian profession with cloisters of Antichrist's own generation, oppressed the true religion with pilgrimages to dead stokes and stones of men's handiwork . . . and "with a purgatory of material fire."

Henry is the David again who with the sling this time of the *regal authority* and the pebble of God's word felled the Goliath of the papacy stone dead. Henry is the archangel Michael who cast the old serpent and his angels out of England. Henry is Hercules who slew the seven headed hydra. King John had cut off one head but it had grown again.

When then the Roman anti-Christ was expelled God raised up Edward's mother, the noble Queen Jane, who as soon as she had born the king took her leave of life, as if to say "I have done the office I was born for. Now fare ye well." We may be sure that God took her at once to confer upon her an eternal crown, lest we "being inebriated with our insatiable felicity" might have been made proud.

The father was in his time peerless, but now the son must surmount him.

Such excellent beginnings being furthered by the daily prayers of all your faithful and true hearted subjects, cannot but have still better and better degrees of continuance and increase, especially since God has graciously supplied the boy king with such sapient counsellors.

Let him take heed to the examples of two boy kings in the Old Testament. Manasses was beguiled by evil counsellors and did not walk in the ways of his father Hezekiah, but Josiah, though but eight years old at the commencement of his reign, gave heed to his "sapient" advisers and did that which was pleasing in the eyes of the Lord.

O happy king are you to have such wise counsellors. O happy counsellors of such a toward king. Whereas Hezekiah and Josiah were able to establish the true religion only during their reigns may your Majesty establish it forever in the bowels of all your most tender and loving subjects.

Then a word of praise to Catherine for giving England God's Word winnowed by Erasmus from all scholastic chaff.

One observes that this time Henry is no longer Hezekiah or Josiah. The altars of Baal have not been pulled down from their high places. Edward is the one to accomplish the demolition.

Is this what Catherine wished? One notes that in her *Lamentation* she passed swiftly from a reference to a visible idol to reproach herself for making an idol of herself. This is the inwardness of Erasmus who disparaged the outward expressions of religion, though to remove them would not use outward means.

The collection of prayers compiled by Catherine voice the aspirations of the ages.[16] They came to her from the ages. The selection rather than the phraseology reveal her leanings. One finds lamentation over the sinfulness and miseries of man, prayers for forgiveness, help and comfort. Here are a few excerpts from a modernized version:

O Lord Jesus, most loving spouse, who shall give me wings of perfect love that I may fly up from these worldly miseries to rest in Thee? O when shall I ascend to Thee, to see and feel how sweet Thou art? I beseech Thee, Lord Jesus, that the sighings and desires of my heart may move and incline Thee to hear me. . . .

Let not flesh and blood overcome me, nor yet the world with his vain glory deceive me, but give me spiritual strength in resisting them, patience in suffering them, constancy in persevering. . . .

O everlasting light, far passing all things, send down the beams of Thy brightness from above and purify and lighten the inward parts of my heart. . . .

O good Lord who hast lordship over all, and power of the sea to assuage the rages and surges of the same, arise and help me, destroy the power of mine enemies, which always make battle against me. Show forth the greatness of Thy goodness, and let the power of Thy right hand be glorified in me, for there is to me none other help or refuge but in Thee only, my Lord and my God; to Thee be honor and glory everlasting.

We outlaws, the children of Eve, weep and wail the bitter tediousness of our day, that is, of this present life, short and evil, full of sorrow and anguish, where man is oftentimes defiled by sin, encumbered with affliction and disquieted with troubles, wrapped in cares, busied with vanities, blinded with errors, overcharged with labors, vexed with temptations, overcome with vain delights and pleasures of the world and grievously tormented with penuary and want. O when shall the end come of all these miseries? Send forth the hot flames of Thy love to burn and consume the hot fantasies of my mind. . . .

Lord give me peace, give me inward peace, give me inward joy and then my soul shall be full of heavenly melody. . . . It is good to me O Lord, that Thou hast meekened me, that I may thereby learn to know Thy righteous judgments and to put from me all honor of presumption and stateliness of heart. . . . Lord, I yield thanks to Thee that Thou hast spared my sins, but hast punished me with the scourges of love, and hast sent me affliction and anguish within and without. . . . Turn not Thy face from me, defer not visiting me, withdraw not Thy comforts, lest haply my soul be made as dry earth without the water of grace.

The note of world weariness, though characteristic of traditional piety, may well have been a reflection of her own mood. One observes the similarity to the poems of Marguerite of Navarre. Such eagerness to be released is the most understandable in her case seeing that she had lost her idolized brother and saw the hopes of her life belied. But Catherine did not live to see the execution of her husband, and the reforms for which she labored were in the ascendant. But where is the mortal who has no need of consolation? A touch of solace fell to Catherine when Princess Elizabeth at the age of eleven translated the *Miroir de l'Ame Perchereuse* of Marguerite of Navarre and presented it to Catherine Parr.[17]

BIBLIOGRAPHY

The works of Catherine Parr are reproduced in modernized form in a volume published by the Presbyterian Board of Publication, Philadelphia, n.d., entitled *Writings of Edward Sixth, William Hugh, Queen Catherine Parr, Anne Askew, Lady Jane Grey, Hamilton and Balnaves.* Her religious position is assessed by William F. Haugaard, "The Religious Convictions of a Renaissance Queene," *Renaissance Quarterly* XXII, 4 (Winter, 1969), 346-359. Her Protestant leanings are underplayed. The devotional writings are evaluated by Helen C. White, *Tudor Books of Private Devotion* (University of Wisconsin Press, 1951). Catherine receives notice *passim* in James McConica, *English Humanists and Reformation Politics* (Oxford, 1965).

NOTES

1. John Foxe, *The Acts and Monuments,* V (Reprint New York, 1965), 553-561.

2. Lacey Baldwin Smith, "Henry VIII and the Protestant Triumph," *American Historical Review,* LXXXI, 4 (July, 1966) 1237-1263.

3. See Helen White and Conyers Read, *Mr. Secretary Cecil and Queen Elizabeth,* (New York, 1955), 43.

4. *Ibid.,* 220.

5. The *Beneficio* was published in Italian accompanied by a French translation and the English translation of Edward Courtenay by Churchill Babington under the title *The Benefit of Christ's Death,* (London, 1855). A new translation with notes has been published by Ruth Orelowski in *Italian Reformation Studies in Honor of Laelius Socinus,* (Florence, 1965). The *Corpus Reformatorum Italicorum* in 1972 published *Il Beneficio di Cristo,* edited by Salvatore Caponetta, who discovers indebtedness not only to Calvin but also to Luther and Melanchthon.

6. Haugaard, 347 note 8 citing Agnes Strickland, *The Life of Queen Elizabeth,* (Everyman ed., London, 1906), 15.

7. Valdo Vinay, "Die Schrift *Il Beneficio di Giesu di Christo,*" *Archiv für Reformationsgeschichte,* LVIII, 1 (1967), 29-72. McConica observed a similarity to the *Beneficio* in a manuscript poem attributed to Catherine.

8. Biographies of these men in the *Dictionary of National Biography.*

9. On Udall's constancy Ruth H. Blackburn, *Biblical Drama under the Tudors,* (The Hague, 1971), 65 note 3.

10. McConica, 241.

11. Udall's preface to Edward VI, *Paraphrases,* I, fol. X verso. At the bottom of the page Bii verso. The passage on Mark XI is fol. LXXVI verso, bottom Kiiii verso.

12. See my article "Erasmus and Luther and the Dialog Julius Exclusus," *Festschrift für Franz Lau, Vierhundertfünfzig Jahre lutherische Reformation,* (Göttingen, 1967), 17-26.

13. On Matthew 6:7, *Paraphrases,* I, fol. fv verso.

14. Thomas Key's dedication to Catherine is before Mark in volume I.

15. Udall's prefaces precede Luke and Matthew in volume I.

16. See the comments in White.

17. *The Mirror of the Sinful Soul,* facsimile ed., Percy W. Ames, (Royal Society of Literature, London, 1897).

10.

Lady Jane Grey
(1537-1554)

Lady Jane, England's nine day queen, made a deeper impact on her countrymen by her death than by her reign. She was virtually canonized by the Protestants, who portrayed her as comely, charming, devout, learned, demure and gentle. They called her in the words of the prophet Isaiah "a lamb that is led to the slaughter," [1] but did not add the verse "like a sheep that before its shearers is dumb, so she opened not her mouth." That assuredly she did not do. Writing at the age of fourteen to the Swiss theologian Bullinger, she depreciated herself in the approved humanist style, saying that to laud his excellence she lacked the eloquence of Demosthenes and Cicero.[2] She need not have been so disparaging, for, confronted by the torrential flow of her periods, they would have doffed their headgear.

Because of royal lineage Jane was given the education of a princess. She was the granddaughter of Mary Tudor, the sister of Henry VIII and of Charles Brandon, that duke of Suffolk, commissioned by Henry to remove Catherine. Jane's mother was the daughter of this couple. Her father became the next duke of Suffolk. These parents were of the domineering sort and the mother looked like a termagant.[3] Out of ambition the parents imposed on their daughter a stiff educational regime, which actually she loved. In her early teens she became proficient in Latin, Greek, French and Italian and corresponded with Bullinger as to the best way of learning Hebrew. Her tutor, Ayl-

181

mer, was an engaging enthusiast. Another great educator, Roger Ascham, has given a charming account of Jane at her studies. About to go abroad, he tells us, he came to take

> leave of that noble Lady Jane Grey, to whom I was exceeding much beholden. Her parents, the duke and the duchess, with all the household, gentlemen and gentlewomen, were hunting in the park. I found her in her chamber, reading *Phaedon Platonis* [the *Phaedo* of Plato] in Greek, and that with as much delight, as some gentlemen would read a merry tale in *Boccace*. After salutation and duty done, with some other talk, I asked her, why she would leese such pastime in the park. Smiling she answered me, "I wisse, al their sport in the park is but a shadow to that plesure that I find in Plato. Alas! good folk, they never felt what true plesure meant."
>
> "And how came you, madam," quoth I, "to this deep knowledge of plesure, and what did chiefly allure you unto it, seeing not many women, but very few men, have attained thereunto?"
>
> "I will tell you," quoth she, "and tell you a troth, which perchance ye will marvel at. One of the greatest benefits that ever God gave me is, that he sent me so sharp and severe parents and so gentle a schoolmaster: for when I am in presence either of father or mother, whether I speak, keep silence, sit, stand or go, eat, drink, be merry or sad, be sewing, playing, dancing, or doing any thing else, I must do it as it were in such weight, measure and number, even so perfectly as God made the world; or else I am so sharply taunted, so cruelly threatened, yea presently sometimes with pinches, nipps, and bobbs, and other ways, (which I will not name for the honour I bear them) so without mesure misordered, that I think myself in hell, till time come that I must go to Mr. Aylmer, who teacheth me so gently, so pleasantly, with such fair allurements to learning, that I think all the time nothing whiles I am with him. And when I am called from him, I fall on weeping, because whatsoever I do else but learning, is full of grief, trouble, fear,

and wholly misliking to me. And thus my book hath been so much my plesure and more, that in respect of it, al other plesures in very deed be but trifles and troubles unto me." [4]

Jane's intense Protestant convictions may very probably have been imbibed from Aylmer, who was an eminent divine and also from Martin Butzer, to whom she confessed herself much indebted. He was a refugee from Strasbourg teaching at Cambridge. He it was, said she, who "led me forward in all probity, piety and sound learning." [5] Jane was for a time in the household of Catherine Parr, who might temper but would not quench her ardor. The degree of Jane's Protestantism is evidenced by an occurrence, when, with her parents, she was the guest of the Princess Mary, who in defiance of the law had mass said in her private chapel during the reign of her brother Edward. Jane, in company with Lady Wharton, was out for a walk when they passed by the chapel. Lady Wharton curtsied. Jane asked why. Was the Lady Mary in the chapel? "No. I curtsied to Him that made us all" [that is the host reserved upon the altar]. "And how," asked Jane, "can He that made us all be there seeing that the baker made Him?" This being reported to the Lady Mary she misliked Jane thereafter.[6]

When the Protestant chaplain to her father turned Catholic on the accession of Mary, Jane sent him a remonstrance replete with the imagery of the Apocalypse and reverberations of Demosthenes. Here are some excerpts:

> So oft as I call to mind the dreadful and fearful saying of God, That "he that layeth hold upon the plough, and looketh back, is not meet for the kingdom of heaven" and, on the other side, the comfortable words of our Saviour Christ to all those that, forsaking themselves, do follow him, I cannot but marvel at thee, and lament thy case, who seemed sometime to be the lively member of Christ, but now the deformed imp [the word then meant simply a child] of the devil; sometime the bountiful temple of God, but now the stinking and filthy kennel of Satan; sometime the unspotted spouse of Christ, but now the unshamefaced

paramour of anti-Christ; sometime my faithful brother, but now a stranger and apostate; sometime a stout Christian soldier, but now a cowardly runaway. Yea, when I consider these things, I cannot but speak to thee, and cry out upon thee, thou seed of Satan and not of Judah, whom the devil hath deceived, the world hath beguiled, and the desire of life subverted, and made thee an infidel.

Wherefore hast thou taken the testament of the Lord in thy mouth? . . . Wherefore hast thou instructed others to be strong in Christ, when thou thyself does now so shamefully shrink, and so horribly abuse the Testament and law of the Lord? . . . Why dost thou now show thyself most weak, when indeed thou oughtest to be most strong? The strength of a fort is unknown before the assault, but thou yieldest thy hold before any battery be made.

O wretched and unhappy man, what art thou, but dust and ashes? and wilt thou resist thy Maker that fashioned thee and framed thee? . . . Wilt thou refuse the true God, and worship the invention of man, the golden calf, the whore of Babylon, the Romish religion, the abominable idol, the most wicked mass? Wilt thou torment again, rend and tear the most precious body of our Saviour Christ, with thy bodily and fleshly teeth? Wilt thou take upon thee to offer up any sacrifice unto God for our sins, considering that Christ offered up himself, as Paul saith, upon the cross, a lively sacrifice once for all? . . . And wilt thou honour a detestable idol invented by Romish popes, and the abominable college of crafty cardinals? Christ offered himself up once for all, and wilt thou offer him up again daily at thy pleasure?

But thou wilt say, thou doest it for a good intent. Oh sink of sin! O child of perdition! Dost thou dream therein of a good intent, where thy conscience beareth thee witness of God's threatened wrath against thee? . . . Wilt thou for a good intent pluck Christ out of heaven, and make his death void? . . .

But thou wilt say, "I will not break unity." What? not the unity of Satan and his members? not the unity of darkness, the agreement of Antichrist and his adherents? Nay, thou deceivest thyself with a fond imagination of such a unity as is among the enemies of Christ. Were not the false prophets in a unity? . . . The agreement of ill men is not a unity but a conspiracy.

Thou hast heard some threatening, some cursings, and some admonitions, out of the Scripture, to those that love themselves above Christ. . . . Well, if these terrible and thundering threatenings cannot stir thee to cleave unto Christ, and forsake the world, yet let the sweet consolations and promises of Scripture . . . encourage thee to take faster hold on Christ. . . . Return, return again into Christ's war. . . . Throw down yourself with the fear of his threatened vengeance . . . and comfort yourself with the mercy, blood, and promise of him that is ready to turn unto you, whensoever you turn unto him. Disdain not to come with the lost son. . . . Be not ashamed to come home again with Mary, and weep bitterly with Peter, not only with shedding the tears of your bodily eyes, but also pouring out the streams of your heart—to wash away, out of the sight of God, the filth and mire of your offensive fall. Be not ashamed to say with the publican, "Lord be merciful to me a sinner." [7]

Ascham was very right when he said that Jane was happier reading about the martyrdom of Socrates than rejoicing in her descent from kings and queens, for from this arose her own martyrdom. During the minority of Edward VI, the government at the end of his reign was in the hands of the duke of Northumberland, who realized, when the sixteen-year-old king was obviously dying, that when he was gone the power would pass to Mary or Elizabeth unless their succession were annulled. In consequence he induced Edward to change the succession in favor of Jane, already married to the duke's own son, Guilford, who presumably would be king. On the king's death high dignitaries came and made obeisance to Jane. She wept, swooned, and protested that if one should scruple to steal a shilling how much more to usurp a crown.[8]

Northumberland informed her that by a previous act Mary and Elizabeth had been declared illegitimate and Edward had conferred upon her the succession. Young Guilford belabored Jane with entreaties and caresses, saying that she should make him to be king. That she flatly refused. A duke he might be, a king never. His parents were infuriated and forbade him to sleep with her. Her parents interposed their authority. Here was a conflict between obedience to father and mother and to the laws of the realm, because the change in succession lacked parliamentary authorization. Jane yielded to her parents and trembling allowed the crown to be placed upon her head. She was sixteen.[9]

Mary, with the utmost intrepidity, rallied forces against the duke. Jane, exercising her royal authority, commanded him to leave London and head his troops in the field. But what was then needed was not a general but a demogogue. He obeyed the authority he had created, though perceiving that to leave the capitol would be his undoing. It was. He and his cohorts, Jane's father and husband, and Jane herself were arraigned for treason and given the sentence of death. Judge Morgan, who pronounced the sentence on Jane, went mad, raving that she be taken from his sight.[10]

But judicial sentence did not mean execution in case of executive clemency. Mary did not pardon Northumberland, but she released Jane's father. She and her husband were neither pardoned nor executed but kept in custody. Mary was moved to refrain from extremities by Jane's letter in which she freely confessed that she had committed a crime in accepting from those deemed wise by all the realm, a crown which was not theirs to bestow.

> My crime is great and I confess it to be so, nevertheless, I am accounted more guilty than in truth I am. For although I took upon me that of which I was unworthy, yet no one can say that I ever sought to obtain it for myself, nor ever solaced myself therein, nor accepted of it willingly.

Then follows an account of the pressures to which she was made subject. "Thus, in truth, was I deceived by the

duke and the council, and ill treated by my husband and
his mother." [11]

Mary kept Jane and Guilford in the Tower. They might well
in time have been released had not Jane's father, pardoned and
released, then joined in Wyatt's conspiracy to dethrone Mary.
The queen and the council now believed that there would be
no tranquility in England so long as Jane and her husband were
alive. Dates were set for the executions of the duke of Suffolk,
his son, and Jane.

A short respite was granted out of concern for Jane's soul.
Mary sent her own confessor, Fecknam, an able and kindly
Catholic theologian, to bring her back to the church outside of
which there is no salvation. He began to talk with Jane of this
and that and gradually led into the subject of religion. Discussion centered on the Eucharist. Jane countered the orthodox
Catholic interpretation by the usual Protestant rejoinders. When
Christ said "This is my body," he no more intended to be taken
literally than when he called himself a vine and a door. Besides,
when those words were pronounced, he was standing right there
in his living body and how could he have said that the bread
and wine were that body? Fecknam's appeal to tradition left
her unmoved. He took his leave with sorrow, "For I am sure
that we two shall never meet." She agreed, being persuaded that
in the beyond he would be in less attractive quarters.[12]

Jane wrote to her father, whose second revolt was the occasion not only of his death but of her own:

> Father, although it hath pleased God to hasten my death
> by you, by whom my life should rather have been length-
> ened, yet I can so patiently take it, as I yield God more
> hearty thanks for shortening my woeful days, than if all
> the world had been given unto my possession. . . . And
> yet, I must needs acknowledge that I grievously offended
> the queen and her laws: yet I do assuredly trust that this
> my offence towards God is so much the less (in that being
> in so royal estate as I was) mine enforced honour blended
> never with mine innocent heart. And thus, good father, I

have opened unto you the state wherein I at present stand; whose death at hand, although to you perhaps it may seem right woeful, to me there is nothing that can be more welcome, than from this vale of misery to aspire to that heavenly throne of all joy and pleasure with Christ our Saviour. In whose steadfast faith (if it may be lawful for the daughter so to write to the father) [She admonishes him not to recant] the Lord that hitherto hath strengthened you, so continue you, that at the last we may meet in heaven with the Father, the Son and the Holy Ghost.

To her sister she wrote:

I have here sent you, good sister Catherine, a book, which although it be not outwardly trimmed with gold, yet inwardly it is worth more than precious stones. It is the book, dear sister, of the law of the Lord. . . . Rejoice in Christ, as I do. Follow the steps of your Master Christ, and take up your cross. Lay your sins on his back, and always embrace him. And as touching my death, rejoice as I do, good sister, that I shall be delivered of this corruption, and put on incorruption. For I am assured, that I shall, for losing of a mortal life, win an immortal life.

A prayer of Lady Jane as the end approached, is recorded. It consists in part of verses from the 77th Psalm:

O merciful God, consider my misery, best known unto thee. Suffer me not to be tempted above my power, but either be thou a deliverer unto me out of this great misery, or else give me grace, patiently to bear thy heavy hand and sharp correction. . . . Let it therefore, likewise seem good to thy fatherly goodness, to deliver me, sorrowful wretch (for whom thy Son Christ shed his precious blood on the cross) out of this miserable captivity and bondage, wherein I am now. How long wilt thou be absent? Forever? O Lord, hast thou forgotten to be gracious, and hast thou shut up thy lovingkindness in displeasure? Wilt thou be no more entreated? Is thy mercy clean gone for ever, and thy promise come utterly to an end for evermore? Why dost thou make so long tarrying? Shall I despair of thy mercy, O God? Far be that from me. I am thy workmanship, created in Christ Jesus.

Give me grace, therefore, to tarry thy leisure, and patiently to bear thy works, assuredly knowing, that as thou canst, so thou wilt deliver me when it shall please thee, nothing doubting or mistrusting thy goodness towards me; for thou knowest better what is good for me than I do. Therefore do with me in all things what thou wilt, and plague me what way thou wilt. . . . Only, in the meantime, arm me, I beseech thee, with thy armour, that I may stand fast . . . praying always with all manner of prayer and supplication, that I may refer myself wholly to thy will, abiding thy pleasure, and comforting myself in those troubles that it shall please thee to send me; seeing such troubles be profitable for me, and seeing I am assuredly persuaded that it cannot be but well, all that thou doest. Hear me, O merciful Father! for his sake, whom thou wouldest should be a sacrifice for my sins, to whom with thee and the Holy Ghost, be all honour and glory. Amen.

As the hour approached for her and for her husband, he requested that he might see her. She replied that their grief would thereby be the more increased and shortly they would meet in the beyond. She stood at the window and watched as he passed. As the cart returned with his severed body she cried out, "O Guilford! Guilford!" [13] When her turn came, beside her stood Fecknam, the queen's chaplain. She spoke briefly to the crowd asserting that she washed her hands in innocency of unlawful intent. She turned to the chaplain and asked whether she should recite the fifty-first psalm. He answered "Yea," and held her hand as she repeated to the end: "Have mercy upon me, O God, according to thy lovingkindness." She thanked the chaplain that he had delivered her from terror, embraced him and mounted the scaffold.[14]

BIBLIOGRAPHY

The best study of Lady Janes is that of Hester W. Chapman, *Lady Jane Grey* (Boston, 1962). She relies rather unduly on the late work of the Catholic historian Pollini, mentioned below, though he alone preserves a letter from Lady Jane to Mary.

The official acts of the reign are in *Public Documents,* ed. J. C. Nichols (Camden Society Publications, 1850).

Foxe refers to John Foxe, *Acts and Monuments* (reprint, 1965).

NOTES

1. Michelangelo Florio, *Historia de la Vita e la Morte de l'Illustriss. Signora Giovanna Graia* (1607). Although the publication is late, Florio was personally acquainted with Jane's father and with Wyatt, 51. Reference to the lamb, 61.

2. *British Reformers,* III, *Writings of Edward VI* and others (Philadelphia, n.d.), 299.

3. See the painting reproduced by Hester Chapman, *Lady Jane Grey* (Boston, 1962), facing p. 48.

4. John Strype, *Life of Bishop Aylmer,* 3-4, from Ascham's *Schoolmaster,* fol. II b.

5. Jane to Bullinger in *British Reformers,* III, 295.

6. Ralph Holinshed, *Chronicles* (London, 1808), 23.

7. Foxe VI, 418-422 and *British Reformers,* III, 34-41.

8. *British Reformers,* II, 280.

9. M. l'Abbé de Vertot, *Ambassades de Messieurs de Noailles en Angleterre* (1763). I, 211.

10. Foxe, VI, 283.

11. *British Reformers,* III, 300-304 translated from Girolamo Pollini, *Historia Ecclestiastica della Rivoluzione d'Inghilterra* (Rome, 1594).

12. This and the following documents are in Foxe, VI, 315-324 and *British Reformers,* III, 304-316.

13. *Ibid.,* 131 note 1.

14. Fecknam's presence attested by Foxe. The embrace related by Raviglio G. Rosso. *Historia delle cose occorse nel regno d'Inghilterra.* (Venice, 1558), 58, and borrowed from him by Pollini.

11.

Mary I
(1516-1558)

Mary I, called "the most merciful of the Tudors," is popularly referred to as "Bloody Mary." She would have subscribed to a passage in Oliver Cromwell's *Souldier's Pocket Bible,* which joins the verse "But I say unto you 'Love your enemies' " (Matt. 5:44) with the words of the Psalm (139:21-22), "Do I not hate them, O Lord that hate thee. . . . I hate them with an unfeigned hatred, as they were mine utter enemies." The superscription is: "A souldier must love his enemies as they are his enemies, and hate them as they are God's enemies." Mary was magnanimous toward those who would exclude or expel her from the throne, but unsparing of those who by heresy assailed the majesty of God. If the same persons were both God's enemies and her enemies, woe betide.

Her happiest years were the earliest. Her mother, Catherine of Aragon, doted over this her only surviving child and lavished upon her the affection so often frustrated by the early deaths of her other children. Henry was fond of Mary and said proudly to the Venetian ambassador, *Per Deum immortalem, ista puella numquam plorat,* "By the immortal God, this little girl never cries." [1]

The mother took personal charge in part of her daughter's education and tutored her in Latin and Spanish. The most distinguished scholars of the day wrote treatises on how she should be trained. Erasmus and Vives recommended familiarity

Mary I

with humane letters for ladies. Erasmus stressed gentleness in discipline.[2] Vives inveighed against such frivolities as dancing and adornment. Let not the doves of Christ be turned into venus birds and think not that baptism which makes all Christians brothers makes them also kissing kin.[3] Mary heeded the counsels as to the humanities and became proficient in Latin, French and Spanish, with an understanding of Italian. She was skilled also on the virginals, lute, and harpsichord. But she did not follow her mentor as to diversions and display and when arrayed in all the gems "as it were of the eighth sphere," she dazzled the company with her beauty.[4]

Mary, as heiress to the English crown, was of course, a matrimonial pawn and for a time was betrothed to her cousin, Charles of Spain. As heiress she bore the title "Princess of Wales." To give reality to the Welsh connection, she was at the age of nine transferred to Ludlow castle and placed under the tutelage of the countess of Salisbury. There was no deliberate attempt at that time to separate her from her mother and correspondence between them was unimpeded.

But then came "the king's great matter": the setting aside of Catherine, the breach with Rome, the marriage with Anne Boleyn and her coronation. The English would be disinclined to accept Anne as queen so long as Catherine had not resigned her title and Anne's expected child would hardly be received as England's sovereign if Mary did not relinquish the title of Princess of Wales. The mother must be only dowager and the daughter only Lady Mary. She was fifteen when this drama began to unfold. Already she was as stubborn as her mother in insisting on the titles of queen for the one and princess for the other. Never would she admit that her parents had lived in sin and that she was a bastard.

But Henry's whole plan for the succession depended on the acquiescence of the pair in their demotion and to drive them to it extreme pressures were applied. One device was to isolate each from the other and from whatever support might come from Spain. Both relied heavily on the advice of the Spanish ambassador, the emissary of Charles, the emperor. Henry took every precaution to prevent communication and every precaution was to a degree eluded. Another device on his part was the threat of death. Catherine believed that her life and that of her daughter were in jeopardy. Henry was claimed to have been overheard saying that he would have Mary's head. The possibility that he might send even his own daughter to the block did not seem absolutely fantastic in view of all the other heads that fell. The remark was transmitted to Mary. In utter desperation she contrived to contact the Spanish ambassador. Visits were permitted by her physician, who at one time had tutored her in Latin. Allowed to be with him only in the presence of others, she began by saying in English that her Latin was rusty and she would like to practice. Then she disclosed to him the king's threat. The doctor played the game, kept his composure and when she had finished told her in English that she was indeed right. Her Latin was not too good.

When the word reached the Spanish ambassador he tried to stir up Charles to invade England.[5] Mary herself intimated that she would look upon such intervention as a holy war. "Unless his majesty, the emperor," she told the ambassador, "for the service of God, the welfare and repose of Christendom, as well as the honor of the king, my father, takes pity on these poor afflicted creatures, all and everything will go to total ruin." She hoped the emperor would apply a prompt remedy. "The work itself will be highly acceptable in the eyes of God, and no less glory will be gained by it than by the conquest of Tunis, or even of Africa." [6] But Charles would have none of it. He did believe that Catherine had been wronged. He did believe that Mary was being cheated. He did lament England's separation from Rome. But he did not relish war.

Another suggestion was that Mary should escape to the continent. She said she would be willing to sail over in a sieve. A fleet of Spanish galleons was anchored off the mouth of the Thames. The ambassador planned that she should be rowed down from Greenwich and then wafted abroad. The emperor perceived that if Mary fled England she would probably never be England's queen, and would not give his approval. A rumor of the plan may have leaked because Mary was moved farther inland. She suggested that while taking her walk in the woods she might be kidnapped by armed horsemen and conveyed to a ship.[7] The emperor again did not approve.

The pressures on Mary were intensified. In January of 1534, the king sent Thomas Cromwell to urge her to renounce the title. She replied that "neither bad treatment, nor rudeness, nor even the chance of death, would make her change her determination."[8] In February she was reported to be nearly destitute of clothes.[9] In March Anne Boleyn substituted cajolery for coercion, signing herself "queen." Mary replied that she would call no one queen but her mother. Anne then resolved to "bring down this unbridled Spanish blood."[10] In April came the report that Henry had threatened her head.[11] In May, Henry also shifted to cajolery and told her that if she would "lay aside her obstinacy" he would give her "a royal title and dignity." She answered "that God had not so blinded her as to confess for any kingdom on earth that the king, her father, and the queen, her mother, had so long lived in adultery, nor would she contravene the ordinances of the church and make herself a bastard."[12] Cromwell was really trying to find a way out for her. She told him in June that she regarded him as one of her chief friends, but all of his advice was in terms of political expediency, for which she cared not a fig. She informed him that she had "done the uttermost her conscience would permit."[13]

Sometime, still in June, Henry sent emissaries who said that her obstinate disobedience was "so unnatural" that they could scarcely believe she was the bastard of the king. Were she their daughter "they would beat her and knock her head so violently against the wall that they would make it as soft as baked apples." Mary devised a way to inform the Spanish ambassador, who transmitted the advice of the emperor that if her life were in danger she should submit, seeing that on her "depended the peace of the realm and the redress of the great disorders." Let her dissemble for a time, knowing that God regards the intention rather than the act.[14]

The king, hearing that she still refused, grew desperate with anger. Cromwell, fearful for his own life, sent Mary a peremptory letter:

I have received your letters, whereby it appeareth you be in great discomfort, and do desire that I should find the means to speak with you. Your discomfort can be no greater than mine, who upon your letters have spoken so much of your repentance for your wilful obstinacy against the King, and of your humble submission to obey his pleasure and laws in all things without exception or qualification. Knowing how diversely and contrarily you have proceeded at the late being of his Majesty's Council with you, I am ashamed of what I have said and afraid of what I have done. What the sequel shall be God knows.

With your folly you undo yourself, and I say to you, as I have said elsewhere heretofore, it were pity you should not be an example in punishment, If you will make yourself an example in the contempt of God, your natural father and his laws by your only fantasie, contrary to the judgments and determinations of all men that ye must confess do know and love God as well as you. To be plain with you, I think you the most obstinate woman that ever was, and I dare not open my lips to name you unless I have such a ground thereto that it may appear you were mistaken, or at least that you repent your ingratitude and are ready to do your duty.

I have therefore sent you a book of articles to subscribe, on receiving which from you again, with a letter declaring that you think in your heart as you have subscribed with your hand, I will venture to speak for your reconciliation. If you do not leave all sinister counsels, which have brought you to the point of undoing, I take leave of you for ever, and desire you to write to me no more; for I will never think you other than the most ungrate, unnatural, and most obstinate person living, both to God and your most dear and benign father. And I advise you to nothing, but I beseech God never to help me if I know it not so certainly to be your bounden duty, by God's laws and man's laws, that I must needs judge that person that shall refuse it not meet to live in a Christian congregation.[15]

Mary, her mother dead and the emperor advising submission, capitulated, declaring that with all her heart she promised "due conformity of obedience to the laws of the realm. . . . . I do most humbly beseech the King's Highness, my father, whom I have obstinately and inobediently offended . . . to forgive mine offenses . . . and to take me to his most gracious mercy." On three counts she yielded: 1) She acknowledged the king as her sovereign; 2) and as the supreme head of the Church of England under Christ and repudiated the pretended authority of the bishop of Rome . . . ; 3) and acknowledged that marriage between the king and her mother, the late princess dowager, to have been 'by God's law and man's law incestuous and unlawful.' [16] To each of the three she appended in her own hand, "Marye."

But like Peter, after the denial of his Lord, she wept bitterly. The Spanish ambassador wrote to the emperor that she was "much dejected. . . . . But I immediately relieved her of every doubt, even of conscience, assuring her that the pope would not only not impute to her any blame, but would hold it rightly done." Let the emperor give her "the marvelous consolation" of a letter in his own hand, assuring her of his approval. She entreats the ambassador to procure for her "an absolution from the Pope. Otherwise her conscience could not be at perfect ease." [17] It never was. And this may well explain why every subsequent attempt to make her renounce the faith met with unflinching refusal.

Henry now showered her with favors. He had long been fond of her. In the midst of his blustering about her "Spanish obstinacy," when the French ambassador reminded him that she had been well brought up, "tears rushed to the king's eyes." [18] Now he gave unbridled scope to his affection. And the court likewise. Cromwell sent her a horse. Queen Jane Seymour, always a supporter of Mary, sent a diamond ring. Mary was godmother at the christening of the baby Edward, and mourner at the obsequies of Jane. Catherine Parr brought together, as far as convenient, all three of the children of her lord and engaged Mary to translate the *Paraphrase* of Erasmus on the Gospel of John.

But the clouds did not altogether lift. There was an uprising in the north consisting of Catholic disaffection and Plantagenet challenge to the Tudors. Strongly implicated was the family of the Poles. The matriarch of the clan was the countess of Salisbury, the one time governess of Mary. Henry at first treated these representatives of the rival house with magnanimity. But the son of the countess was Reginald Pole, who from the safety of the continent, launched a vehement attack upon the divorce. His family besought him to be more circumspect. He was intransigeant and the pope made him a cardinal. One brother went to the stake. One died of remorse for having betrayed the other. The countess was imprisoned. Cromwell delayed her execution for three years. Then the stately dowager of the Plantagenets went to the block. Her last prayer was for the Princess Mary.[19]

When Henry died, Mary, who had so suffered at his hands, declared that "his soul God would pardon," and that he "is yet very ripe in my own remembrance." [20] Her father was succeeded by her brother the "regal imp," Edward VI. The word "imp" was not then derogatory, but meant simply a child. He was nine. She was twenty-one years his senior. His reign was marked by progressive moves in a Protestant direction. There were two periods of three years each under two regencies, the first that of the king's uncle, the duke of Somerset with the title of protector, and the second that of the earl of Warwick, soon to be made the duke of Northumberland.

Somerset was the most tolerant ruler of the century. Under him there were no executions for religion. The heresy laws of Henry were repealed. The mass was, however, replaced by the *Book of Common Prayer* in 1549, in which the words for the consecration of the Eucharist were susceptible of a Lutheran interpretation. The coincident Act of Uniformity required that this liturgy be used in all of the churches. Thus was inaugurated the policy of comprehension which prevailed in England until the Act of Toleration in 1688. The term "comprehension" is applied to a system which seeks to comprise all the inhabitants of an area in one form of religion. The term "toleration" refers to the allowance of diversity. The England of the sixteenth century was in accord with the general assumption that one region must have one religion. The emphasis in England was not, however, so much upon unity of belief as on uniformity of practice. Englishmen might believe largely as they wished, provided they worshipped as they were told. The Prayer Book must be used. The mass must, therefore, go.

But there came the rub. Mary would not give up the mass in her private chapel. A protracted interchange ensued between her and the government, represented by her brother, the protectors, and the Privy Council. Their main argument was that enactments issued in the name of the royal supremacy must be enforced with utter impartiality. Several of the other considerations adduced were curious inversions of the Catholic attack on the Protestants. One was that in the name of private judgment the Lutherans should not contravene the consensus of Christendom. Now Mary was told that in the name of private judgment she should not contravene the consensus of the Church of England. Another plea began by twisting an idea developed in the interests of religious liberty. The point was that the number of doctrines necessary to be believed for salvation being small, on all other points freedom should be allowed. The argument was reversed when the emperor told the Lutherans that on all points on which they would not be damned they should conform to his decree. Now Mary was told that with respect to the *adiaphora*—the points of indifference—she should submit to the royal supremacy.

Here is a running summary of the events and the interchanges. June 22, 1549: Mary tells the council she perceives they are sorry over her failure to conform to his majesty's laws. She answers that she has disobeyed no law save one of their own making. The law is that enacted by her father and sworn to by the very persons by whom it is now abrogated. No innovations in religion should be introduced during the tender years of her brother. She begs them "no more to unquiet me with matters touching my conscience." [21]

The council at once replied telling her that for the king's sister to disobey the law is much worse than in the case of any other subject. A law superseded by another law is no longer a law. The king is indeed of tender years. But Scripture shows that by God's special ordinance children were kings and good kings in ancient Israel. The members of the council would not disquiet her were it not for their consciences.

June 27th, 1549: Mary answered that since the death of her father "I never took you for other than my friends. But in this it appeareth contrary. . . . I pray almighty God to illuminate you all with his Holy Spirit."

The council was right that Mary's disobedience was not just a private affair. There were risings in Devon and Cornwall, chiefly on account of economic grievances but the Cornishmen demanded the restoration of the mass and their leader had been one of Mary's chaplains. She kept scrupulously aloof from any alliance with the rebels. Warwick subdued them and then ousted and replaced Somerset in July of 1549. He succeeded by at first currying Catholic favor and some supposed he would restore the authority of Rome. Mary had no illusions, calling him the "most inconstant" man in England. Once in the saddle he cultivated the ultra-Protestants and renewed the attack on Mary. Jan. 24th, 1550: The king, no doubt under dictation, writing in the official first person plural, addressed his sister: "You were dealt with leniently at first that you might learn to obey. We know we are young but this matter is so plain that we could have judged of it six years passed. It grieveth us that you who should give us comfort cause so much discomfort. You say yours is the faith of Christendom but you are a member of the Church of England. You would make no alteration, but our father made alterations and we have the same authority. We exhort you to do your duty." Feb. 3, 1550: Mary answered: "Your letter troubles me more than any bodily sickness though it were even unto death. I know you are advanced for your years but until you are grown you should stay in matters touching the soul. For conscience I would lose all that I have including my life."

She grew hysterical and began considering flight once more. The emperor was informed that she was afraid of being murdered by her brother's counsellors when he should be on the point of death, but if she were out of the country all England would rally to her standard. This time the emperor acquiesced.[22] The ambassador left for Holland lest the emperor appear to be implicated, and there shortly died. The execution of the plan was then entrusted to a certain Dubois. Sailing from Holland in a large ship he put off to the English shore in a small craft and offered grain for sale to the villagers. Time was consumed in haggling over the price. Contact was at length made with Mary's controller, who intimated that she was losing her nerve. Dubois should come and talk with her. Fretting over the delay, he went.

Confidants had indeed sapped her resolution. She said she could not get off right away because of packing. He told her to leave the stuff and get a move on. Everything would be supplied on the other side. Her friends advised him to get back to Holland on the next tide, for if he were discovered the game would be up. Mary whimpered, "What will become of me?" And then promised to make another attempt in about a fortnight. Dubois made the tide. Mary lost her chance. News of the attempt leaked and she was left to face the infuriated Northumberland.[23]

He changed his tactic. If he could not persuade Mary to abandon the mass he could keep her from having it by removing her chaplains. One of them was that Malet who, when Mary was ill, took over the translation of Erasmus' *Paraphrase* of the Gospel of John. Mary protested against the arrests (Dec. 4, 1550) and appealed to the promise made to the emperor that she would not be molested as to her faith.[24]

The council replied (Dec. 25th) that when the emperor made the request they had pointed out to him "the discommodities that should follow the grant thereof . . . were a private fancy to prejudice a common order." As a concession they had agreed "it should be winked at, if you had the private mass used in your own closet for a season, until you might be better informed. The king's majesty and his whole realm had their consciences well quieted . . . by reducing the mass to the order of the primitive church." To allow otherwise would be "an offense against God, and a very sin against a truth known. Our greatest change is not in the substance of our faith. . . . Only the difference is that we use the ceremonies, observations, and sacraments

of our religion, as the apostles . . . did." You use that which
"the corruption of time brought in, and very barbarousness and
ignorance nourished; and seem to hold for custom against the
truth, and we for truth against custom. . . ." Where has she
found warrant "to think common prayer in the English church
should not be in the English tongue? . . . We do perceive great
discommodity to the realm by your grace's singularity . . . in
opinion. . . . For God's sake we beseech your grace, let nature
set before your eyes the young age of the king your brother. . . .
Can it be a love in you to forsake him, his rule and law, and
take a private way by yourself? . . . Your grace cannot love
him as your brother, but you must obey his majesty as his
subject." If any of your chaplains turn up you should deliver
them to the sheriff of Essex.

Mary, bristling with truculence, came before the council, but
when she saw Edward was in tears and he as well. "I was sorry
for having caused him to weep; and his Majesty benignly requested me to dry my tears, saying he thought no harm of me." [25]

The council sent her chaplain, Malet, to the Tower. She demanded to know why. "For disobeying the king's laws," said
they. "For saying mass," said she. "He did it at my command.
I told him he would not suffer. You make me a liar." They told
her again that to allow contempt of the ecclesiastical orders of
this Church of England would incur the great displeasure of God.
Mary then pleaded with Edward to let her have the mass on
which they were both brought up under their father. She was
sure the letters sent in his name were not really his but those
of his advisers, "by whom I understand not to rule my conscience. . . . Otherwise I offer my body at your will and death
shall be more welcome than life with a troubled conscience."

Edward answered (or was it really he?) to his "Right dear
and right entirely beloved sister" that he was grieved to perceive in her no amendment. Though she had given such occasion to diminish natural love, "we be loath to see it decay."
"Wherefore lest he be found guilty in his conscience to God for
having omitted his bounden duty" he is sending three well beloved counsellors to instruct her as to the conduct of her household. And their instruction was that no harm was intended to

her body but her chaplains were forbidden to say mass and her household to attend and if she found any priests or other persons disobedient to this order she should commit them "forthwith to prison." So matters stood for two years. Mary was thus circumvented by the removal of her priests. Then Edward died on July 6, 1553.

There followed the abortive attempt to forestall her succession in favor of Lady Jane Grey. Mary was proclaimed queen on July 19, 1553. A great many of the hats thrown up in delirious joy at her accession were Protestant. An orderly succession in the direct Tudor line bade better for the tranquility of the land than recourse to a more remote claim in order to exclude a Catholic. Besides no one then knew how far Mary would go. Initially she did no more than revert to the status under the last days of her father. Her first act was one of clemency toward those imprisoned for various reasons. When she visited the Tower all of the prisoners knelt in supplication for mercy, including that Courtenay who had translated the *Benefit of Christ's Death.* He was released.

Among the pardoned churchmen was Gardiner, now made the chancellor. This was a move in a Catholic direction. But Mary told the Spanish ambassador, a new ambassador named Renard, that "she would force no one to go to mass, but meant to see that those who wished to go should be free to do so." And again that she would have her mass without compelling any one to assist who did not feel inclined. However, she also said that such freedom would obtain until enactment of law by parliament.[26]

From the outset Mary undoubtedly did aspire to return England to Rome and that would unquestionably entail the prosecution of heretics. The emperor advised her to move slowly, to dissemble and first ingratiate herself with her subjects. He was more concerned to ally England with Spain by Mary's marriage to his son Philip than in the restoration of Rome obedience. There were, however, many in England of Catholic leanings like Gardiner who considered a Hapsburg alliance highly distasteful and schemed rather to get Mary married to Courtenay. But the Spanish ambassador described Philip so glowingly that Mary fell in love with his unseen image. Besides, she was herself half Spanish. The announcement of the marriage agreement precipitated Wyatt's rebellion. It was promptly suppressed and only a few of the leaders were executed. The hysteria of the hour caused the beheading of Lady Jane and her husband. Philip arrived and the marriage took place in July, 1554. Only after this alliance was cemented would the emperor allow Cardinal Pole to come to England to receive her submission to Rome.

The cardinal reached London in November, 1554. Both houses of parliament went down on their knees while he pronounced the words of absolution in the name of the Father, the Son and the Holy Ghost. "Amen" resounded throughout the hall. The response would not have been so unanimous if the cardinal had not brought from Rome a dispensation from obligation to restore confiscated monastic properties. The earl of Bedford, turned Catholic, at the word of restoration, "broke his rosary beads and flung them into the fire declaring that he valued the sweet abbey of Woburn more than the fatherly counsel that should come from Rome." [27] Mary herself restored as much as she could of the spoils which had passed to the crown and in consequence became more dependent upon parliament for subsidies. The clergy likewise, deprived of much of their landed income, grew more dependent on the state and in consequence more subservient.

But Mary's power was never absolute. The doctrine of the royal supremacy was a supremacy of the king in parliament. And parliament thwarted her ardent desire to have the matrimonial crown bestowed upon her husband. The fear that a Spaniard might be England's king prompted a plot to unseat Mary and Philip in favor of Elizabeth to be married to that Courtenay who earlier had been envisioned for Mary. The plot was nipped. The evidence was insufficient to convict Elizabeth and Courtenay of complicity, but both for a time were sent to the Tower.

But what now of those who refused to accept the religious settlement as enacted by the crown in parliament? Mary had said that she was reverting to the policy of her father, but he certainly had used constraint. She had restored the authority of

Rome and Rome would not refrain from constraint. Her avowed intent collapsed. The number of those burned at the stake for heresy during her reign is estimated as roughly 273. The Catholic historian, Hughes, comments that the execution of so many in so short a time was unparalleled in English history. "Never before and never since, was there anything quite like it." [28] And that is why she is known as "Bloody Mary."

This extensive persecution was a phase of the stringent application of the royal supremacy. Mary, if not the supreme head of the church, was the supreme head of the state, and it was in the name of the state that heresy was ferreted out. Arrests were made not by the bishops but by the sheriffs for non-attendance at mass as commanded by law. Of course heresy was involved, because recantation would bring release. The procedure differed from the ideal conduct of the Inquisition which was supposed to have jurisdiction only over Catholics who had fallen away from the faith. The younger generation in England could not be accused of falling away. They never had been Catholics. What

An Execution at Smithfield

we have here is a coalition of state absolutism and Catholic orthodoxy. For a parallel we must look to Spain, where for the sake of national and religious solidarity, the Inquisition prosecuted Jews and not simply *marranos,* that is converted Jews.

Various attempts have been made to exculpate Mary. One is that she was not directly responsible. How could anyone so kind have been so cruel? Together with a companion she would go disguised as a peasant and mingle with the common folk to learn whether they had legitimate complaints of the government, which would then be corrected. She was extravagantly prodigal in her benefactions and on the annual occasion of washing the feet of poor women was lavish in her largesses. How then could she deserve to be called "bloody?"

Others then must have pushed her. But who? Cardinal Pole? He was so gentle and besides he was himself suspected of heresy and had received a summons to answer at Rome. Had not death released him he might have spent the remaining years of his life in the chambers of the Inquisition as did Cardinal Carranza, the primate of Spain.

The bishops then? Gardiner actually gave money to Peter Martyr to enable him to leave England. Gardiner did preside over the trials of Hooper, Latimer, Ridley and Cranmer, then sickened of it all and withdrew. Bonner, called by Foxe "Bloody Bonner," professed to have had no heart for the business. Under Elizabeth he excused himself on the ground that he acted to "obey his betters." Eichmann's excuse! But Bonner may have been right that his heart was not in it, because Mary's government sent him a reprimand for leniency toward those arrested by the sheriffs.[29]

Who then remains to be saddled with the responsibility unless parliament? But the Commons, at the insistence of Cecil, defeated the enactment of the Lords to confiscate the goods of the Marian exiles. The responsibility rests with Mary and Pole. They could have extinguished the fire had they wished. This, however, may be said for them that their holocaust differed only in numbers from what was done by some of their victims when in power. Cranmer, as archbishop of Canterbury, signed the death warrants of Joan Boucher and George Parish, charged with Anabaptism. Latimer preached the sermon at the burning of Friar Forest. Calvin instigated the execution of Servetus. Butzer and Melanchthon applauded. On the Catholic side Thomas More assisted in the racking of a heretic. The saints burn the saints. Those who believe strongly enough in an idea to die for it may be willing also to kill for it.

One may add that in Mary's case political considerations played a part. The refugees on the continent, subsidized by France, aspired to displace Mary. After the discovery of a plot she became more stringent. At the beginning, the flight of the ultra-Protestants was openly or clandestinely encouraged. Cranmer and Latimer could have saved themselves had they not felt obligated not to desert their flocks. But when conspiracy was unearthed, attempts were made to get the refugees back in order to keep them under surveillance, if not indeed to send them to the stake. John Cheke, for example, the one time tutor of Prince Edward, was kidnapped on the continent and brought back to England. He saved his life by recantation and died very quickly of remorse. But granted all this, the judgment is just that politically speaking Mary would have done better to hang more traitors and spare more heretics.

Her last years were embittered by the blasting of her hopes. England was alienated by the Spanish alliance. This alliance brought her into conflict with France, resulting in the loss of Calais. Her Spanish husband lost interest when he was denied the matrimonial crown. He went over to the Netherlands, where his father's abdication made him Philip II of Spain. He returned briefly to England but in July, 1557 left definitively. Mary went down to Dover to bid him goodbye, wept copiously and never saw him again. Perhaps she might have held him had she been able to present an heir, whom England would have accepted as half Tudor. She thought she was pregnant and compared her meeting with Pole on his arrival in England with that of the Mary and Elizabeth when "the babe leapt in her womb." A concourse of noblewomen gathered at Hampton Court to be present at the delivery, but the swelling was only a premonition of death.

Her breviary is stained with tears at the prayer for the safe delivery of a woman with child.

Mary alienated England, lost her husband, lost her adviser Cardinal Pole. If the joy at her accession proved that England was not solidly Protestant, the revulsion at the burnings at Smithfield proved that England was not solidly Catholic. The conflicts of the reigns of Henry, Edward and Mary had been between the royal supremacy and the individual conscience, whether Catholic or Protestant. For the time being the only solution was that the strong should impose, and the weak should suffer. This was the problem bequeathed to Elizabeth.

BIBLIOGRAPHY

Prescott, H. M. F., *A Spanish Tudor* (New York, 1940), is the best treatment and the source of statements not otherwise documented in the notes.

Stone, J. M., *A History of Mary I, Queen of England* (1901), contains some documentation not in other works.

Hughes, Philip, *The Reformation in England,* II (New York, 1954) discusses Mary's persecutions.

Jordan, W. K., *Edward the Young King* (1967) has a good account of the clash between Mary and Edward.

Abbreviations:

Foxe, John, *Acts and Monuments* (reprint, 1965).

LP, Letters and Papers Foreign and Domestic.

LB, Opera Omnia of Erasmus, Leiden edition.

Span., Calendar of State Papers, Spanish.

NOTES

1. Henry Clifford, *Life of Jane Dorner,* 80-81.
2. LB, V, 711 C-D, 712 C, 716 D. Compare my *Erasmus of Christendom* (New York, 1968).
3. Io. Lodovici Vivis Valentini, *De Institutione Foeminae. Christianae,* liv.
4. Stone, 30. *Venetian Calendar* IV, 105.
5. *Span.,* V, 1, No. 45, pp. 129-130. Ap. 1534.
6. *Ibid.,* V. 1, No. 218, pp. 559-560, Oct. 1535.
7. *Ibid.,* V, 2, No. 21 and *LP,* X, No. 307.
8. *LP,* VII, No. 83, p. 31.
9. *Ibid.,* No. 214.
10. *Ibid.,* No. 296.
11. *Ibid.,* No. 530.
12. *Ibid.,* No. 662, p. 254.
13. *Ibid.,* X, No. 1108.
14. *Ibid.,* XI, No. 7, pp. 7-8.
15. *Ibid.,* X, No. 1110, pp. 467-468.
16. *Ibid.,* X, Nos. 1136 and 1137, June 15, 1536.
17. *Ibid.,* XI, No. 7, p. 8, July 1, 1536.
18. *Span.,* V, i, No. 10, pp. 32-33 and *LP* VII, No. 171, p. 68.
19. John E. Paul, *Catherine of Aragon and her Friends* (New York, 1966), 232-252.
20. Prescott, 115.
21. Foxe, the following references run from 7-13.
22. *Span.,* X, 80-82 and 111.
23. *Ibid.,* 124-135.
24. Foxe, the following references run from 13-24.
25. *Span.,* X, 206.
26. *Ibid.,* XI, 131, 169-170. Cf. Hughes, II, 196.
27. Stone, 340.
28. Hughes, II, 255.
29. Foxe, V, 611 and 86.

Title page of Foxe's *Actes and Monuments* in the editions of 1563 and 1570

12.

John Foxe and the Women Martyrs

John Foxe's *Acts and Monuments of these latter and perilous dayes* is said to have been only slightly less influential than the Bible and Bunyan's *Pilgrim's Progress* for the shaping of the mind of Protestant England. All three give a high place to women. The Bible relates that the first to bring to the disciples the news of the risen Lord was a woman, Mary Magdalene. *Pilgrim's Progress* is in two parts. The first relates the adventurers of Christian and the second of Christina. John Foxe tells us more about the women of the Reformation in England than does any other source. All of the royal and noble personages receive copious treatment but space is devoted also to many whose only memorial is the listing of a name.

One has the feeling that Foxe derived a special relish from relating the tart, smart, pert, audacious, and superbly defiant words and deeds of these women to illustrate the point that the weaker vessel when filled with the Holy Spirit is powerful to pull down strongholds. He reports with gusto the retort of a woman who when asked what she thought of the see of Rome replied that it was "a sea for crows, kites, owls and ravens to swim in." [1] A woman, shedding tears at the burning of a martyr, was asked why she wept for a heretic and answered that actually she saw more reason to weep over the priests attending the execution.[2] One woman dared to call Queen Mary Jezebel.[3] Another asked

Beholde now here by,
J bringe to Boners stall:
Whose thursty throtes so dry,
For more bloude styll dothe call.

Arrests

The Burning of
Two Women

why she would not let St. Nicholas into her house at Christmas replied, "St. Nicholas is in heaven." [4] One there was who instead of absenting herself from mass, attended and did everything contrary. When the congregation rose she sat, when they sat she rose.[5]

Mistress Dolly said to her servant John Bainton (I'm going to look him up in the heavenly places if I ever get there) that prayer in her chamber had as much merit as going on a pilgrimage to Walsingham. The women, said she, go and make offerings to the saints to show off their fine gear and the people go on pilgrimages more "for the green" than for devotion. Images are a "carpenter's chips." [6] An image in the rood loft was dubbed "Block Almighty." [7] A woman in the early days of Henry VIII got into trouble for knowing too much Scripture. How delightful was the version she learned! "Blessed are the mild men for they shall weld the earth." [8]

Whenever the available documents sufficed, Foxe reported examinations *in extenso* for women as well as for men. The questions put to the accused became stereotyped. There is a neat summary of the points of non-conformity in the letter to a woman exhorting her to reject all practices which Christ did not observe. "Christ," said the writer, "ought to be regarded as a heretic because he never "went in procession with cope, cross or candlestick: he never censered images, nor sang Latin services. He never sat in confession: He never preached on purgatory; nor on the pope's pardons. He never honored saints nor prayed for the dead: He never said mass, matins, nor evensong; he never commanded Friday fast, nor vigil, Lent, nor Advent; he never hallowed church nor chalice, ashes, nor palms, candles, nor bells." [9] The reference to the mass covers also the doctrinal points that the mass is not a sacrifice and that Christ's body and blood are not substantially present in the bread and the wine.

Now let us turn to the examinations. The records for our purpose are here considerably abridged and slightly paraphrased. The first is that of Anne Askew, a woman born of such stock that she might have lived in great prosperity. She suffered in the year 1546 during the "Tudor reaction" of the last days of Henry VIII. Among the examiners were Wriothesley, the chancellor, Gardiner, bishop of Winchester, a priest named Shaxton, who had recanted and tried to persuade her to do the like, and others who need not be enumerated. The report of her examinations comes from her own pen.[10] The first was in March of 1545.

I was asked how I interpreted the passage of the Book of Acts which says that God dwells not in temples made with hands. I replied that I would not cast pearls before swine. Acorns are good enough. Did I say that five lines out of the Bible are better than five masses? "Yes, I get something out of the Bible, nothing out of the masses." I was accused of saying that if an evil priest administers the sacrament it is of the devil. I never said anything of the sort. I said that without faith I cannot receive worthily. What did I think of confession? I replied that to confess one's faults is salutary. "Do private masses profit the dead?" I answered that it is idolatry to trust the masses more than to Christ. I was sent back to prison for eleven days. One priest visited me.

At the next examination I was asked whether if a beast ate the sacrament it would eat God. I told the examiner to answer himself. He said it was not the custom of the schools for the questioner to answer the question. I told him I was not versed in the custom of the schools. My cousin came to bail me out. He was told that the consent of a churchman was necessary and I was, therefore, taken to the bishop of London. He set the hour for three o'clock and then sent sudden word that I should come at one. I sent word that friends were coming with me at three and three it should be.

I was asked why I was in trouble. "You tell me," I said. It is "because of that book you have read by a man already burned." I told him that "such unadvised hasty judgment is a token of a slender wit." I showed him the book and he could find nothing wrong with it. The bishop of London told me to bare my conscience. I told him there was nothing to bare. I was asked to interpret a text of Paul. I answered that a woman should not presume to interpret Paul.

I was accused of making mock of the Easter communion. "Produce the accuser," said I. I was asked, "If Scripture says that the bread and wine are the body of Christ will you believe it?" "I believe Scripture." "If Scripture says they are not the body of Christ will you believe it?" "I believe Scripture. I believe all things as Christ and the apostles did leave them." I was asked to sign a confession that the body and blood of Christ are in substance in the mass. I said, "in so far as Holy Scripture doth agree unto."

At the third examination she was told that the king's pleasure was that she should open her mind to the examiners. "I will answer to the king." "He is too busy to be bothered." "Solomon was not too busy to be bothered with two women." I was asked to say that the sacrament is the flesh, blood and bone of Christ. The bishop asked to speak familiarly with me. I told him that was the way Judas betrayed Christ. He would like to speak alone with me. I said that the truth is established out of the mouths of two or three witnesses. I was threatened with the fire and answered that Christ and the apostles put no one to death. God would scorn their threatenings.

I asked to be allowed to speak to Dr. Latimer and was refused. I wrote out for them my confession of faith: "That the sacramental bread was left to us to be received with thanksgiving, in remembrance of Christ's death, the only remedy of our soul's recovery; and that thereby we also receive the whole benefits and fruits of his most glorious passion." I told them that if the bread is left in a box for three months it will be mouldy, so it cannot be God. "I wish neither death nor fear his might." Shaxton tried to persuade me to recant as he had done. I told him it were better he had never been born.

I was moved to another prison. An attempt was made to compel me to inform on others. The chancellor and another took off their gowns and racked me " 'til the bones were almost plucked asunder." I had to be moved in a carriage.

At the stake she had to be chained up to keep her limp body from sagging. The chancellor sent her a pardon if she would recant. She refused to open it saying, "I did not come here to deny my Lord and Master." Three men suffered with her and were "boldened by her invincible constancy."

While in prison she had composed a poem of which this is the first verse:

> Lyke as the armed knyghte
> Appointed to the fielde,
> With thys worlde wyll I fyght
> And fayth shall be my shielde.

Our second example is the examination of Elizabeth Young in the year 1558. She was the mother of three children and had gone to Holland to bring back for sale Protestant books there printed in English. One of the books was entitled *Antichrist*. Of her thirteen examinations nine have been recorded. Here is an abridgement. The examiners are not differentiated in this summary.[11]

FIRST EXAMINATION

Examiner: Where were you born and who were your father and mother?

Elizabeth: This has nothing to do with the case. Come to the point.

Examiner: Why did you leave the country?

Elizabeth: For conscience.

Examiner: When were you last at mass?

Elizabeth: Not for three years.

Examiner: And before that?

Elizabeth: Another three years and another three years.

Examiner: How old are you?

Elizabeth: Forty and upwards.

SECOND EXAMINATION

Examiner: What are the books you brought from over the sea?
I hear you won't swear. If you are stubborn you will be racked
by the inch, you traitorly whore and heretic.

Elizabeth: I don't know what it is to swear. As for the books you
have impounded them.

Examiner: Yes, and you have sold some of them already. We
know every place where you have been. We are not fools.

Elizabeth: No, you are too wise for me.

Examiner: I'll make you tell to whom you sold those books.

Elizabeth: Here is my carcass. Do with it what you will. You cannot take more than my blood.

Then the examiner gave order that Elizabeth should be
given bread on one day and water the next.

Elizabeth: If you take away my meat I hope God will take away
my hunger.

THIRD EXAMINATION

Examiner: Give me the names of those in exile on the continent
or you will be racked.

Elizabeth gave no answer.

FOURTH EXAMINATION

She was sent to the bishop of London who told her that the
refusal to swear was the mark of an Anabaptist. One present,
seeing her courage, bet twenty pounds she was a man.

Elizabeth: I am not a man. I have children.

He was evidently convinced, for he called her a whore.

She was examined as to her belief with respect to the sacrament of the altar and declared:

Elizabeth: I believe in the holy sacrament of Christ's body and
blood. . . . When I do receive this sacrament in faith and
spirit I do receive Christ.

Examiner: Nothing but spirit and faith, is it? Away with the
whore.

She was told that being a woman she should stick to the
distaff and spindle and not meddle with Scripture.

FIFTH EXAMINATION

Examiner: What is your belief? Do you believe that Christ's
body is present really, corporately, substantially?

Elizabeth: I don't understand really and corporately and if by
substantial you mean his real human body I say that he is at
the right hand of God and cannot be in two places.

Examiner: If you don't have this faith you are damned.

Elizabeth: Can you give me this faith?

Examiner: No, only God can do that.

Elizabeth: Well, he hasn't. "The Spirit gives life, the flesh profits
nothing."

SIXTH EXAMINATION

Examiner: You accept only what is in Scripture? How about the
seven sacraments? Is marriage a sacrament?

Elizabeth: No, it is a holy estate.

Examiner: What about purgatory? You have only skimmed the
Scriptures. The doctrine of purgatory is there.

Elizabeth: Sir, that could never be found in Scripture.

Examiner: If you accept only what is in Scripture what about
the Sabbath? In Scripture it is Saturday.

Elizabeth: Is there anything in Scripture to prove that it cannot
be Sunday?

Examiner: You know so much about Scripture you must be a
priest's woman or wife.

Elizabeth: I am not a priest's woman or wife.

Examiner: Have I touched your conscience?

Elizabeth: No, you'd better look after your own.

SEVENTH EXAMINATION

Examiner: Do you believe that the pope of Rome is the supreme
head of the Church?

Elizabeth: No, Christ is the head.

Examiner: Haven't you prayed that God deliver you from the
tyranny of the bishop of Rome and all his detestable enormities?

Elizabeth: Yes, I have.

Examiner: Aren't you sorry?
Elizabeth: Not a whit.

EIGHTH EXAMINATION
Now come some who offered to go surety for her.

NINTH EXAMINATION
Examiner: Are you any wiser than last time?
Elizabeth: I haven't learned much since.

The two women who came to offer surety were asked whether
they also "did not smell of the frying pan of heresy?" This they
denied. They why did they come? "Because," said one, "she has
three children who are like to die. I got a nurse for one. I'll
have to look after her children and that's why I want her out."
The death of Queen Mary brought about her release.

Foxe was by no means inhibited from telling ghastly tales both
of routine and of wanton cruelties. Mother Seaman, aged three
score and six, for refusal to go to mass had to sleep in bushes,
groves and fields or sometimes in a neighbor's house. Her eighty
year old husband fell sick. With no regard for her safety she
came and nursed him to the end and shortly followed him in
death. She was denied Christian burial and her friends had to
lay her in a pit by the moat's side.[12]

Elizabeth Folkes, when she came to the stake, took off her
petticoat to give it to her mother, who came and kissed her,
but the gift was not permitted.[13]

Alice Benden, about to be delivered up by her own husband,
to save him shame, went of her own accord. The sheriff allowed
her to be taken to prison by a lad. There she lay without change
of raiment for nine weeks and when she was cleansed the skin
peeled off.[14]

Joan Waste, twenty-two years old, had been blind from birth.
She had learned to "knit hosen and sleeves and to turn ropes."
She had saved enough to buy a New Testament and from listening had learned portions by heart. Refusing to confess that the
bread and wine on the altar were the body and blood of Christ,

she was told that she was blind not only in body but also in soul and that her body would be burned with material fire and her soul with fire everlasting. None should be permitted to pray for her. During her execution the bishop dozed.[15]

In the case of Rose Allin, a certain Master Tyrrell had come to arrest her parents. The mother thereupon felt sick and asked for a drink. Rose took a stone pitcher in one hand and a candle in the other to fetch water. But Tyrrell interrupted her, saying that she should instruct her parents. She answered the Holy Ghost would do that. He perceived that she was of their mind and told her she would burn, too, "for company's sake." "For Christ's sake," she corrected him. To show her how she would burn he grasped her wrist, took the candle and burned cross-wise over the back of her hand "until the very sinews cracked asunder." Rose reported, "I had the stone pot in the other hand and might have laid him on the face with it. I thank God I did it not." [16]

After the recitation of such cases one can understand why Foxe should gloat over calamities which befell the persecutors. He had

The burning of Rofe Allins hand, by fyr Edmond Tiryll, as fhe was going to fetche drynke for her Mother, lyeng fycke in her bed.

behind him a venerable tradition in this regard. In the days of Constantine, Lactantius had written his *De Mortibus Persecutorum, (On the Deaths of the Persecutors),* and Tertullian thought that one of the delights of the martyrs would be to look down from heaven on the torments of their persecutors. Foxe relates instances of divine retribution.

In the days of Henry VII, at the instance of Chancellor Whittington, a woman was burned for heresy. A great concourse assembled to witness her death, among them Chancellor Whittington. Now while she was being burned a butcher was slaying a bull, and being less adept in slaughtering beasts than papists in murdering Christians, struck too low. The bull with a mighty lurch broke his tether and rushed out as the crowd was coming from the burning. The people parted. The bull paid no heed but went straight for the chancellor "and, pricked with sudden ve hemency, ran full butt, gored his paunch and careened through the street with the entrails on his horns, to the great admiration and wonder of all that saw it." Some might attribute this to chance but who can be so dull "which seeth not herein a plain miracle of God's mighty judgment?" [17]

Another instance occurred in the first days of Mary's reign when a curate continued to use the Prayer Book of Edward VI. As he was so engaged, a bailiff seized him in the pulpit, saying, "Will you not say mass, you knave? Or by God's blood, I will sheathe my dagger in your shoulder." The curate set himself to say mass. As the bailiff was on his way home a crow, sitting in a willow tree, flew up directly over his head, cawing "Knave! knave!," and let go a dropping, which falling on his nose, ran down over his beard. "The scent and savor so noyed his stomach that he never ceased vomiting till he came home, where he got him to bed" and in a few days died without repentance. This story, we are assured, was testified by credible witnesses.[18]

But Foxe derived greater satisfaction from deliverances than from retributions. He relates the case of Agnes Wardell. She and her husband were suspect. He went to sea. She, left with a babe and a maid, took in a woman and child as tenants. The queen's men came by night to arrest Agnes who was asleep. At the first and second knocks the tenant did not answer. At the

third she called to know who was there. Why had she not responded sooner? "Because," said she, "there are spirits and if
one answers to the first or the second knock there is peril." They
laughed but would not be put off. Let her open. "There is no
candle," said she. "Open, or we'll take off the door." During
this stalling the maid had wakened Agnes who came down in a
buckram apron and was locked in a closet in the parlor. The
queen's men, having obtained a candle from a neighbor, were
admitted and began the search, first in the tenant's room. "The
bed's warm. Who's been in it? "The child and I." "None other?"
"None other." Then they came into the parlor. "There's a fair
cupboard," said one. "She may be in it." "Yea, she may," agreed
another, but they did not pry. In the yard they found a horse
eating shorn grass. "Whose horse is this?" they asked the maid.
"Hers. She came in before night and went away again. I know
not whither." They took the maid in custody and went to search
the grounds.

In the meantime Agnes in the closet began to think burning
would be preferable to suffocation and asked the tenant to let
her out. "Where are the keys?" "In the hamper." The lock
would not yield. "Then break the door." The tenant went for
a chisel and hammer but found none. "Try again with the key.
I trust God will give you the power to open it." He did. Agnes
slipped out into the garden, pushed back two loose pales on the
fence, threw herself into a ditch of nettles and at the approach
of searchers concealed herself beneath the buckram apron.
Thus she escaped.[19]

But where to? and what became of the babe, and the maid and
did she ever find her husband again?

Another instance of deliverance was the case of one Cross-
man's wife. Her own name is not even known. For not going to
mass she was sought in her own home by the constable. She hid
herself with a babe in arms along side of a chimney. The child,
though wailing before, did not cry and she was saved.[20]

Babes more than once proved a convenience. There was the
case of Moon and his wife. The bishop said, "Is this your wife,
Moon?" "Yea, my lord." "O good Lord, how may a man be deceived in a woman!" The wife broke in. "None can charge me

with dishonesty of body." "No, not that," quoth the bishop, "Better to have given your body to twenty sundry men than to pluck the king and the queen's majesties out of their royal seats." Then Moon yielded and his wife followed. Hearing her child crying below, she said she must leave to give suck. The bishop granted permission on condition that they report again on the morrow, but he was called away and they were not again summoned.[21]

Highly gratifying was an act of restitution when Elizabeth became queen. The wife of Peter Martyr had died during Edward's reign and had been buried in the cemetery of Corpus Christi College at Oxford. On Mary's accession complaint was made to Cardinal Pole that the bones of this heretic should not be allowed to repose in holy ground. Sufficient evidence could not be produced to warrant the burning of her remains. Nevertheless the cardinal would not suffer them to lie in close proximity to the relics of St. Frideswide. Madame's bones were disinterred and left on a dunghill. On Elizabeth's accession they were restored and so mixed up with the relics of the saint that if any future cardinal were so mad as to move them again he would not know which were which.[22]

One is amazed at the measure of communication between those in and out of prison, both men and women. In the case of the women this was chiefly by way of visitation and the supplying of material needs, in the case of the men by way of correspondence.

We have Latimer's letter of thanks to a Mrs. Wilkinson of London, who prior to her own exile, did much to aid the bishops imprisoned by Mary including Hooper, the bishop of Hereford, Coverdale, Cranmer and Latimer himself, who wrote: "If the gift of a pot of cold water shall not be in oblivion with God, how can God forget your manifold and bountiful gifts, when he shall say to you, 'I was in prison, and you visited me?' God grant to us all to do and suffer, while we be here, as may be to his will and pleasure. Amen." [23]

We have a letter in like vein from a William Tyms who suffered in 1556. He was really a lay preacher, though called a deacon, ministering to a congregation in the woods. When the

DE KATHE-
RINÆ NVPER VXO-
ris doctissimi viri D. Petri Marty-
ris vermilij Florentini, regij Theologiæ
apud Oxonienses tempore Ed-
wardi sexti pro-
fessoris,
Cardinalis Poli mandato, regnante Maria, effossæ
exhumatione, ac eiusdem ad honestam sepul-
turam sub Elisabetha regina restitu-
tione, studiosorum quorundam
tam Oxoniensium quàm
aliorum
Carmina, cum præfatione quadam
totam rei gestæ seriem
depingente.
(∴)

EXCVSVM LONDINI
in officina Ioannis Day.

CVM PRIVILEG
Regiæ Maiestatis.

Anno Do,
1561.

Title page of *The Res-
toration of the Bones of
Katherine Vermigli* (the
wife of Peter Martyr)

¶ A letter sente to Maystres Wyl-
kinson of Soper lane in London, wydowe,
she being at the maner of Englysh in Oxforde
there from M. Hughe Latimer out of
Bocardo in Oxford, where he
was prisoner for the testi
mony of Christ.
An. 1555.

F the gifte of a pot of colde
water shall not be in ob-
lyuion with God, how can
God forget your manifold
and bountifull gifts, when
he shall saye to you: I was in pryson,
and you visited me. God graunt vs all
to do and suffer while wee be here, as
maye bee to hys wyll and pleasure.
Amen.

Yours in Bocardo,
Hugh Latimer.

Latimer's letter.

owner learned that his woods were polluted by sermons to as
many as a hundred, the preacher was apprehended and in a garment white above and sheep's russet below was brought before
Winchester who thought his attire did not resemble that of a
deacon, to which he retorted that it more nearly resembled that
of a deacon than the bishop's the attire of an apostle. Tyms had
children and a wife brought again to bed during his captivity.
To the women of his parish he wrote:

> Dear sisters, I have me most heartily commended unto
> you, thanking you for the great kindness showed unto me
> in this time of mine imprisonment, and not only unto me,
> but also unto my poor wife and children; and also for the
> great kindness that you show unto all the living saints that
> be dispersed abroad, and are fain to hide their heads for
> fear of this cruel persecution. . . . I do believe that when
> the Lord shall send his angel to destroy these idolatrous
> Egyptians here in England, and shall find the blood of the
> Lamb sprinkled on the door-post of your hearts, he will go
> by you, and not hurt you, but spare your whole households
> for your sakes.[24]

We have an instance of a man visiting a woman prisoner in
grave disturbance of mind. Agnes Bonger was not permitted to die
with her fellow prisoners because her name had been misspelled
as Bowyer and the jailor required confirmation of her iden-
tity. She was grieved because she had made herself a smock for
the occasion and had already engaged a wet nurse for her babe.
The man consoled her that God accepted Abraham's readiness
to sacrifice his son, though excusing him from doing it. "Yes,"
she objected. "But it's not my son. It's me." "And your babe," he
reminded her. Thereat she began "to stay herself" by reading
and prayer until the time of her offering up.[25]

Great was the distress of those guilty of recantation, whether
men or women. Elizabeth Cooper made amends by going to St.
Andrew's church while the people were at their "popish service"
and renouncing her recantation, for which she suffered accord-
ingly.[26] Agnes Glascock had gone to mass under pressure from

her husband and now reproached herself bitterly. A letter of assurance came from John Careless lying in prison, saying:

> Your foot hath chanced to slip forth of the way, to the great discomfort of your soul, and the heaviness of your heart. But, my good sister, the Lord will raise you up again, and make you stronger than ever you were. For if you had not by this proved the experience of your own strength, or rather your own weakness, you would have stood too much in your own conceit, and have despised and condemned other weak persons that have committed the like offence. Do not think that God will cast you clean away. It is a greater sin to mistrust the mercy and goodness of God than to commit the greatest offense in the world. Know for a surety that all your sins be utterly forgiven you for Christ's sake, be they never so many, so grievous and so great. The thing that is done cannot be undone, and you are not the first that hath offended. There is with the Lord "mercy and plenteous redemption." He maketh backslidings many times turn to profit, as doubtless, dear sisters, yours shall do, if you put your whole faith, hope and trust, only in his infinite and eternal sweet mercies.[27]

When she visited him in prison he wrote some verses in her book with the concluding lines:

> "And think on me, I do you pray,
> The which did write this for your sake.
> And thus to God I you betake,
> Who is your castle and strong Rock;
> He keeps you, whether you sleep or wake;
> Farewell, dear Mistress A. Glascock!" [28]

Here are a few lines written from prison by Ralph Atherton to Agnes Smith, widow:

> We are spoiled of our labors. The holy sanctuary of God's most blessed word, is laid waste and desolate, so that the very foxes run over it. Yet it is the food of our souls, the lantern of our feet, and a light unto our paths, and where it is not preached the people perish.[29]

Richard Woodman wrote to Mistress Roberts of Hawkhurst:

> For when I have been in prison, wearing onewhile bolts, otherwhile shackles, otherwhile lying on the bare ground; sometime sitting in the stocks; sometimes bound with cords, that all my body hath been swollen; much like to be overcome from the pain that hath been in my flesh; sometime fain to lie without in the woods and fields, yet for all this I praise my God. All this that hath happened unto me hath been easy, light, and most delectable and joyful of any treasure that ever I possessed. Fear hath painfulness, but perfect love casteth out all fear; which love I have no mistrust but God hath poured it upon you so abundantly, that nothing in the world shall be able to separate you from God. Neither high nor low, rich nor poor, life nor death, shall be able to put you from Christ; but by him I trust you shall enter into the new Jerusalem, there to live forever.

There are many tributes to women. Here is one to Mother Benet, who was not allowed to be buried in a churchyard. Her benefactions were so great that her husband chided her and said she might have saved him a hundred marks. She answered, "I could not firkin up my butter and keep my cheese in the chamber and wait a great price, and let the poor want." Foxe comments, "This good woman, of that vice of covetousness, of all that knew her was judged least to be spotted of any infirmity she had." [30]

We have noted before that the Protestants and Catholics would have marriage only within the faith and that this insistence tended to break down the system of family-arranged marriages in favor of unions grounded in conviction. The above mentioned John Careless wrote to his wife that when the daughters came of age he hoped they might be provided with husbands "as fear God, and love his holy word. I charge you take heed that you match them with no papists, and if you live and marry again yourself (which thing I would wish you to do, if need require, or else not) good wife, take heed how you bestow yourself, that you and my poor children be not compelled to wickedness." [31]

This same John Careless sent the following counsel to a friend about to embark upon matrimony:

> First and above all things you must be very circumspect to keep the band of love, and beware that there never spring up the root of bitterness between you. If at any time there happen to rise any cause of unkindness between you (as it is impossible always to be free from it), see that you weed up the same with all lenity, gentleness and patience; and never suffer yourself, nor your wife, to sleep in displeasure.
>
> If you have cause to speak sharply, and sometimes to reprove, beware that you do not the same in the presence of others, but keep your words until a convenient time, and then utter them in a spirit of meekness, and the groaning spirit of perfect love; which you must also let sometimes to cover faults, and wink at them if they be not intolerable. Whatsoever loss and mischance shall happen unto you, take it patiently, and bear it merrily; and though the same should come partly through your wife's negligence, yet let it rather be a loving warning to take heed in time to come, than a cause of sorrow for that which is past and cannot be holpen. I know by mine own experience, that we are in this life subject to many inconveniences, and that of nature we are prone to displeasure, and ready to think unkindness of every little trifle, and specially with out our best friends, yea soonest with our loving wives, which be most loath to displease us. But let us beware of this cankered corruption, and consider that we ought most of all in love to bear with them, according to Christ's example.[32]

NOTES

All of the references are to John Foxe *Actes and Monuments* in the modern reprint, AMS Press, Inc., New York, 1965. An instructive chapter is devoted to Foxe by Helen C. White, *Tudor Books of Saints and Martyrs* (University of Wisconsin Press, Madison, 1967). The book by V. Norskov Olsen, *John Foxe and the Elizabethan Church* (U. of California, 1973), appeared too late to be consulted.

1. VIII, 391
2. VIII, 429
3. VIII, 493
4. VIII, 579
5. VIII, 553
6. IV, 239
7. IV, 243
8. IV, 225
9. VIII, 115-116
10. V, 537-550
11. VIII, 536-548
12. VIII, 467
13. VIII, 392
14. VIII, 327
15. VIII, 247
16. VIII, 385-386
17. IV, 128
18. VIII, 633
19. VIII, 219
20. VIII, 556
21. VIII, 224
22. VIII, 296
23. VII, 517
24. VIII, 113-114
25. VIII, 422-423
26. VIII, 381
27. VIII, 193-196
28. VIII, 195
29. VIII, 414
30. VIII, 467
31. VIII, 174, Cf. VII, 117
32. VIII, 197

Elizabeth I

13.

Elizabeth I
(1533-1603)

When Mary was dying she assured Elizabeth of her willingness to confer upon her the succession if she would not change the privy council, if she would not alter religion and if she would pay Mary's debts. Elizabeth's reply was that the succession was not Mary's to confer, that the complexion of the privy council would be her own prerogative, that religion would not be changed save in accord with the word of God.[1] The debts would of course be discharged. Elizabeth meant to be untrammeled by the past but the past could not be escaped.

Especially was this true of religion. Her father had cast off the "usurped primacy of the bishop of Rome" without diverging markedly otherwise. Her brother had moved first to Wittenberg and then to Zürich. Her sister had reverted to Rome. The modern solution would be religious pluralism. Elizabeth hinted at it when she said she "would not make windows into men's hearts," [2] but she did mean to control their bodies. She was England's queen. In accord with the universal assumption she regarded England as a Christian nation. All citizens were Christian and should worship alike for the sake of concord and national unity. There might be pluralism among the states but each state or region should have its own religion. Comprehension rather than toleration was the policy. But if all England were to be comprised in one system the requirements must not be too exacting. Elizabeth's problem was to know what to command and what to condone.

Elizabeth's Coronation Procession

She made the decision to return to the status of the last years of her father and again cast off "the usurped primacy of the bishop of Rome." Some judge her motive to have been purely secular. She was simply a *politique*. But what she did was not politic. In the year 1558, the year of her accession, France and Spain made peace with the mutual resolve to exterminate heresy in their respective domains. Either might find Protestantism a pretext for falling upon England. France in league with Scotland could exert pressure from the south and from the north. Spain would be neutral. Germany was quiescent after the Peace of Augsburg had granted toleration to the Lutherans. England would have to try to enlist Spain, but the Spanish alliance had been ruinous for Mary. Elizabeth took the risk. She reminds one of William of Orange, who, when told that he must make an alliance with a foreign potentate, declared that he had made an alliance with the mightiest of potentates, the Lord of Hosts.

Here is her own statement:

> When first I took the scepter, my title made me not forget the giver, and there [I] began as it became me, with such religion as both I was born in, bred in, and I trust, shall die in; although I was not so simple as not to know what danger and peril so great an alteration might procure me

—how many great Princes of the contrary opinion would attempt all they might against me, and generally what enmity I should thereby breed unto myself. Which all I regarded not, knowing that He, for whose sake I did it, might and would defend me.[3]

What, then, were her religious convictions? She told the Spanish ambassador that she would like the Augsburg Confession to be maintained in her land, though she would not introduce exactly that. (This would link her too obviously with the Germans). "She differed little from us [the Catholics] as she believed God was in the sacrament of the Eucharist and only dissented from three or four things in the mass." [4] She did, then, believe in transubstantiation.

At the same time she had come under the influence of the evangelical Catholicism in vogue early in the century. At the age of ten she had translated into English *The Mirror of the Sinful Soul* of Marguerite of Navarre.[5] One finds in Elizabeth no rhapsodic flights but one does find the note so poignantly expressed by Marguerite of the tedium of this mortal life and the sighing for deliverance. Elizabeth as queen declared herself to live for the sake of her subjects, but "as for me I assure you I find no great cause I should be fond to live, nor conceive such terror in death that I should greatly fear it." They are "happiest that are soonest hence." This has "taught me with better mind to bear these treasons, than is common to my sex—yea with better heart perhaps than is in some men." [6]

Another influence in her youth was that of Melanchthon [7] who made much of the distinction basic for her policy between the beliefs necessary for salvation and those indifferent, called the *adiaphora*. Another with whom she was personally friendly was the Italian exile Bernardino Ochino who dedicated to her his *Labyrinth* in which he set forth four dilemmas of the determinist and four of the indeterminist, then extricated himself from the first set and from the second set and left the question at the end as it had been at the beginning. She likewise did not relish prying into the inscrutable.

This same Ochino struck another note appearing in her utterances of disregard for *prudenza humana,* human prudence. She declared:

> If policy had been preferred before truth, would I, trow you, even at the first beginning of my rule, have turned upside down so great affairs, or entered into tossing of the great waves and billows of the world: [I] that might, if I had sought mine ease, having harbored and cast anchor in a more seeming security?

Worldly wisdom dictated a marriage alliance with some great power.

> But all those means of leagues, alliance, and foreign strength I quite forsook, and gave myself to seek for truth, without respect, reposing my assured stay in God's most mighty grace, with full assurance. Thus I began, thus I did proceed, and thus I hope to end.[8]

Her prayers bespeak the same spirit. After the defeat of the Armada, unlike her father, she did not forget to thank God.

> And not the least for that the weakest sex hath been so fortified by Thy strongest help that neither my people might find lack by my weakness nor foreigners triumph at my ruin.
> Such hath been Thy unwonted grace in my days, although Satan hath made holiday in busy practices both for my life and state. Yet Thy mighty hand hath overspread both with shade of thy blessed wings so that both neither hath been overthrown nor received shame, but obtained victory to Thy most great glory and their greatest ignominy. For which, Lord, of Thy mere goodness grant us grace to be hourly thankful and ever mindful. And if it may please Thee to pardon my request, give us the continuance in my days of like goodness, that mine eyes never see change of such grace to me, but specially to this my kingdom, which, Lord, grant to flourish many ages after my end. Amen.[9]

Elizabeth did have convictions. One might call her already an Anglo-Catholic. She was also England's queen, with no fanatical inclination to plunge the land into wars of religion. The

Protestants owed their very existence to her rule, and she, having renounced the pope, was dependent upon them. All of the Marian bishops, save two, refused to serve. They were replaced by the ardent Protestants returning from exile. They were an aristocratic elite—able, educated and passionately in earnest. Counting families, the number of those returning was about 800. Of these only about a third were of the cloth. A number of the laity entered parliament. Of the 404 members, over a hundred were vehemently Protestant. Elizabeth could not carry on without them. Her father's rule had been largely personal. Hers became parliamentary. Henry manipulated legislative bodies. Elizabeth, blustered, wheedled, revised public documents with incredible diligence and often gave in. The Protestants were intensely loyal to her but not averse to inflicting the wounds of love.

Her initial procedure was in line with the advice that glasses with small necks reject liquid too rapidly poured. "Howbeit, if you instill water into them by a little and little, they are soon replenished." [10] The first move was to place a moderate Protestant in the key post of the church. Matthew Parker was made the archbishop of Canterbury. As a student at Cambridge he had been associated with the reforming party, but under Mary instead of going to the continent he had retired to his books. Called upon by the queen to head the church, he protested his unworthiness and yielded partly out of loyalty to the queen's mother, for Anne Boleyn a week before her execution had entrusted to him the care of the baby Elizabeth.[11] Parker was prepared out of loyalty and conviction to implement the queen's program. For civil affairs the chief secretary was William Cecil, made Lord Burghley. He had contemplated exile during Mary's reign but had stayed to mitigate the severities. When the fires of Smithfield burned he retired to his estate. He could be counted on for moderation and sometimes embarrassed the queen by his complacency toward heretics.[12]

Despite the resolve not to pour the new wine too rapidly down the narrow neck she summoned parliament during the first year of her reign, the year 1559. The chief acts of the Anglican settlement were then promulgated. By the *Act of Supremacy* she was made not the supreme head, but the supreme governor of the church. The title, though less pretentious, did not inhibit her governing. But she was not obstinately arbitrary and on matters of state could brook sharp dissent. Another secretary, Sir Francis Walsingham, castigated her niggardliness with respect to the salaries of public servants: "If this sparing and unprovident course be held on still, the mischiefs approaching being so apparent as they are, that no one that serveth in place of a Councillor . . . would not wish himself rather in the farthest part of Ethiopia than the fairest palace in England." [13]

Elizabeth accepted this as a wound of love, but the case was very different when Bishop Cox remonstrated with her for expropriating to the use of the crown some of the possessions of his see. She crushed him with peremptory brevity: "You know what you were before I made you what you are now. If you do not immediately comply with my request, I will unfrock you, by God." [14]

When it came to the religious settlement the queen wished to revert to the last days of her father and the first of her brother. She wished to restore the Prayer Book of 1549 which was Lutheran in tone. The Protestant party desired the book of 1552 which was Zwinglian. They won but the queen made certain alterations. The prayer to be delivered "from the tyranny of the Bysshop of Rome and al hys detestable enormities," came out, for it would offend not only English Catholics, but also Catholic countries. The Black Rubric which forbad kneeling at the reception of Holy Communion, lest it should imply adoration of the "reall essential presence there beeing of Christ's natural fleshe and bloude," was likewise removed, as not only anti-Roman but anti-Lutheran.

As for the administration of the Eucharist the book of 1552 prescribed: "Take and eate this, in remembrance that Christ dyed for thee, and feede on him in thy hearte by faythe, with thanksgiving." This suggests that the Lord's Supper is only a memorial and a spiritual experience. The version of 1549 read: "The body of our Lorde Jesus Christe whiche was given for thee, preserve thy bodye and soule unto everlasting lyfe." [15] These words are patient of a Lutheran and even a Catholic interpretation. The queen simply put them together.

The *Injunctions* permitted the marriage of the clergy as a remedy for sin. Elizabeth did not approve of sin but she did not like this remedy.[16] Her beloved Archbishop Parker wrote to Cecil:

> I was in an horror to hear such words to come from her mild nature and christianly learned conscience, as she spake concerning God's holy ordinance and institution of matrimony. I marvelled that our states in that behalf cannot please her Highness, which we doubt nothing at all to please God's sacred Majesty, and trust to stand before God's judgment and in a good conscience therewith. Princes have ever held their clergy in esteem, but we alone of our time [are] openly brought in hatred, shamed and traduced before the malicious and ignorant people, as beasts without knowledge to Godward, in using this liberty of his word, as men of effrenate intemperancy, without discretion or any godly disposition worthy to serve our state. The Queen's Highness expressed to me a repentance that we were thus appointed in office, wishing it had been otherwise. But in patience and silence we leave all to God. In the mean time we have cause all to be utterly discomforted and discouraged.[17]

The *Act of Uniformity* required every person within the queen's dominions to attend divine services on Sundays and holy days on pain of penalties to be imposed by the bishops and the justices of the peace.[18] State and church were thus combined. But the imposition of conformity did not insure uniformity. There were ambiguities in the enactments which gave rise to diversities. The *Act* said that the ornaments of the church should be retained as they were in the second year of Edward, that is in the book of 1549, but exactly what were the ornaments? The *Injunctions* of the same year called for the extinction of "shrines, tables, candlesticks, rolls of wax, paintings, pictures on walls and windows in churches and houses." But another injunction said that images were not to be "set forth and extolled." [19] If they were not set forth how could they be extolled? And if they could be extolled must they not have been set forth?

There was no explicit prohibition of the crucifix or the cross without the body. The queen had a silver crucifix in her chapel and before it a lighted candle. When Bishop Cox officiated in her chapel he did it with trembling and addressed to her an agonized petition saying:

> In trembling fear of God I humbly sue . . . prostrate and with wet eyes, that ye will vouchsafe and peruse the considerations, which move that I shall not minister in your Grace's chapel, the lights and cross remaining. The Scripture says God suffered no similitude, nor likeness of anything to be seen. How durst man, dust and ashes, set up an image in the temple of God? [20]

The reply of those who defended the images was that their prohibition was only an appendage to the command to have no other God. If images were not worshipped they did no harm. The objectors made the command to make no image into a second commandment with the result that all those coming after had to be renumbered. In all of this there were emotional concomitants stemming from the Marian persecution. Those whose friends had gone to the stake, those who themselves had forsaken goods and friends to sing the Lord's song in a strange land, now came home with a deep repugnance to everything which reminded them of the "detestable enormities of the bishop of Rome." The historian, Strype, records that "not long from the queen's entrance upon her government, crucifixes were so distasteful to the people that they brought many of them unto Smithfield and there broke them to pieces and burnt them; as it were to make atonement for many holy men and women that were not long before roasted to death there." [21]

But the queen had a silver crucifix in her private chapel and a candle burning. When she was touring the provinces the crucifix and candle were removed. On her return they were replaced. In 1562 a vandal broke the crucifix and the candlesticks. They were again replaced. In 1567 a zealot threw down the crucifix and the candlesticks during a service. A tapestry took their place for a time but in 1571 they were put back and the queen never gave up her silver crucifix.[22] By so doing she defied her own royal supremacy. To be sure the *Injunctions* of 1559 did not expressly forbid the cross but an order of 1561 called for the erection of a crest consisting presumably of the queen's arms on the roods instead of the cross and in the years 1569-75 a series of episcopal visitation articles issued with royal approval called for the removal of rood lofts, altars, altar stones, images, crosses, candlesticks, censers and bells, together with "all other monuments of idolatry." Yet the queen kept her silver crucifix.[23]

But after all, this was only in her own chapel. Elsewhere the relics of the Amorites disappeared. The image controversy subsided to be succeeded by the vestarian dispute. Protestant passion was increasingly enflamed by the intensified Roman menace. In 1570 the pope excommunicated Elizabeth and absolved Catholics from the oath of political allegiance. In this year the Jesuits arrived. There were two attempts to remove Elizabeth in favor of Mary Queen of Scots, the Ridolfi conspiracy of 1572 and the Babington plot of 1586. The massacre of St. Bartholomew came in 1572 and the attack of the Armada on England in 1588. These events caused Elizabeth to forsake her earlier leniency toward the Catholics, but she did not on that account abate the campaign against the Puritans.

Already in 1565 she outlined her position to Archbishop Parker. The Puritans, she told him, were given to a "vain love of singularity" which "must needs provoke the displeasure of Almighty God and be to us, having the burden of government, discomfortable, heavy and troublesome; and finally we must needs bring danger of ruin to our people and country." There must be uniformity to avoid "the breeding of contentions." "We have not," said she, "taken it upon us . . . to define, decide or determine any article of the Christian faith and religion." Nor would we make an inquisition into matters of faith or ceremonies, so long as our subjects "shall in their outward conversation show themselves quiet and conformable . . . to the laws of the realm." [24] This sounds as if she were saying, "You may believe as you please provided you do as you are told."

In pursuance of her attitude Parker issued his *Advertisements* in 1566.[25] They stipulated that the clergy must wear the cope at the altar, the surplice in the pulpit and a cap on the streets. Then flared up anew the controversy which was thought to have been settled in King Edward's day. Hooper had then refused to be consecrated if he must wear the Aaronic vestments. He yielded to the extent of agreeing to wear them *sometimes*. The new universal edict brought the issue again to the fore and all the arguments used in the image controversy were again hurtled back and forth. If the vestments, as all agreed, were not necessary to be worn for salvation, why, asked the insurgents, should the government require them? Conversely, asked the government, if they are indifferent why should the stubborn decline to put them on for the sake of national solidarity? [26]

The continental divines were consulted. Zürich and Geneva gave essentially the same answers. Peter Martyr from Zürich said that if the altars had been removed, indicating that further reform was in store, the vestments might be worn.[27] Beza from Geneva thought that over non-essentials the shepherds should not leave the sheep to the wolves and the sheep should not refuse to be fed by the vested shepherds. This was a real point because some of the clergy feared to appear in the rags of popery lest the sheep turn and rend them. Beza concluded with the hope that "the merciful Lord, taking pity on human infirmity, would effectually direct the Queen's Majesty with his Holy Spirit." [28] But the Holy Spirit did not restrain the Queen's Majesty.

She even went so far to meddle with doctrine. The *Thirty Nine Articles* received her scrutiny and revision. To the Thirty Ninth she added that "The Church hath power to decree rites and ceremonies and authority in controversies of faith." She expunged Article Twenty Nine that "the wicked and such as be void of a lively faith, though they do press with their teeth, the sacrament of the body and blood of Christ, yet in nowise are partakers of Christ." [29] That is a doctrinal statement.

If, then, the queen would not listen, if the archbishop would not listen—he talked about the "fantastical spirits and the stubborn multitude" [30]—then the recourse would have to be to parliament. This is one of the stages by which the government of England came to be in fact that of the crown in parliament. In 1572 an *Admonition* was addressed to parliament. There was a long comparison between the church in Elizabeth's day with that of the apostles:

> Then ministers were placed with the consent of the congregation, now by the bishop; then the ministers were preachers, now mere readers of homilies; then they prayed as the Spirit moved; now out of the *Book of Common Prayer,* containing many things contrary to the word of God; then at the communion they used common bread, now wafer cakes; they received sitting, we kneeling; they ministered plainly, we pompously with surplice and cope; they received with conscience, we with custom; they simply, we sinfully. Fie upon this stinking abomination.

The archbishop's court is "the filthy quagmire and poisoned plash of all abominations that do infect the whole realm." and the Commisaries' court is "but a petty little stinking ditch that floweth out of that former great puddle." [31]

Parliament did not redress the grievances. Very well then, address the nation. There followed a freshet of tracts and a notable satire under the pseudonym of *Martin Marprelate.* The lampoon inveighed against the "proud, popish, presumptious, profane, paultry, pestilent and pernicious prelates." Their incompetence was ridiculed by the story of the vicar of Trumpington who coming upon the words in Aramaic spoken by Jesus on the cross *"eli, eli lama sabachthani?"* exclaimed, "Eli, Eli! If the bishop of Ely *(eli)* sees this he will say it is his book. It ought to read 'Trumpington, Trumpington *lama sabachthani!'*" Seven such salvos were fired in as many months. The type was lugged about in baskets to five different places. Copy would be dropped under a hedge to be picked up by another. Women unbeknownst to their husbands harbored the perpetrators. The tracts were smuggled inside clothes or parcels. The press was finally discovered and suppressed.[32]

If propaganda failed then there "should be no tarrying for any" that "the walls of Jerusalem should be rebuilt and the blood of the martyrs should not have been shed in vain. [33] As a matter of fact the blood of the martyrs worked potently through

the *Acts and Monuments* of John Foxe issued first in 1563 and
appearing in seven editions during the reign of Elizabeth. No
work did so much to fashion the mind of Protestant England
save the Geneva Bible of 1560. But there were no immediate
results. Consequently attempts were made to erect the walls of
Jerusalem beyond the walls of the establishment, or at least to
a degree. Lecturers on religious subjects were engaged and supported by the congregations. They were not subject to the jurisdiction of the bishops. This measure was in part an effort at lay
autonomy, but gave scope also for Puritan propaganda.[34]

Then there was the device of "prophesyings," for a greater
freedom of expression. Here the conflict was not between the
Puritans and the establishment but between the establishment
and the crown. Parker had been succeeded as archbishop by
Grindal, one of the Marian exiles who had compiled materials
for Foxe's *Book of Martyrs.* He looked with favor on meetings
of the clergy which began with a prayer from the *Book of Common Prayer.* Then sang "an hymne unto the Holy Ghost" and
next expounded Scripture by way of discussion. The leader and
the participants were commonly clergymen, but sometimes lay-
men participated and the laity were encouraged to attend, including the common folk and justices of the peace.

Grindal invited opinions from a number of bishops who
reported that these exercises were edifying and useful for the
instruction of the inferior clergy, who were also thereby kept
from gaming, drinking and "wanderyne upe and downe." [35] But
the queen claimed that such discussions "lead to divided opinions upon pointes of divinity farre unmeete for vulgar people."
She would like to abolish the "prophesyings" altogether and
restrict the clergy to reading homilies instead of preaching. On
the one hand she needed preaching as a propaganda instrument
for her legislation, but on the other hand was appalled by
Puritan preachers who said that she "had no religion and was
enough to make God vomit." [36]

Grindal sent her a vehement protest which deserves to be
excerpted as an example of the reformatory spirit within the
establishment. He wrote:

With remembrance of my humble duty to your Majesty, it may please the same to be advertised that the speeches which it pleased you to deliver unto me concerning abridging the numbers of preachers and the utter suppressing of all learned exercises and conferences have exceedingly dismayed and discomforted me. Madam, first of all I must confess that there is no earthly creature to whom I am so much bounden as to your Majesty. I do, with the rest of all your good subjects, acknowledge that we have received by your government many and most excellent benefits, as amongst others freedom of conscience, suppressing idolatry, sincere preaching of the gospel with public peace and tranquillity. I am even persuaded that even in the chief matter which you seem to urge, your zeal and meaning is for the best.

Alas, Madam, is the Scripture more plain in any one thing than that the gospel of Christ should be plentifully preached? There was appointed to the building of Solomon's material temple a hundred and fifteen thousand artificers and laborers, besides three thousand three hundred overseers and shall we think that a few preachers may suffice to build the spiritual temple of Christ? Public and continual preaching of God's word is the ordinary means and instrument of the salvation of mankind.

Now as concerning the learned exercises and conferences amongst the ministers of the church, I have consulted with divers of my brethren, the bishops, by letters, who think the same as I do that these are profitable to the church and therefore to be continued. Samuel did practice such like exercises in his time. St. Paul also doth make express mention that the like in effect was used in the primitive Church.

If it be your Majesty's pleasure to remove me out of this place I will with all humility yield thereto. What should I win if I gained, I will not say a bishropic but the whole world, and lose mine own soul? Bear with me, I beseech you Madam, if I choose rather to offend your earthly Majesty than to offend the heavenly Majesty of God. Remember,

Madam, you are an earthly creature. Look not only upon the purple and princely array wherewith you are apparelled, but consider withal what it is that is covered therewith: is it not flesh and blood? Is it not dust and ashes? Is it not a corruptible body which must return to this earth again? Wherefore I beseech you, Madam, in the bowels of Christ, when you deal in these religious causes, set the majesty of God before your eyes, laying all earthly majesty aside. And if ye so do, although God have just cause many ways to be angry with you and us for our unthankfulness, yet I doubt nothing but that for his own names sake and for his own glory sake, He will still hold his merciful hand over us, shield and protect us under the shadow of his wings." [37]

After this salvo Elizabeth would have been glad to be rid of Grindal. She hesitated to unfrock the archbishop of Canterbury, but sequestered him. After six months he begged to be restored that he might pass on the huge accumulation of unsettled cases. Both the queen and he were soon relieved of the dilemma by his death. He was succeeded by Whitgift to whom Cecil wrote that his articles to be imposed on the clergy "be so curiously penned, as I think the Inquisitors of Spain use not so many questions to trap their prey." [38]

The opposition grew more radical. If the establishment with its hierarchy of bishops would not reform, then away with the hierarchy. This was the cry of the Presbyterians. Their most outstanding representative, Cartwright, a one time fellow student of Whitgift, was now locked with him in vehement controversy. What was now demanded amounted to a revolution. If the bishops went, the royal supremacy would go, because the supreme governor appointed the bishops. James I was not exactly right when he said "No bishop, no king." Elizabeth stated the case more precisely to James telling him that there

had arisen both in your Realm and mine, a sect of perilous consequence, such as would have no king but a presbytery. . . . Yea look well unto them. When they have made in

our people's hearts a doubt of our religion, and that we
err if they say so, what perilous issue this may make I
rather think than mind to write. . . . Suppose you, my
dear brother, that I can tolerate such scandals in my sincere
government? No, I hope, howsoever you be pleased to bear
with their audacity towards yourself, yet you will not suffer
a strange King receive that indignity at such caterpillars'
hand, that instead of fruit, I am afraid will stuff your
Realm with venom.[39]

The Presbyterians did achieve a rudimentary organization.
Yet their program, though it would destroy the royal supremacy,
still left intact the concepts of uniformity and conformity. They
still regarded England as a Christian nation which as a whole
should be made to conform to the pattern of God's word. The
Presbyterians in power were no more tolerant than the Angli-
cans. Then arose a much more radical movement, separatism.
The concept of a church coterminous with the nation was shat-
tered. All England, said the separatists, is not Christian. The
true Christians should be gathered into congregations. Hence
the term "the gathered church." Its government should be congregational. Separatist congregations came into being especially
in the latter years of the queen's reign.[40]

An interesting aspect of the movement is the part played in
it by women. In the area around London, says a recent historian,
"It was the women who occupied the front line in defense of
their preachers, with a sense of emotional engagement hardly
exceeded by the suffragettes of three and a half centuries later."
When a preacher was suspended by Grindal, six women de-
scended upon him in his house. He was hooted. A preacher
who had deserted the cause was assaulted by "a certain number
of wives." When two preachers were sent over London Bridge
into exile in the country two or three hundred women feted
them with exhortations and goodies. "There were more women
than men imprisoned in Bridewell in 1568." The government
clamped down. The three leaders Penry, Barrow and Greenwood
went to the scaffold to Lord Burghley's "impotent sorrow." [41]

The Arrest of a Priest and of the Lady who harbored him,
together with the ransacking of her house

Monks in England hanged, drawn, and quartered

In the meantime there was the question of the papist recusants. All faithful Catholics were made traitors by the pope's bull excommunicating Elizabeth and absolving Catholics from political obedience. A codicil was later added that she not be extinguished *at once*. But what about later on? The Jesuit mission began in 1570. The first priests, such as the martyrs Campion and Parsons, were occupied only in the cure of souls, but Cardinal Allen was fomenting actual rebellion. The two conspiracies to supplant Elizabeth and install Mary Queen of Scots enflamed opinion. Priests were hanged, drawn and quartered.[42]

Nevertheless subterranean activity continued. Many of the laity practiced what Calvin in a reverse situation called Nicodemism after Nicodemus who came to Jesus only by night. Sufficient outward conformity was practiced to escape detection while clandestine masses were celebrated in country estates. One of the greatest obstacles to the extermination of the "traitors" lay in the wives of the gentry who harbored the priests. Skilled craftsmen constructed "hiding holes" for the secreting of priests and the paraphernalia of the mass when houses were raided. We have the diary of a Jesuit by name Gerard who in his own eyes was not deemed worthy of martyrdom and lived to bequeath the record.[43] Four days he lay in a hole with only a few scraps of bread and a mite of jelly slipped to him by the hostess as he hustled into concealment. He could hear the pursuers knocking against walls, and pulling off plaster. When they gave up he emerged weak and wasted.

Many were caught and imprisoned. One at Bridewell had barely enough bread to sustain life. The cell was narrow with thick walls. He had to sleep in a sitting posture on a window ledge. His clothes were not removed for months. The straw on the floor swarmed with vermin and the open pail for excrements gave a stifling stench.

The underground contrived a system of communication. This Gerard explains the relative merits of orange and lemon juice for secret writing. Orange can be brought up by heat only once and therefore precludes the possibility of interception and forwarding to the unsuspecting. Lemon juice can be brought out several times and is better if the message is to go to one friend after another. Gerard, imprisoned in the tower, asked the warden for a quill for a toothpick, oranges to make rosaries out of the peel and paper in which to wrap the rosaries for friends who were allowed to bring him supplies. With the quill as a pen, the orange juice as ink and the wrapping paper for a letter he contrived to set up an escape by letting a string from the window to be attached to a rope below. This pulled up, the prisoner let himself down to a boat waiting in the moat. A letter was left exonerating the jailer, but lest nevertheless he should feel unsafe word was brought to him that a horse was waiting should he wish to flee. He did.

The Rucusants like the Puritans carried on an extensive propaganda campaign with a secret press in England and publishing establishments abroad.[44] There are striking parallels between the Papists and the Puritans as to their methods and their trials. At the end of the queen's reign both types of opposition appeared to have been crushed. But they were like those trick candles on birthday cakes which having been snuffed out burst again into flame. The queen succeeded to this extent that Anglicanism survived. So also did Catholicism and Puritanism. And the queen herself contributed to the collapse of comprehension and the triumph of toleration by her stubborn defiance of the royal supremacy in keeping on her altar the silver crucifix.

If there be any who doubt the sincerity of her religious sentiment let them ponder this her private prayer.

O Most Glorious King, and Creator of the whole world, to whom all things be subject, both in heaven and earth, and all best Princes most gladly obey, Hear the most humble voice of thy handmaid, in this only happy, to be so accepted. How exceeding is thy goodness, and how great mine offences. Of nothing hast thou made me not a worm, but a Creature according to thine own image, heaping all the blessings upon me that men on earth hold most happy. Drawing my blood from kings and my bringing up in virtue; giving me that more is, even in my youth knowledge of thy truth: and in times of most danger, most gracious deliverance: pulling me from the prison to the palace: and placing me a Sovereign Princess over thy people of England. And above all this, making me (though a weak woman) yet thy instrument, to set forth the glorious Gospel of thy dear Son Christ Jesus.

Thus in these last and worst days of the world, when wars and seditions with grievous persecutions have vexed almost all Kings and Countries, round about me, my reign hath been peaceable, and my realm a receptacle to thy afflicted church. The love of my people hath appeared firm, and the devices of mine enemies frustrate. Now for these and other thy benefits (O Lord of all goodness) what have I rendered to thee? Forgetfulness, unthankfulness and great disobedience. I should have magnified thee, I have neglected thee. I should have prayed unto thee, I have forgotten thee. I should have served thee, I have sinned against thee. This is my case. Then where is my hope?

If thou Lord wilt be extreme to mark what is done amiss, who may abide it? But thou art gracious and merciful, long suffering and of great goodness, not delighting in the death of a Sinner. Thou seest whereof I came, of corrupt seed: what I am, a most frail substance: where I live in the world full of wickedness: where delights be snares, where dangers be imminent, where sin reigneth, and death abideth. This is my state. Now where is my comfort?

In the depth of my misery I know no help (O Lord) but the height of thy mercy, who hast sent thine only Son into the world to save sinners. This God of my life and life of my soul, the King of all comfort, is my only refuge. For his sake therefore, to whom thou hast given all power, and wilt deny no petition, hear my prayers. Turn thy face from my sins (O Lord) and thine eyes to thy handiwork. Create a clean heart, and renew a right spirit within me. Order my steps in thy word, that no wickedness have dominion over me, make me obedient to thy will, and delight in thy law. Grant me grace to live godly and to govern justly: that so living to please thee, and reigning to serve thee I may ever glorify thee, the Father of all goodness and mercy. To whom with thy dear Son, my only Saviour, and the Holy Ghost my Sanctifier, three persons and one God: be all praise, dominion and power, world without end. Amen.[45]

NOTES

Abbreviations:

> Gee and Hardy—*Documents Illustrative of English Church History* (London, 1914).
>
> *Letters*—G. B. Harrison, *The Letters of Queen Elizabeth* (London, 1935).
>
> Meyer—Carl S. Meyer, *Elizabeth and the Religious Settlement of 1559* (St. Louis, 1960).
>
> Neale—J. E. Neale, *Elizabeth and her Parliaments*, 2 vols. (London, 1953 and 1957).
>
> *ZL*—*Zurich Letters*, 2 vols. (Parker Society, 1842 and 1845).

1. Meyer, 9-10, *ZL*, I, No. 2, pp. 3-4.
2. Powell Wells Dawley, *John Whitgift* (New York, 1954), 48.
3. Neale, II, 128.
4. *Ibid.*, I, 79. *Spanish Papers*, I, 61-62.
5. *A Godly Medytacyon of the christen Sowle*, 1548. Reprint ed. Percy Ames (1897) with the title *Mirror of the Sinful Soul.*
6. Neale, II, 118.
7. Meyer, 5.
8. Neale, I, 365.
9. Tucker Brook, "Queen Elizabeth's Prayers," *Huntington Library Quarterly*, II, 1 (Oct. 1938), 72.
10. Neale, I, 37.
11. V. J. K. Brook, *Life of Archbishop Parker* (Oxford, 1962).
12. Conyers Read, *Lord Burghley and Queen Elizabeth* (New York, 1960).
13. *Letters*, XXX, 49.
14. *Ibid.*, XI, 120-121.
15. *The First and Second Prayer Books of King Edward the Sixth* (Everyman's Library, 1910).
16. Gee and Hardy, No. XXIX, 431.
17. *Correspondence of Matthew Parker* (Parker Society, Cambridge, 1853) No. CXIV, 156.
18. Gee and Hardy, No. LXXX, 463-464.
19. *Ibid.*, No. LXXVIII, 428 and 419.
20. John Strype, *Annals of the Reformation* I, 2. App. XXII, 500-502.

21. *Ibid.*, I, 1, p. 260.

22. William P. Haugaard, *Elizabeth and the English Reformation*, (Cambridge, 1968).

23. Great Britain, *Laws and Statutes*, III, 210, 226, 255, 311, 333, 381.

24. Parker, *Correspondence*, 223-227, and Joseph M. Levine, *Elizabeth I* (Prentice-Hall, 1969), 71-73.

25. Gee and Hardy, No. LXXXI.

26. John Henry Primus, *The Vestments Controversy* (Kampen, Holland, 1960).

27. *ZL*, II, xiv.

28. John Strype, *Edmund Grindal*, App. XVI, 507-516.

29. Text in Philip Schaff, *Creeds of Christendom* vol. III and John H. Leith, *Creeds of the Churches* (New York, 1963).

30. Parker, *Correspondence* CCLXXXIV, 377, and CCCXXXI, 434.

31. Walter Howard Frere, *Puritan Manifestoes* No. X (New York, 1907).

32. Henry Martin Dexter, *Congregationalism* (New York, 1880), 129-202. Text ed. E. Arber, *English Scholar's Library*.

33. Neale, I, 83.

34. Paul S. Seaver, *The Puritan Lectureships* (Stanford, Cal., 1970).

35. Stanford E. Lehmberg, "Archbishop Grindal and the Prophesyngs," *Historical Magazine of the Protestant Episcopal Church*, XXXIV (1965), 87-145.

36. Neale, II, 70.

37. The text is given in modern spelling in Strype's *Edmund Grindal*, a more accurate text in the old spelling in Lehmberg. I have used his text in modern spelling, and have excerpted without dots.

38. Dawley, *Whitgift* from Strype, *Whitgift*, III, 104-107.

39. *Letters*, No. XIV, 203-204.

40. William A. Clebsch, *England's Early Protestants* (New Haven, 1964).

41. Patrick Collinson, *The Elizabethan Puritan Movement* (University of California Press, 1967), 93 and 428.

42. Patrick McGrath, *Papists and Puritans under Elizabeth I* (London, 1967), covers both movements admirably.

43. *John Gerard*, tr. Philip Caraman (London, 1951).

44. Leona Rostenberg, *The Minority Press and the English Crown 1558-1625* (Nieuwkoop, Holland, 1971).

45. *A Book of Devotions composed by Her Majesty Elizabeth*, tr. Adam Fox (Colin Smythe, 1970), a collection of Elizabeth's private prayers, two in English, the others translated from French, Italian, Latin and Greek.

The Duchess of Suffolk

14.

Catherine Willoughby, The Duchess of Suffolk
(1519/20-1580)

Catherine Willoughby, the duchess of Suffolk, was the daughter of Maria de Salinas, that Spanish lady in waiting to Catherine of Aragon, who with such defiant intrepidity forced herself past the guards to the chamber of the queen and attended her to the death.[1] The queen and the lady both had daughters. The queen named hers Mary, quite possibly for Maria. The lady named hers Catherine undoubtedly for the queen. Yet when the queen's daughter became Mary I of England and restored Catholicism, the lady's daughter fled as a Protestant refugee to the continent. Another anomaly is that the prelate who became godfather to the daughter of the lady, Stephen Gardiner,[2] was chiefly responsible for precipitating the flight.

Maria de Salinas married the English Lord Willoughby. Their daughter Catherine was not long with her parents, for at an early age she became a maid in waiting in the household of the sister of Henry VIII, another Mary Tudor, the widow of King Louis XII of France and the wife of Charles Brandon, the crony of Henry VIII. He it was upon whom was forced the unpalatable mission of moving the "dowager" Catherine of Aragon to a less salubrious spot. When Brandon lost his wife he married Catherine, the maid.[3] She was fourteen, he was forty nine. Theirs was a happy union of a dozen years. She bore him two sons, one named Henry for the king, the other Charles for his father. Since Brandon was the duke of Suffolk Catherine became the duchess.

In this role she mingled with the high aristocracy and had a part in the christenings of the royal children, Elizabeth and Edward. With Princess Mary she was friendly and beguiled her loneliness by playing cards in the days when she was badgered by her father and her brother.[4] Catherine's two sons shared the schooling of Prince Edward. The Suffolks did a great deal of entertaining, whether at their estate at Grimsthorpe in Lincolnshire or in their home near London. On one occasion Henry VIII and his bride Catherine Howard enjoyed their hospitality.[5] But entertaining royalty was more expensive than paying them to stay away. The Suffolks received a mandate to play hosts to Margaret, the dowager of Scotland, another sister of Henry VIII.[6]

A very different assignment was foisted upon Catherine following the death of Catherine Parr, who on the decease of the king had married right speedily her one time lover, had borne to him a daughter and had died very soon thereafter. No one seemed more appropriate than the duchess to care for the child of the dowager, whom in life she had honored by publishing her devotional tract the *Lamentation of the Sinful Soul*. The duchess might well have taken over had not the babe been accompanied by a horde of retainers without stipend. Catherine addressed a letter of remonstrance to William Cecil, at that time secretary to the Lord Protector. The letter commences with a jocose pomposity and then drives to the point. The original spelling is here retained for a touch of flavor.

The Two Sons of Catherine and Charles Brandon

It is said, that the best mean of Remedy to the Sick, is first plainly to confess, and to disclose the Disease. Wherefore both for Remedy, and again for that my Disease is so strong that it will not be hidden, I will discover me unto you. First, I will . . . in high Secresie, declare unto you, that all the World knoweth, tho' I go never so coverly in my Net, what a very Beggar I am. The Sickness, as I have said, I Promise you, increaseth mightily upon me, amongst other the Causes thereof, if you will understand not the least, the Queens Child hath layn and yet doth lye at my House with her Company, wholly at my Charges, &c. Wherefore I cease, and commit me and my Sickness to your diligent care, with my hearty Commendations to your Wife. At my Manor of Grimesthorp, the xxvii of August [1548].

> Your assured Loving Friend,
> K. Suffolk.[7]

There was another reason why the assignment was too oner-ous. When this letter was written in 1548 Catherine had been a widow for three years. Another solution was found.

The duchess was not always gracious. On an earlier occasion when the ducal couple were giving a grand party the duke pro-posed that each lady should ask the gentleman for whom she most cared to escort her to dinner, excepting himself as host. The duchess, having perforce to choose another, turned to her godfather, Bishop Stephen Gardiner, saying that since she could not have her husband for whom she most cared she would invite the bishop for whom she cared least.[8] The barb rankled for years. One said of her: She is "a lady of sharp wit, and sure hand to drive her wit home, and make it pierce where she pleases." [9] Another said that "the Lady Suffolk's heats oft cum-bered him. It is a pity that so goodly a wit waiteth upon so froward a will." [10]

She certainly did not alienate every one. The protector es-teemed her so highly as to propose that his daughter be be-trothed to her son. Here is her reply, addressed again to Cecil as the intermediary.

No unadvised bonds between a boy and a girl can give such assurance of good will as has been tried already. And now, they, marrying by our orders, and without their consents, as they be yet without judgment to give such consent as ought to be given in matrimony, I cannot tell what more unkindness one of us might show one another, or wherein we might work more wickedly, than to bring our children into so miserable a state not to choose, by their own likings.

There is none she would rather have him take than the duke's daughter, but the daughter might not want it, nor he. Let the parents be friends and "suffer our children . . . to begin their loves themselves, without our forming." If they were to marry under constraint they would not feel so bound to each other. "I doubt not . . . my son and his daughter shall much better like it, to make up the matter themselves. And so my good Cecil, being weary, I leave you to the Lord." [11]

This letter supports the suggestion made in our introduction that the individualizing of faith led to the personalizing of marriage. The duchess here insisted that the marriage must rest on the personal choice of the couple. By this time she had already made a personal choice as to religion. We do not know the exact stages.

Reference has already been made to her publication of Catherine Parr's devotional tract. The influences to which the duchess was subject in the home of her first husband are somewhat a matter of inference. The duke, dutiful to his master, supported him in the repudiation of the "usurped primacy of the bishop of Rome," but this meant little. Gardiner, the conservative, did the same. There are indications, however, that the duke was leaning to the left.

One of his chaplains was Alexander Seton,[12] a refugee for religion from Scotland at that time still Catholic. In England he preached openly that good works do not save. Under pressure he recanted and bore a faggot at St. Paul's cross in 1541. He was one of the many who in the first years of intimidation like Peter denied their Lord, then wept bitterly and embraced the cross. Another chaplain was John Parkhurst, who under Mary fled to the continent and under Elizabeth returned to be a prickly bishop, lax in enforcing conformity.[13] Another evidence of Catherine's interest in the reform is the hospitality afforded to John Foxe, the later martyrologist, on the occasion of his ordination.[14]

Unquestionably the reformer who influenced her most was Hugh Latimer. She referred to him with great affection years after his martyrdom.[15] During the period of her widowhood, between the death of Charles Brandon in 1545 and her remarriage with the ardent Protestant, Richard Bertie early in 1553,[16] Latimer was her mentor and from November 1551 to the spring of 1552, her chaplain at Grimesthorpe.[17] A series of his sermons delivered in her chapel became available in printed form, bearing her coat of arms in the editions of 1548 and 1549, and in the latter also a dedication by the editor which in part read:

> Tis my rude laboure of another mans swet (most verteous lady) I offer most humbli vnto iour grace, mouid there vnto of godli zeale, thorough the godli fame, that is disperst vnyuersally of your most godly disposicion, and vnfayned loue towards the lyuynge, almyghtye, eternall God and hys holye word, practysed dayly both in your graces most vertuous behauour, and also godly charitie towardes the edification of euery membre graffed in Chryste Iesu, most humbly desirying your grace to accept fauorably thys my temerous interprise.[18]

One cannot say, of course, that the duchess endorsed every opinion of Latimer. For that matter, he himself went through changes of mind. For long he held to the doctrine of transubstantiation and only in his latter years, under the influence of Cranmer, came to interpret the words "This is my body" in a purely spiritual sense. But the general marks of his stance are evident also in hers. He was not greatly interested in theology, though there was one cardinal doctrine to which he clung with tenacity and that was the all-sufficiency of Christ's sacrifice for the forgiveness of sins to the complete exclusion of any good

Latimer Preaching before Edward VI

"The *Fyrste Sermon* of Mayster Hugh Latimer . . .
Preached before the Kynges Grace," 1549
With the coat of arms of the Duchess of Suffolk and a dedication to her

works on the part of man, for, though highly commendable, these are superfluous and irrelevant for salvation.

> All the passion of all the martyrs that ever were, all the sacrifices of all the patriarchs that ever were, all the good works that ever were done, were not able to remedy our sin, to make satisfaction for our sins, nor anything besides, but this extreme passion and blood letting of our merciful Savior Christ.[19]

Certain theological deductions, however, followed of necessity from the doctrine of justification by faith solely in the meritorious passion of Christ. Monasticism became useless as a way of gaining merit and earning salvation. Purgatory could not be regarded as a place to atone for sin or accumulate credit. Examined as to his view of purgatory, Latimer answered that he would rather be there than in the Lollard's Tower, for in purgatory one could not be strangled and reported to have committed suicide.[20] The merits of the Virgin and the saints were superfluous and their intercessions needless. Such statements differed obviously from Roman orthodoxy and Latimer could rejoice that England had been delivered from "the stormy surges and dangerous rocks of the Roman sea." [21] But the English sea was not to prove calm.

Passing lightly over dogma, he indulged, like the Franciscan preachers, in social criticism. In their style he inveighed against avarice, extortion, pomp, gaming, guzzling and wenching. Commenting on the shepherds at the nativity he threw in the aside that the angels would never have reached them with the good news if they had been tippling in the ale house.[22] The clergy drew constant strictures. "Once," he related, "when the townsfolk did not announce the arrival of a bishop by the ringing of a bell, saying that the clapper was broken, the bishop, pointing to the pulpit, said, 'There's a bell that hasn't had a clapper in twenty years.' " [23]

Latimer was in the wake of Erasmus in disparaging such externals as the cult of relics, images and pilgrimages, but more radical in desiring to root them out. The following excerpts from the *Sermon on the Plough* are a fair sample of his style and message:

> Who is the most diligent bishop and prelate in all England? I will tell you. It is the Devil. He is never out of his diocese. Where the Devil is resident the cry is, "Away with Bibles, up with beads. Away with the light of the gospel, up with the light of candles, yea at noon days. Down with Christ's cross, up with purgatory. Away with clothing the naked. Up with decking of images.[24]

Such preaching might well have inspired the reformatory activity of the duchess in her domain. We have this description of her efforts:

> She was very active in seconding the efforts of government to abolish superfluous Holy Days, to remove images and relics from the churches, to destroy shrines, to put an end to pilgrimages, to reform the clergy, to see that every church had provided, in some convenient place, a copy of the large Bible, to stir up the Bishops, Vicars and Curates to diligence in preaching against the usurped authority of the Pope; in inculcating upon all the reading of the Scriptures and especially the young, the Pater Noster, the Articles of Faith and the Ten Commandments in English.[25]

Her zeal for the reform made her the more hospitable to the strangers within the land. The Augsburg Interim on the continent in 1548 cut athwart the reign of Edward VI in England. In the biographies of Katherine Zell and Frau Wibrandis we learned that Martyr migrated to Oxford, Butzer to Cambridge. The duchess at that time, having lost her husband, was living near Cambridge to be close to her two sons. She saw a good deal of Butzer, who at first was by himself. A friend, we recall, wrote to his wife still at Strasbourg, saying, "She had better come to care for Butzer else he might marry some one else. The duchess of Suffolk would have him. She is a widow."[26] When Frau Wibrandis and some of the children did come the duchess provided them with a cow and a calf. Once Butzer was watching them in a pasture when a wag suggested that they were his teachers.

"Yes," he laughed, "though they speak not French, German, Latin, Greek or Hebrew." [27] During Butzer's last illness he was nursed by his wife and the duchess.

Another refugee who enlisted her devotion was Bernardino Ochino the one time luminary of Franciscan preaching in Italy. After his apostasy the Spanish ambassador reported that in the judgment of the Italian Catholics in London his eloquence had so far deserted him that soon he would have no followers save the marquis of Northampton and the duchess of Suffolk.[28]

Her assistance to refugees was more extensive. There were some two thousand in London: French, Italians, Spaniards, German, Dutch and Poles. Through the good offices of the duchess they were given a church and a constitution exempting them from the *Act of Uniformity* in the hope that for all England they might set up a model church purged of all the dregs of popery. The accompanying illustration shows King Edward conferring the charter on the Pole, Lasco, as superintendent for the whole. The pastor of the French speaking Walloon congregation was named Perussel. We shall meet him again. The reputation of the duchess abroad was such that Tyndale, still in exile, and the French pastor Viret dedicated to her some of their works.[29]

Edward VI conferring the Charter of the Church of the Strangers on Lasco. Pictured here are Cranmer, Edward VI, Somerset, Lasco, Ridley, and Latimer.

Opposition to Catherine's reforms had long been building up. The chief instigator was her godfather Stephen Gardiner, in high favor as the bishop of Winchester under Henry, in high disfavor under Edward because of his resistance to reforms aggressively promoted by the duchess. A visitation was decreed in the name of the crown. Gardiner heartily detested the effort to stamp out relics, pilgrimages, candles, holy water, beads and crosses of wood.[30] Images, said he, are instructive for the illiterates who are a hundred to one in England. The cross is not worshipped. A sacristan carrying a cross for a Good Friday procession, while taking a drink at the ale house, tucked it under his gown.[31] Was that worship? But for all Gardiner's sputtering the visitation in his diocese was carried through with the "helping forwardness of that devout woman of God, the Duchess of Suffolk." [32]

Gardiner was finally deprived and sent to the Tower. His bishopric was conferred on John Ponet, who had had the misfortune to marry unwittingly the wife of a butcher. She was returned to her husband. When Gardiner was asked whether he ever expected to get back his bishopric he replied, "Why not? The butcher got back his wife." [33] Gardiner got back more than his bishopric. On the accession of Mary he became the chancellor of the realm with jurisdiction over heresy.

The policy of the government with respect to the heretics was not at first stringent. The foreigners were assisted by the queen's officers in leaving the country. The English Protestant leaders were given time enough to escape. Gardiner told the Spanish ambassador that his tactic was to summon a suspect to appear, whereat he would be frightened and disappear.[34] The leniency was ended by a rebellion and the disclosure of a conspiracy. The rebellion led by Wyatt caused the execution of Lady Jane. Then the Dudleian conspiracy, nipped in time, brought to light a plot abetted by refugees and financed by France to unseat Mary and Philip in favor of Elizabeth and her consort. It was led by Edward Courtenay, the one who translated *The Benefit of Christ's Death*. He and Wyatt were sent to the Tower.

The fear that the refugees abroad might be fomenting conspiracies was rendered the more plausible by what they continued to proclaim. Ponet in 1556 declared that the lawfulness of killing a tyrant is "grafted in the hearts of men." Christopher Goodman in 1558 declared that the common people are duty bound to cut off the rotten member "even if it be their rulers and magistrates. If death be deserved, then death." [35] John Knox came out with the *Faithful Admonition unto the Professors of God's Truth in England* saying that Mary's "usurped government" was "a rage without reason."

> Jesabell never erected halfe so manie gallowes in all Israel, as mischeevous Marie hath done within London alone. She declareth herself an open trateresse to the realme of England, contrarie to the just lawes of the same, to bring in a stranger, and mak a proud Spaniard king, to the destruction of the nobilitie and subversioun of the realme.

To Gardiner, Knox apostrophized:

> O thou beast . . . more cruel than any tiger, ashamest thou not, bloody beast, to betray thy native country? Fearest thou not to open such a door to all iniquity that the whole England shall be made a cannon stew to Spaniards?" [36]

The leading reformers were already in the Tower. Efforts began to be made to bring back the refugees from abroad to burn them if they did not recant, in any case to keep them under surveillance. Sir Peter Carew and Sir John Cheke were kidnapped at Antwerp and carted home.[37] Catherine, still with the title of duchess, was married to the Protestant Richard Bertie. Still in England, they were suspect. Ridley from the Tower wrote to a friend that the prisoners, meaning Hooper, Latimer, Cranmer and others, lacked neither "meat, money, nor shirts" because though "strictly watched by bailiffs and our hosts" friends eluded such vigilance. "I have received," he wrote, "my Lady's alms. I desire you to render her grace hearty thanks." [38] The lady was the duchess of Suffolk. When Parkhurst, her one time chaplain, fled to the continent, he expressed his anxiety for Elizabeth and his "patroness, the good duchess of Suffolk." [39]

In the case of the Berties, Gardiner still had recourse to his devise of frightening out of the country. Richard Bertie received a summons to appear.[40] He did appear. The chancellor came around tactfully to the subject of religion and particularly the religion of the duchess. He recalled not so tactfully her rude remark to him at the party and now sarcastically asked whether she was ready to set up the mass as formerly to pull it down. Bertie assured him that she was no "masking Christian. You know, my Lord, one judgment reformed is worth more than a thousand transformed temporizers. To force a profession of religion by mouth, contrary to that in the heart, worketh damnation." "I pray you," inquired the bishop, "think you it possible to persuade her?" "Yea verily, with the truth, for she is reasonable enough." Bertie was dismissed.

He suspected that this was not the end and employed a ruse. Returning to the chancellor he requested permission to go to the continent to collect a debt owing by the emperor to his wife's late husband. "I like your device well," said the bishop, "but think it better to tarry the prince's coming." (The reference is to Philip of Spain who was coming to marry Queen Mary.) "Nay," answered Bertie. When the marriage is consummated the emperor will have no further reason for obliging England. "By Saint Mary, you answer shrewdly," answered Gardiner and gave him a pass to go and come as often as he wished. Gardiner may have seen through the ruse and would have been glad enough to have him gone together with his truculent lady.

He betook himself abroad not to collect the debt but to make arrangements for the coming of his wife and child. Her two sons by Brandon had been swept off in a day by the sweating sickness while at Cambridge. Catherine had in arms a babe, Susan, by Bertie and was pregnant. With her she took a few menials: four men, a Greek who exercised horses, a joiner, a brewer and a fool, that is, a court jester whose wit may well have been as sharp as her own. There were three women, a cook, a gentlewoman and a laundress. All, including the duchess, were dressed as servants. They set out from London between four and five in the morning. The keeper of the house, hearing a noise, came out with a torch. Catherine eluded him by abandoning a pot of milk and her portmanteau, containing clothes for her daughter. The man, instead of making search for her, rummaged in her luggage. Retaining but two women with herself, she instructed the others to make separately for a rendezvous at a quay on the Thames.

The junction was effected. The boatman because of fog was loath to take off but was persuaded. At Gravesend they were put up for the night by a friend with whom Bertie had made arrangements. The duchess was able to sew some more clothes for her child. Accompanied now by Bertie the company boarded for the crossing but contrary winds drove them almost to the coast of Zeeland. Returning to England they had to send a man ashore for provisions. He was questioned as to whether the duchess was aboard and answered that he had seen none but menials. The passage was effected and once in Brabant the women changed into the "hukes" native to the region.

They journeyed toward the town of Wesel in Cleves where Bertie had secured permission of residence from the magistrate through the good offices of Perussel, now pastor there of a French speaking refugee congregation. He was not unmindful of the "courtesy of the Duchess' hand" shown him while in London. The party on the way stopped at the town of Stanton. Here the inhabitants became suspicious that the duchess and her husband were "greater personages than they gave themselves forth." The magistrates and the bishop of Arras ordered an examination "of a sudden." Bertie having wind of this, took the wife and child but only two of the servants for a stroll "as it were." At three o'clock in the afternoon on a February day they set out on foot fearing to hire a horse or carriage. The other servants were left to fend for themselves and join up as they might.

At this point let the martyrologist John Foxe continue the narrative:

> After the duchess and he were one English mile from the town, there fell a mighty rain of continuance, whereby a long frost and ice, before congealed, was thawed, which doubled more the weariness of those new lacquies. But, being now on the way, and overtaken with the night, they

The above illustrations are from a ballad of Elizabeth's day with embellishments of Foxe's account. In the ballad Bertie gets the keys to a church porch and there kindles a fire for Catherine and the baby Susan. The sexton wrenches the keys from Bertie and cracks him over the head so that the blood spurts. The officers arrive and take him before the governor to whom Bertie makes such a brave, bold, gallant speech in Latin that all is adjusted. Here are two of the stanzas:

When all in vain her speech
    was spent
And they could not House-Room
    get,
Into a Church-Porch then they
    went
To Stand out of the Rain and Wet;
Then said the Duchess to her Dear,
O that we had some fire here.

Then did her husband so provide
That fire and coals they got with
    Speed
She sat down by the Fire-Side,
To dress her daughter that had
    need,
And while she dressed it in her Lap,
Her husband made the infant pap.

sent their two servants (which only went with them) to villages as they passed, to hire some car [carriage] for their ease, but none could be hired. In the mean time master Bertie was forced to carry the child, and the duchess his cloak and rapier. At last, betwixt six and seven of the clock in the dark night, they came to Wesell, and repairing to the inns for lodging, and some repose after such a painful journey, found hard entertainment; for going from inn to inn offering large money for small lodging, they were refused of all the innholders, suspecting master Bertie to be a lance-knight, and the duchess to be his woman. The child for cold and sustenance cried pitifully; the mother wept; the heavens rained as fast as the clouds could pour.

Master Bertie, destitute of all other succour of hospitality, resolved to bring the duchess to the porch of the great church in the town, and so to buy coals, victuals, and straw for the miserable repose there that night, or at least till by God's help he might provide her better lodging. Master Bertie at that time understood not much Dutch, and by reason of evil weather and late season of the night, he could not happen upon any that could speak English, French, Italian, or Latin; till at last going towards the church-porch, he heard two striplings talking Latin, to whom he approached, and offered them two stivers to bring him to some Walloon's house.

By these boys, and God's good conduct, he chanced at the first upon the house where master Perusell supped that night, who had procured them the protection of the magistrates of that town. At the first knock, the good man of the house himself came to the door, and opening it, asked Master Bertie what he was. Master Bertie said, "An Englishman, that sought for one master Perusell's house." The Walloon willed master Bertie to stay a while, who went back, and told master Perusell, that the same English gentleman, of whom they had talked the same supper, had sent by likelihood his servant to speak with him. Whereupon master Perusell came to the door, and beholding master Bertie, the duchess, and their child, their faces, apparels, and bodies so far from their old form, deformed with dirt, weather, and heaviness, could not speak to them, nor they to him, for tears. At length recovering themselves, they saluted one another, and so together entered the house, God knoweth full joyfully; master Bertie changing his apparel with the good man, the duchess with the good wife, and their child with the child of the house.

Within few days after, by master Perusell's means, they hired a very fair house in the town, and did not let to show themselves what they were, in such good sort as their present condition permitted. It was by this time through the whole town what discourtesy the innholders had showed unto them at their entry, insomuch as on the Sunday following a preacher in the pulpit openly, in sharp terms, rebuked that great incivility toward strangers, by allegation of sundry places out of holy Scriptures, discoursing how not only princes sometimes are received in the image of private persons, but angels in the shape of men; and that God of his justice would make them strangers one day in another land, to have more sense of the afflicted heart of a stranger.

Their presence in Wesel was soon noised abroad and other English refugees began to arrive to the number of about a hundred in the end. Their pastor for a time was Miles Coverdale, the translator of the Bible into English.[41] Under such circumstances the location of the Berties could not be concealed from the English government. The ambassador in the Netherlands circumvented his own government by tipping off Bertie that he was being sought.[42] The news was correct. The Lords passed an order that if the duchess and her husband did not return, their goods would be confiscated. Inventories were taken of their possessions in Lincolnshire and around London. The Commons, however, vetoed the order.[43] But this did not stop efforts to bring them home. A still more disquieting piece of news was that the duke of Brunswick was in the area in command of Austrian troops. This was none other than Erich of Braunschweig whose brutality towards his mother has been described elsewhere.[44] He was in the service of the emperor and his son Philip of Spain, the consort of Mary in England. Since the duchess was half Spanish, Spain might claim jurisdiction over her. Another move appeared imperative and it was harder now because while at Wesel Catherine had given birth to a son, named Peregrine, because born on a peregrination.[45]

Foxe tells us that they set out for a place called Windsheim "in high Dutchland under the Palsgrave's dominion." The term "high" was applied to south Germany. The area was the Palatinate. Windsheim was near Heidelberg, where lately Calvinism had been infiltrating.[46] This region also was not remote from the arm of the English government. An agent named John Brett was sent by Philip and Mary with letters missive to a number of refugees including the duchess and her husband.[47] Here is a section from his account:

> I repayred to the Duches of Suffolk and her husbande Richarde Barteue which persons resyde in Germany in an old Castell scytuate upon the topp of a hill nighe unto a towne of the Palsegraves callyd Weinheim. At that Towne I arryved on Fryday the xth of July afore mentioned and leavinge my horses there in an Inne I went uppe the hill a good half englysshe myle highe a foote accompanyed with myne owne servaunte and a man of the Towne to shew us the waye. When I came afore the Castell gates I founde them faste shitte [shut] and a stryplynge lyke an englisshe lakey standing afore them. Of hym I demaunded if the sayde Duches and Barteue were within. The said lackey aunsweryd me yea and had scarsely spoken this worde but one loking out of a Grate in the gate asked who I was and what I wolde haue. I toldde hym that I wolde gladly speake with the saide Duches and Barteue and that I had letters to delyver them from certayne of their fryndes: he demaunde me eftsones my name and I tolde it hym. Then he badde me to tary at the gate and he wolde goe tell the Duches of me.

While he waited someone from a turret above dropped a stone.

My hap was that it missed my heade but it hat me so bigge a blowe on the right hande that I colde not rule my forefynger and thombe a fortenighte after. And ymmediately certen of the Duches servauntes russhed oute of the gate with great fearsenes. I wat not howe many so that yt seemed vnto vs highe tyme to retyre thence or to tary there by force.

The upshot of it all was that when communication was established the duchess and her husband demanded to be told whether the letters were missives, that is simply messages, or processes, that is subpoenas. If the latter they would not receive them "sithen they were within an other Prynces domynyons." He refused to tell. They refused to receive. He returned to his sovereigns and to this day we do not know what those missives contained.

Obviously the Palatinate was no secure and tranquil refuge. At that point arrived an invitation to go to Poland. The hand behind it was that of Lasco, whom the Berties had known as the head of the Church of the Strangers in London. On invitation from King Sigismund he was returning to his native heath in order to establish there a reformation after the manner of Edward's England. The king invited also the Berties. They set out from Windsheim in April of 1557 going by way of Frankfurt. Let Foxe here pick up the story: [48]

In the which their journey it were long here to describe what dangers fell by the way upon them and their whole company, by reason of their landgrave's captain who, under a quarrel pretensed for a spaniel of master Bertie's, set upon them in the highway with his horsemen, thrusting their boar-spears through the waggon where the children and women were, master Bertie having but four horsemen with him. [This sounds as if the four men servants had caught up with them.] In the which brabble it happened the captain's horse to be slain under him.

Whereupon a rumour was sparsed immediately through towns and villages about, that the landgrave's captain

should be slain by certain Walloons, which incensed the
ire of the countremen there fiercely against master Bertie,
as afterward it proved. For as he was motioned by his
wife to save himself by the swiftness of his horse, and to
recover some town thereby for his rescue, he, so doing,
was in worse case than before; for the townsmen and the
captain's brother, supposing no less but that the captain
had been slain, pressed so eagerly upon him, that he had
been there taken and murdered among them, had not he
(as God would), spying a ladder leaning to a window, by
the same got up into the house, and so gone up into a
garret in the top of the house, where he with his dagger
and rapier defended himself for a space; but at length, the
burgomaster coming thither with another magistrate which
could speak Latin, he was counselled to submit himself to
the judgment of the law, upon condition that the magistrate would receive him under safe-conduct, and defend
him from the rage of the multitude. Which being promised, master Bertie putteth himself and his weapon into
the magistrate's hand, and so was committed to safe custody, while the truth of his cause should be tried.

Then master Bertie, writing his letters to the landgrave,
and to the earl of Erpach, the next day early in the morning the earl of Erpach, dwelling within eight miles, came
to the town whither the duchess was brought with her
waggon, master Bertie also being in the same town, under
custody.

The earl, who had some intelligence of the duchess before, after he was come and had showed such courtesy as
he thought to her estate was seemly, the townsmen perceiving the earl to behave himself so humbly unto her,
began to consider more of the matter; and further, understanding the captain to be alive, both they, and especially
the authors of the stir, shrank away, and made all the
friends they could to master Bertie and his wife, not to
report their doings after the worst sort.

Foxe at this point completely omits all that happened at

Frankfurt. He may well have regarded it as an unedifying tale. The contention among the English exiles there gathered was "so boiling hot, that it ran over on both sides, and yet no fire quenched." [49] The debate centered around whether to use the second prayer book of Edward VI. Despite its Zwinglian leanings on the Lord's Supper it was held to have retained some of the dregs of Rome. Calvin said that it contained "tolerable ineptitudes." The intransigeants at Frankfurt considered them intolerable.

This prayer book allowed vestments, the very "rags of Antichrist," as the Puritans were wont to call them. It used the ring in marriage, implying that marriage was a Christian sacrament instituted by Christ, whereas it was instituted by God in the garden of Eden. Kneeling at the altar was held to imply bread worship. Godparents were permitted at baptism. Knox and Foxe worked out an acceptable compromise till Cox arrived from Cambridge insisting that Englishmen abroad should use the form enacted at home by the late king. Knox was disposed of, when his jibe, that the emperor was worse than Nero, was communicated to the magistrates who shipped him off to Geneva.

The quarrel involved also the seat of churchly authority, whether residing in the congregation (congregationalism), or in the ministers and elders (presbyterianism), or in the magistrates (Erastianism). They did take a hand and appointed three arbiters consisting of Cox, Sandys and the lately arrived Richard Bertie. The dissidents would accept no arbiters appointed by the magistrates. The wrangling ceased only on the accession of Elizabeth. Among the signatories to several documents was one John Browne, who will appear again. This little teapot tempest anticipated the Puritan revolution.

The Berties were no doubt relieved to find Lasco at Frankfurt, for their Polish benefactor had not yet returned home. His hopes were high because the king was favorable and the Calvinists, Lutherans and Bohemians were working in unison. The idyllic period was brief. The Berties arrived during a propitious interlude. Bertie was made the governor of the district of Crozan.[50] Of his year's administration no record is available.

On the accession of Elizabeth the duke and the duchess returned to England.

The duchess sent a letter of congratulation to the queen whose christening she had witnessed. It read in part:[51]

> The almighty and ever-living God so endue your Majesty with his Spirit, that it may be said of you, as of his prophet David, 'He hath found one even after his own heart.' . . . Now is our season of rejoicing, and to say, after Zachery, 'Blessed be the Lord God of Israel.' which hath visited and delivered your Majesty, and by you us, his and your miserable and afflicted subjects. . . . We generally ought to praise, thank, and honour Him in you, and you in Him, with an unfeigned love and obedience all the days of our lives. It is comfort enough to all your subjects, that you do the will of Him that hath raised you up, spite of His and your enemies; but unto the heavy hearts of your persecuted subjects, these tidings distil like the sweet dew of Hermon; and though I have my portion of this gladness equal with the rest, yet I cannot choose but increase it with the remembrance of your gracious good will towards me in times past, and with hope, continuance of the same in time to come: only I greedily wait and pray to the Almighty to consummate his consolation, giving me a prosperous journey once again presently to see your Majesty, to rejoice together with my countryfolks, and to sing a song to the Lord in my native land. God for His mercy grant it, and to your Majesty long life, with safe government, to His glory, your honour, and subjects comfort. From Crossen, in Sanogelia, the 25th of January /1559/.
>
> Your Majesty's
Most humble, loving and obedient subject,
K. Suffoulk.

To Cecil she wrote in a different vein three months later. News had reached her that Elizabeth was being held back from her good inclination in fostering the reform "among whom you are especially named." She reminds him of what happened to Somerset when he followed worldly devices.

Wherefore I am forced to say with the prophet Elie, how long halt ye between two opinions? . . . If the mass be good, tarry not to follow it nor take from it no part of that honour which the last queen, with her notable stoutness, brought it to and left in (wherein she deserved immortal praise seeing she was so persuaded that it was good) but if you be not so persuaded, alas, who should move the Queen's Majesty to honour it with her presence, or any of her counsellers?

There is no fear of innovation in restoring old good laws and repealing new evil, but it is to be feared men have so long worn the Gospel slopewise that they will not gladly have it again straight to their legs. Christ's plain coat without a seam is fairer to the older eyes than all the jaggs of Germany; this I say for that it is also said here that certain Dutchers should commend to us the confession of Augsburg as they did to the Poles, where it was answered by a wise counsellor [that] neither Augsburg nor Rome were their ruler but Christ, who hath left His Gospel behind Him a rule sufficient and only to be followed.

Thus write I after my old manner, which if I persuade you, take it thankfully and friendly as I mean it; then I will say to you as my father Latimer was wont to say to me, I will be bold to write to you another time as I hear and what I think: and if not I shall hold my peace and pray God amend it to Him. With my hearty prayer that He will so assist you with His grace that you may the first and only seek Him as His eldest and chosen vessel. And so I leave both you and your wife, resting as ready to do you both pleasure if I were able as willing to serve you. With my hearty commendation from our house of Crossen, the fourth of March.

So far yours as you are God's.[52]

This letter makes the striking point that Mary, the persecuting Catholic, was more to be esteemed than Elizabeth halting between opinions.

After the return to England the energies of the duchess were sorely drained by worry over the estrangement of Peregrine from the wife of his own choosing. Reconciliation was achieved, but only after the duchess was dead. Her anxiety was not allowed to distract her from response to those who still looked to her for leadership. One such was a certain Mrs. Locke who for religion had deserted her husband and gone to live in Geneva. After having made a translation of Calvin's commentary on the song of Hezekiah, she dedicated it in these words to the duchess. "This receipte [for the diseases of the soul] God the heavenly Physitian hath taught, his most excellent Apothecarie Master John Calvin hath compounded, and I, your grace's most bounden and humble, have put into an Englishe box and do present unto you." [53]

Aid to dissenters was much needed in the England of Elizabeth, who was striving to establish uniformity and to suppress separatist congregations engaged in "prophesyings" under unauthorized lecturers. Coverdale, active in such movements, became Catherine's chaplain. He reported that she "abhored the popish ceremonies." After a royal visitation in her Suffolk, Cecil noted that "the surplice may not be borne here." In the area called the Minories near Aldgate in London, separatism was rife and in this district we learn that the duchess had extensive holdings.[54]

Two instances are recorded in which she exerted herself stoutly on behalf of Non-conformists.[55] The first is the case of Master Pattenson for preaching without a cure. The bishop of London examining him in September, 1567 received the retort that his cure was "wheresoever I do meet with a congregation that are willing to hear the word of God preached at my mouth." When told that he must not preach without a licence from the archbishop he replied: "But the Archbishop of archbishops hath not suspended me from preaching . . . and hath also given me a congregation that looketh that I should bestow it among them; and therefore I may not disobey Him to obey you." The "talk" continued:

> *Bishop:* I sent for you because the Duchess of Suffolk hath been a suitor to me for you, that you might be at liberty.

And I am contented therewith at her request, so that you will put me in two sureties that you will not preach or minister the Sacraments any more without my license or the Bishop's of Canterbury.

Patterson: Her grace told me of no such sureties, neither do I mind to put in sureties to break the commandments of God. I can do that fast enough without sureties. As you do, neither mind I to make the preaching of the Gospel subject to a popish license.

Pattenson recorded all of this for the duchess.

The second case was that of John Browne, whom the Berties had known at Frankfurt. He was now another of their chaplains. Because of his non-cooperation in the enforcement of the *Act of Uniformity* he was summoned to appear and answer to Parker, the archbishop of Canterbury. The duchess refused to have him go, on the plea that her territory was exempt from the jurisdiction of the archbishop. He replied that no part of her majesty's domain was exempt from his jurisdiction.

We are persuaded that your grace knowing the authority of our commission, and how straitly we are charged to proceed in redressing disorders, will not stay your said servant, contrary to the laws of this realm. . . . We would be loth to use other means to bring him to his answer, as we must be forced to do, if your grace will not like hereof. Thus we bid your grace heavenly farewell. From Lambeth, this 13th of January [1571-2].

Browne did have to appear but was released, presumably because of the intercession of the duchess.

Her work was being progressively undone. She died in 1580. Six years later only a single minister was left in her area who would not conform.[56] The lights appeared to have gone out, but they were yet to burst into flame.

The duchess of Suffolk, the daughter of the most devoted and devout among the ladies of Catherine of Aragon became the high priestess of early English Puritanism.

BIBLIOGRAPHY

There are three biographies of the duchess of Suffolk each of which adds to the others.
Lady Georgina Bertie, *Five Generations of a Loyal House,* (London, 1845).
Lady Cecilie Goff, *A Woman of the Tudor Age,* (London, 1930), detailed.
Evylyn Read, *Catherine Duchess of Suffolk,* (London, 1962), a charming scholarly popularization.
The source for the adventures of the duchess on the continent is:
John Foxe, *The Acts and Monuments* (Reprint, New York, 1965), VIII, 569-576.
Brett's account of his vain attempt to deliver the letters missive is in:
I. S. Leadam, "A Narrative of the Pursuit of English Refugees in Germany under Queen Mary," *Transactions of the Royal Historical Society* Ser. II, XI (1897), 113-131.
The theological wrangle at Frankfurt is described in:
A Brief Discourse of the Troubles Begun at Frankfurt (London, 1846).
Numerous details are supplied in:
Christina Hallowell Garrett, *The Marian Exiles* (Cambridge, Eng., 1938).
A number of references occur in the works of:
John Strype, *Ecclesiastical Memorials,* (abbr. *M*), (Oxford, 1822). *Annals,* (abbr. *A*), (Oxford, 1825).
The Parker Society publications include:
Zurich Letters, 2 vols. (Cambridge, 1842, 1845).
Original Letters, 2 vols. (Cambridge, 1846, 1847).
Sermons and Remains of Hugh Latimer, 2 vols. (Cambridge, 1845).
Letters to Cecil in 1550-1551 in Mary A. E. Wood, *Letters of Royal and Illustrious Ladies,* 3 vols. (London, 1846), III, Nos. CXII-CXVII.

General Histories:

Gilbert Burnet, *History of the Reformation of the Church of England,* ed. Nicholas Pocock, 7 vols. (Oxford, 1865).
Thomas Fuller, *The Church History of Britain,* ed. J. S. Brewer (Oxford, 1845).
Dedications listed in:
Franklin B. Williams Jr., *Index of Dedications,* London Bibliographical Society (1962).

Contemporaries of the duchess:

Hugh Latimer:
Robert Demaus, *Hugh Latimer* (Nashville, Tenn., 1903).
Allen C. Chester, *Hugh Latimer* (Philadelphia, 1954).
Latimer's sermons noted above with the Parker Society Publications.
Several sermons are available in *English Reprints: The Plough* (London, 1868) and *Seven Sermons before Edward VI* (London, 1869).
Bernardino Ochino:
Roland H. Bainton, *Bernardino Ochino* (in Italian, Florence, 1940).
John Foxe:
J. F. Mozeley, *John Foxe, His Book* (London, 1940).
Stephen Gardiner:
James Arthur Muller, *Stephen Gardiner and the Tudor Reaction* (New York, 1926).
References and documents bearing on the activities of the duchess after her return to England:
Patrick Collinson, *The Elizabethan Puritan Movement* (Berkeley, Cal., 1967).
Albert Peel, *The First Congregational Churches* (Cambridge, Eng., 1920).

NOTES

1. Goff, 50 and Read, 40.

2. Foxe, VIII, 570.

3. Read, 28. The marriage was in September 1533.

4. Read, 59-60. Cf. Frederick Madden, *Privy Purse Expenses of the Princess Mary* (London, 1831), 143. For other disbursements to Catherine's servants, 7, 51, 102.

5. Goff, 133 f.

6. Strype, *M.* XI, 1, 502 (Title page II, 1).

7. Strype, *M.* XI, 1, 202 (Title page II, 1).

8. Foxe, VIII, 570.

9. Fuller, 235.

10. Garrett, p. 101.

11. Goff, 187-188 and Wood, III, CXII.

12. Foxe, V, 449, 451, 458, 468 and 832 note.

13. On Parkhurst see Garrett.

14. Mozely, 48-49.

15. Read, 135.

16. Bertie, 12, 92.

17. Demaus, 469.

18. Beinecke Library, Yale University.

19. *Seven Sermons*, 202.

20. Latimer, *Remains*, Parker Society II, 262.

21. *Ibid.*, 47.

22. *Ibid.*, 119.

23. *Sixth Sermon, English Reprints*, 172.

24. *The Plough, English Reprints*, 29-30.

25. Strype *M.*, XI, I, 383. (Title page II, 1).

26. Bainton, *Women of the Reformation*, (Germany and Italy), (Augsburg, Minneapolis, 1971), 91.

27. Strype, *M.*, XI, I, 383 (Title page II, 1).

28. Bainton, *Ochino*, 88, 89, 104.

29. Williams, *Dedications*. On the church of the Strangers: Frederick A. Norwood, "The Strangers' 'Model Churches' in sixteenth century England," *Reformation Studies*, ed. F. Littell (Richmond, Va., 1962), 181-196. On the role of the duchess: A. A. Van Schelven, *De Nederduitsche Vluchtingendenkerken der XVI eeuw* (Hague, 1909), 63. and *Werken der Marnix-Vereenigung*, Ser. III, Deel. I, 12.

30. Strype, *M.*, XI, 1, 72 ff. (Title page II, 1).

31. Muller, 148-150.

32. Strype, *M.*, XI, 1 83 (Title page II, 1).

33. Muller, 203.

34. Garrett, 11, Muller, 232-233.

35. Bainton, *Reformation of the Sixteenth Century* (Boston, 1953), 241.

36. *Brief Discourse*, xii-xiii and Muller, 257.

37. *Original Letters*, I, 132-133.

38. Ridley's *Works*, Parker Society XXXIX, 382.

39. Strype, *A*, II, 1, 347.

40. Foxe, VIII, 569 ff.

41. Strype, *M.*, XII, 1 233 and 410 (Title page III, 1).

42. Foxe, VIII, 574.

43. Burnet, II, 518-519.

44. Bainton, *Women of the Reformation* (Germany and Italy), (Minneapolis, 1971).

45. Bertie, 28 note 3, cf. 487.

46. Émile G. Léonard, *Histoire Générale du Protestantisme* (Paris, 1961).

47. Brett, 121-125.

48. Foxe, VIII, 573 f.

49. *Brief Discourse*, clxxxv.

50. Foxe, 576. Garrett, 89.

51. Bertie, 34-35.

52. Read, 133-135.

53. Patrick Collinson, "The Role of Women in the English Reformation illustrated by the Life and Friendships of Anne Locke," *Studies in Church History*, II (1965), 258-272, p. 265 note 2.

54. Collinson, *The Puritan Movement*, 50, 68, 86.

55. Peel, Document in *Correspondence of Archbishop Parker* (Parker Society XXXIII) No. CCXCVI.

56. Collinson, *Puritan Movement*, 265.

Illustrations

Index